"David, with your book, *DRYLAND*, you've created an excellent tool for hockey players to better themselves. The information is presented in such a way that it teaches players how to effectively train themselves. Bottom line: it's not just a "Simon-Says" training program. A job well-done!

Kirk Olson, MA, CSCS
Strength and Conditioning Coach, Minnesota Wild, National Hockey League (NHL)

"I really liked David Pollitt's book *DRYLAND*. You have all of these great training aspects included and it provides an outstanding resource for any hockey player at any level. Following this program will help you achieve your goals as a hockey player."

Sean Skahan, MS, CSCS
Strength and Conditioning Coach, Anaheim Ducks, National Hockey League (NHL)

"Dave's book (*DRYLAND*) gives a great overview of conditioning for ice hockey. If you want to excel and learn this is a must read!"

Jim McCrossin, ATC, CSCS
Strength and Conditioning Coach, Philadelphia Flyers, National Hockey League (NHL)

"I have taken the time to go through David's manual (*DRYLAND*) and am impressed by how thorough and detailed he has been in researching and organizing this important component of the game. He has made a training manual for hockey players that is simple and clear while still teaching how to train the important physiological systems that need to be strong. This manual will be a good resource for players who train themselves but also for trainers and coaches who want to support their players and teams to work hard and get results."

Steffany Hanlen, BPE
16-Year NHL Skating Coach (Edmonton Oilers & St. Louis Blues), www.quantumspeed.ca

"David Pollitt's (*DRYLAND*) is the most in depth training manual I have ever seen designed specifically for hockey players. What I like is that his innovative training techniques are designed to simulate the movements most commonly seen during a hockey game which is a very important aspect of any training program. As a skill development specialist I see many of Dave's exercises helping my students to develop the necessary strength to create many of the movements required to generate a powerful stride, hard shot, and a solid check. I would highly recommend this training manual to any player who wanted to advance their game to the next level."

Steve Phillips
Former Professional Hockey Player
Hockey Skill Development Specialist, Hockey Contractor, Inc., www.hockeycontractor.com

"Dave's book is a testament to his commitment to seeing athletes become better and better. I have known Dave for many years and have had my athletes work under his guidance for quite some time. The common thread with their feedback is that they keep getting stronger, faster and they appreciate Dave's commitment, passion and drive to make them better. If you are in the game, either as a coach or an athlete, this book will help you achieve your potential. Congratulations, Dave! Keep up the great work!"

William Doherty
President and Director, Banff Hockey Academy, www.banffhockey.ab.ca

"Dave is one of the most unique and sports specific trainers I have ever worked with. His creativeness backed by sound fundamental training principles, have helped me accelerate my own on-ice development to allow me to excel in my career. His writing brings a fresh perspective on what an athlete needs to do to be the best they can be."

Ryan Galloway, BPE
Linesmen #82, National Hockey League (NHL)

"Having used David's training programs for many years I know that his conditioning workouts are awesome and have helped me get to the next level. After reading this book I started to smile as I know that many hockey players will now share my pain (and results) that I have seen from David's training knowledge."

Stephen Margeson
Professional Hockey Player, Lake Erie Monsters, American Hockey League (AHL)

"The *DRYLAND* is the most complete book I've ever seen for training the hockey athlete. With the amount of hockey specific exercises and drills in this book you'll never need another resource to develop a program to meet the specific needs of the hockey athlete at any level. In addition to the hockey specific information this book is chalked full of time tested methods of strength and conditioning that will work for athletes of any sport. If you are an athlete or you train athletes I highly recommend adding *DRYLAND* to your library."

Josh Everett, MS, CSCS
Head Strength & Conditioning Coach, Naval Special Warfare Group 1: SEAL Teams 1, 3, 5, 7
Former Head Strength and Conditioning Coach, University of California Riverside

"Dave, you've done a ton of research with this book and pretty much nailed everything. The book is very comprehensive and definitely a complete spectrum of training and variation. I'm going to get all of my athlete's reading it for sure and especially the "putting it all together section" as this is very informative."

Clint Hazen, BKin, CSCS
Assistant Strength & Conditioning Coach, Simon Fraser University (CIS) & former NCAA goaltender

"As an athlete working with David Pollitt was one of the best experiences I have had with a strength and conditioning coach. Everything we did was extremely innovative and sport specific which enhanced my team-mates and my own performance on and off the ice. With this book David has taken his vast knowledge of hockey specific training and disseminated it for players at any level."

Dan Gableman, BKin, CSCS, USAW
Head Strength & Conditioning Coach at Union University (NCAA Division 1)
Former Goaltender, Boston University Terriers (NCAA Division 1 Ice Hockey)

"Dave, the book *(DRYLAND)* looks amazing! As you know I've been using your programs now for many years as a junior and pro, and have to say the results have been vast. My level of play has improved and I am much stronger on the ice thanks to your help. I highly recommend your training methods and this new book."

Mark Thomas
Professional Hockey Player, Sheffield Steelers, (EIHL) Elite Ice Hockey League
Member of Team Great Britain

"I love it – It takes hockey training to a new level. A lot of information that trainers have to accumulate from many sources is all here in one book – Awesome!!! I train elite athletes every day and this new book has just made my life a lot easier. The DRYLAND will become my summer bible for many young midget and junior aged hockey players!"

Tim Cooper, BSc (Kinesiology)
Strength and Conditioning Coach, Vernon Vipers, British Columbia Junior-A Hockey League (BCHL)
Owner of Cooper Fitness & Rehabilitation

"It's black and white. Too be a successful hockey player in the game today you need a lot of tools. Strength and conditioning is becoming more evident with players becoming bigger and faster. In this book, DRYLAND, Dave has put together a complete manual for players to improve dramatically. Dave's programs will push you in ways words can't describe. But the pain is worth the pleasure in the end when you're winning your races to the puck and skating past your opponent. Dave definitely changed my hockey career and I will always thank him."

Kevin Flather
Dayton Gems, International Hockey League, (IHL), German Professional Player (EHV Schnheide 09)

"I would strongly recommend this book to any hockey player or coach. DRYLAND covers everything you need to know about how to become a better hockey player and athlete. Dave has written a truly complete training manual."

Nicholas Friebel, MS, CSCS, USAW
Strength & Conditioning Coach, & Former Junior Hockey Player

"Dave's training methods have helped me out tremendously. Everything in his book (DRYLAND) from new conditioning techniques and workouts, to the variety of exercises has helped me improve physically and mentally. I owe a lot of my success to Dave, he has truly made a difference in my career so far."

Justin Todd
Professional Hockey Player, ERC 99 Sonthofen Bulls, Germany

"Dave is 100% committed to improving his athlete's performance. His passion for hockey conditioning is unmatched. I have seen his players make big gains in just one season, which goes a long way to help them achieve their athletic goals. This book is a great compilation of his unique ideas and I feel that every hockey player should read this book to help improve their game."

Oly Hicks, MA
Head Coach in Italy SSI Vipiteno/Sterzing (Division II), former 7-Year NCAA Hockey Coach, & former Professional Player

"The book DRYLAND by David Pollitt is simply about the strength training and conditioning of hockey players! In my opinion Coach Pollitt goes beyond the call of duty by creating a systematic approach to achieving a desired result. His ingenuity has produced a lesson plan based on goal and objectives needed by the hockey athlete. Coach Pollitt's work is outstanding and I recommend it to not only hockey coaches and players but to all coaches and trainers in other sports as well. I found drills to enhance skills that I am going to use in my developing of young weightlifters as well as athletes. Great job Coach Pollitt!"

Mike Burgener, MS (Exercise Physiology), CSCS
Senior International Weightlifting Coach (USA Weightlifting)
Head Coach of the Junior Women's USA Weightlifting Team
Director of the Southern California Regional Training Center for USA Weightlifting

"Coach Pollitt has put together THE BEST book on training hockey players! I started training with his pro-group this summer and I have seen gains in my strength, speed and conditioning that I never thought possible. Before I always played on talent alone, but now I have great conditioning and strength to match. I highly recommend his training, and absolutely recommend this book."

Chris Fraterrigo
Fitchburg State Falcons, (NCAA Division III Ice Hockey), Pro-Tryout with Toledo Walleye (ECHL)

"I just wanted to tell you this book is amazing! Everything you have covered talks about the training I have been doing with you for years. The training programs, time and everything you have done for me helped get me into pro hockey with the Vipers. People who read this book will clearly improve their ability to play hockey."

Matt Sellers
Professional Hockey Player, Newcastle Vipers, (EIHL) Elite Ice Hockey League

"With his obvious command in the sport of ice hockey, David Pollitt has compiled a THOROUGH and PRACTICAL book on training. Sport specific can only begin to describe the extent of this book as he has covered hockey training from A to Z with virtually every aspect. It's not a bunch of gimmicky crap you see in other books, but solid training information that is so specific to what these athletes really need. Hockey specific speed & agility training, hockey specific strength training and hockey specific condition is all covered in great detail in this book. He has provided ways to employ hockey specific speed, agility, strength and conditioning exercises to maximize their efficiency to help the reader reach their true potential. It is without a doubt the most complete book on hockey training I have ever come across and every hockey club from peewee's to the Pittsburg Penguins should be using these training methods. If you are a hockey player, at ANY level, you had better kick off those skates and sink your teeth into this book, which is sure to be the key to unlocking your body's true potential"

Todd Bostrom
UCLA Assistant Strength & Conditioning Coach & Author of "Z Last Book You'll Ever Need On Strength Training"

"Being a smaller player on the ice, I need all the help I can get. Not just to perform better, but to avoid injuries. Dave introduced me to off-ice conditioning and made me realize its importance. I noticed a huge difference in my ability to perform on the ice over the time I spent working with you, which helped get me to the D-1 level."

Taka Hoshino
Sacred Heart University Pioneers, (NCAA Division I Ice Hockey)

"Thank you for everything you have done for me. I am a better player thanks to you!"

Tyler Doherty
Professional hockey player, Mississippi Riverskings, Central Hockey League (CHL)
Concordia University (CIS)

"Dave has helped me become an all around stronger player with his innovative training methods that keep me in the gym and excited to workout. He has helped me get to the next level of hockey with his inspiring attitude, and his motivation in the gym. Without his level of expertise I would not be able to perform at the level I am at now. "

Justin Anonas
Wentworth Technical Institute
NCAA Division III Ice Hockey

Dryland
Next Level Hockey Training

www.dphockey.com

Facebook: www.facebook.com/dphockey.dryland

Twitter: www.twitter.com/DP_Hockey_Legit

ISBN: 0-9824256-0-0

Printed in the United States of America
First Edition: 2013

Special thanks to my wife Christine & son Ethan for all of their support, & my awesome mum Carol.

Many thanks to Peggy Underwood, Clint Hazen, Steve Phillips, & Todd Bostrom who provided excellent advice, manuscript reviews and help during this project. A big thank you to all the professional reviewers Steffany Hanlen, Kirk Olson, Jim McCrossin, Josh Everett, Sean Skahan, Mike Burgener, Ryan Galloway, Peter Friesen, Mike Kadar, Reg Grant, Billy Doherty, Scott Arniel, Andrew Volkening, Jay Seals, Nick Friebel, Matt Robinson, Mike Olson, Stephen Margeson, Mykul Haun, Willie Desjardins, Oly Hicks, Mike Panah, Mike Boyle, Tim Cooper, Kevin Flather, Dan Spence and Jan Muirhead who all provided great technical reviews and advice.

Thanks to athletes Justin Todd, Clint Hazen, Dan Spence, Todd Bostrom, Kevin Flather, Cody Kreger, Ryan Galloway, Austin Block, Mark Pustin, Nick Kooiker, Bryce Nielsen, Kayla Nielsen, Carol Henson, Wesley Frietae, John Greiner, Bryan Hodges, Mitchell Hodges, Kyle Jordon, Alec James, John Accardo, Jay Seals, Mark Thomas, Trent Takeuchi, Peter Mercredi, Ryan McInnis, Sean Keating, Matt Korotva, Tyler Doherty, Julie Young, William Young, Stephen Margeson, Mykul Haun, Brandon Stone, Lisa Newcomb, JG Gobeil, Stacey, Mitch Hughes, Brighton MacDonald, Duquesne University and to all my athlete clients (including former students of the Banff Hockey Academy) with whom I used as guinea pigs for all my ideas and training theories.

Special thanks to Revolution Athletics, Town of Banff, Magic Hockey (Langley, BC), the Hockey Contractor (Simi Valley, CA), Canlan Ice Sports (North Vancouver, BC), Easy Street Arena (Simi Valley, CA), Fitness World (Richmond, BC), Gold's Gym (Langley, BC), Fitness Vacation (Richmond, BC), & photographer Dave O.

DISCLAIMER

Table of Contents

Forward

Perhaps there is no relationship in sport more pure than the bond between strength & conditioning coach and athlete. The success of trainer and athlete is one and the same. By definition, the head coach must show preference between players to ensure success. Positional coaches undoubtedly form close ties with their players, but they too may be called upon to favor one athlete or another when the head coach needs an opinion. This is especially true when decisions must be made during tryouts or when new talent arrives and player cuts must be made.

The goal of the strength & conditioning coach is to improve the performance of <u>each</u> athlete with the application of scientific method and knowledge on human performance. Long hours will be dedicated in the gym, at the rink and in the office to plan, prep and execute a solid strength and conditioning program that will yield results. As athletes progress to higher levels of competition, they will seek the help of those who can help them the most. If the athlete improves, the team improves, and if the team improves more than the competition, then the Coach win's more games and the program evolves.

As a young junior hockey player I came to know Coach Pollitt at the Banff Hockey Academy and found that what I thought I knew about training and game preparation was not the same as what he knew about that subject. At first I was hesitant about Dave's advice. I was a young big dumb athlete, and thought I knew everything I needed to know. Coach Pollitt's programs were radically different than expert advice in popular magazines on health and exercise. Our Head Coach Billy Doherty sat me down one day and said he wanted me to speak with Dave about our training program. He thought it would help me play better and improve my athleticism. So I spoke with Coach Pollitt and everything he said sounded reasonable and intelligent. He had clearly done his research and been down this road before. Talking to him and following his advice was one of the best decisions I ever made as every point I listened to helped me improve. Even still, it took years to fully appreciate the quality and depth of Dave's coaching.

Over his 20+ year career as a strength and conditioning coach Dave has proven his knowledge and professional ability by publishing numerous articles and references in the industry. He has served as the associate editor of the *Performance Training Journal* of the National Strength and Conditioning Association, the leading reference of academic knowledge on the topic of human performance. It is important to note however that Coach Pollitt has earned the respect among colleagues and athletes alike due to his ability to teach what he knows and prepare his athletes better than the rest. Each athlete who dedicates himself to Coach Pollitt's methods become known as strong, well-conditioned athletes who show up at training camps and finish at the top of the fitness testing. Coach Pollitt has made his mark in this field by helping hundreds of minor players, aged 12-20, and turning them into elite hockey players. This type of progression is outside normative progress and simply put, is impossible to fake.

Not only are coach Pollitt's athletes the most physically prepared, they also end up among the most knowledgeable athletes on the subject in nutrition, aerobic/anaerobic metabolic conditioning, strength and power training, flexibility, injury prevention, mental preparation and showing up ready to compete.

Again, proof is found in the seven of Coach Pollitt's former athletes who have gone on to become university (NCAA) and professional strength & conditioning coaches. All of them credit Coach Pollitt with making the difference in their training and wanting to give back to new generations of hockey players the way they learned from Coach Pollitt.

Not only has David Pollitt made his mark in athletics and sports competition, but we are starting to see military and US Special Forces members teaming successfully with Coach Pollitt on a career long journey of specialization and physical dominance. Again, it is impossible to fake results against testing methodology based on the philosophy, "100 soldiers we'll test today, only 3 will win the Green Beret."

Across the field of physical education and the application of knowledge in human performance, David Pollitt has made his mark both as a mentor and strength & conditioning coach. I am extremely grateful and lucky to have been one of Dave's athletes for so many years. I believe I speak for all of Coach Pollitt's athletes when I say we are excited to watch his next generation of professional and college athletes on their journey to athletic success.

Clint Hazen, BSc, CSCS
Assistant Strength & Conditioning Coach (Simon Fraser University)
Former University hockey goaltender & All Conference Goalie of the Year

Clint Hazen on the ice for Duquesne University

Introduction

Pro-Hockey player Justin Todd & team-mates line up for the anthem

I know everyone skips the introduction anyway, so I'll keep this short. From age 14 to 22+ (the bantam, midget, junior, college and minor professional level) these are important years in a hockey player's career. It is critical that a solid hockey and dryland training program is put in place that works in a relatively short period of time (and keeps working) to make the most of these important developmental years.

In this book I have taken many of the exercises and workouts developed over the past 23+ years as a hockey strength and conditioning coach, and put them all into one place. Many of these drills and exercises will use minimal equipment and can be performed just about anywhere. The training methodology outlined in this book includes plenty of exercises, photos, workouts and workout suggestions that have been tested with hundreds of hockey players, from amateur to professional, with great success. While there is a lot of information, I felt it necessary to offer you great value and teach you the right methods for maximal player development the way a coach might teach a player over many, many years.

When the book was finished, various NHL strength and conditioning coaches, professional coaches, junior-A coaches, skating experts, university strength coaches and elite players provided technical reviews and offered tremendous feedback to make it better. The end result is the most complete hockey strength & conditioning book on the market. I **guarantee** that if you apply the information in this book to your training it will catapult your physical abilities to the next level.

In addition to this book I am putting together a series of online videos and articles that will demonstrate and explain a lot more information, exercises and programming that is not possible to show in a book format. I have also partnered up with several hockey skills experts to provide more on-ice information that is critical to the success of any hockey player. Look for this on my website, **www.dphockey.com** in the coming year.

As a final thought I want to people to know they can contact me through my website, **www.dphockey.com** via the contact section for questions you might have while reading this book. I will post some of these questions on the website and on the DP Hockey FB page (which will also be the place to find updates, news and new product launches. Good luck with your dryland hockey training and I look forward to hearing from you!

Coach Pollitt.

Chapter 1 - Dryland Introduction

"He who would learn to fly one day must first learn to stand and walk and run and climb and dance; one cannot fly into flying."

~ Friedrich Nietzsche

Great hockey players must work very hard to develop general and specific athleticism off the ice (over a long period of years) so that their on-ice performance can be enhanced to elite levels. Qualities such as speed, strength, power, flexibility, agility, general and specific coordination, and all manner of injury prevention can all be improved to a large extent off the ice.

Combining solid dryland training methods with hockey specific instruction and well planned out hockey practices allow players to play their best during games, and make significant progress towards the next level up the ladder in hockey.

Perhaps the most important element of dryland training for hockey lies in the basic strength to body weight ratio a player must maintain throughout the season. Strength provides a platform for which all other training is developed. In my years as a Strength and Conditioning Coach I have **NEVER** seen a player who is too strong for hockey. Strong muscles act like "armor" to protect against injuries, provide power for fast skating and to help battle opponents during the game. After general and specific strength, players must work conditioning, flexibility, agility, power and of course a great many skills on the ice.

The 5-Critical Dyrland Areas for Players

- Explosive first step quickness and high top end speed.

- High strength to body weight ratio (which means less fat and more muscle)

- Improve overall agility (specifically lateral and spatial agility).

- Train to greatly enhance cardiovascular conditioning and shift to shift recovery

- Develop a solid Injury prevention training plan and work flexibility/Yoga throughout the year

Hockey Specific Training

In hockey the reason why so many areas of the body need to be developed are evident in the pictures below. Players must have a full range of motion and necessary power in the ankles, hamstrings, quadriceps, hips, and shoulders to compete at the highest level. Therefore when a hockey specific strength coach makes up a program for you it is important to note all the variables that go into making it as complete and correct as possible to improve your performance on the ice. Hockey is one of the hardest sports to train for as you need ample strength, power, explosiveness, speed, agility, flexibility, cardiovascular conditioning and mental strength. Therefore, when you train, make each day count as there is a lot of work to do for players looking to skate at the highest levels.

Of particular note, hockey players universally need to work on the muscles of the hip such as the hip flexors (front of the hip) , abductors (groin), adductors (the IT band and glutes) and especially the hamstrings as these are key to power generation. Players need strong quadriceps to help produce power in the skating stride, with agility and when battling opponents. A strong core area helps to transfer the power developed in the legs for skating, passing, shooting and hitting. The upper body must be able to take that developed power from the legs and core, and fully apply that to the stick for shooting and passing, and without the stick when battling opponents. In developing programs the strength coach also needs to worry about injury prevention as they plan training for the neck, shoulders, external rotators, hips and ankles.

*NOTE: All in all a cookie cutter program or pro-program from an NHL or college team will often **NOT** do the job that it is designed for (and in many cases can lead to higher injury levels). Coaches need to consult with true hockey strength and conditioning coaches to design, implement, assess and re-design programs for teams at all levels. If possible, a coach with knowledge of <u>Long-Term Athlete Development</u> is recommended.*

Efficient Application of Force

Notice how players need a full range of motion in many joints of the body, and tremendous strength to play the game at the fastest possible speed. In diagram-1 it shows the application of force in a correct hockey stride, while picture-2 shows how professional Justin Todd (#21) has to cut very hard as part of the fore-check. Both pictures show the need to not only be strong, but hockey strong.

General Dryland Training Guidelines

- Realize that hockey is a fun sport, and if you are not having fun working on the game of hockey (both on and off the ice), then do something else. Life is too short to work so hard if you aren't having fun.

- All training should be done with the idea of safety and injury prevention in mind. Dryland training exists to help prepare players to play the game at a higher level but it should also help them guard against injuries that happen in the game.

- Dryland training for hockey is a very involved activity and should not be taken lightly. Study this manual and then ask a qualified professional strength and conditioning coach for additional guidance on the various lifts or to prepare a customized training program for your specific needs. I offer these online at **www.dphockey.com**.

- Many on-ice skills can be trained with dryland hockey training. Many kids grew up playing the game of hockey on city streets or on playground blacktops. This can be used for development of many skills such as shooting, passing, stickhandling, and positioning. Organized street hockey (Ball Hockey) is a great way for players to formally improve skills while playing a version of hockey. Another good method of dryland development is to play inline (roller) hockey with your friends or in an organized league setting.

- Flexibility training should rank high on every players list of training protocols. Players need a full range of motion in many joints to provide the most power and explosiveness during the skating stride. Flexibility is also a key aspect of injury prevention as most injuries occur from body contact that stretches a joint to the end range of motion before tearing the muscle, ligament or tendon. If players have a higher degree of flexibility, there is a larger range of motion to absorb contact and prevent injury. This is why I have begun to implement Yoga into all my athletes programs as I am convinced it is a cornerstone of hockey training for both flexibility but also recovery and essential for a good post game routine.

- All players will benefit from cross sport conditioning such as squash, racquetball, handball, tennis and beach volleyball. These sports will help develop hand/eye coordination, conditioning and lateral agility in a fun environment.

- Finally, younger players (less than 16-years of age) can benefit greatly from other summer sports such as lacrosse or soccer (among many others). Younger players DO NOT need to go to every summer hockey school, clinic or evaluation camp to move to the next level. Immersing young players into only hockey activities tends to burn them out and zap the fun out of the sport.

The following chapters will include all the information you will need to improve all elements of dryland training which will positively impact on-ice performance. Remember that this information is not enough to get you to the next level...you need dedication, commitment and lots of hard work to make it. This information only provides the tools; but, you'll have to do the work!

Spring time pond hockey in Banff, Alberta, Canada...

Chapter 2 - Long Term Athlete Development

"In youth hockey, in most cases, it's really important for kids to play other sports - whether it's indoor lacrosse or soccer or baseball. I think what that does is two things. One, each sport helps the other sport. And then I think taking time off in the off-season - that three or four month window - really rejuvenates kids so when they come back at the end of August, they're more excited. They think, 'All right, hockey's back, I'm ready to go.'"

~ Wayne Gretzky, excerpt from the Globe and Mail, September 26th, 2008, by Erick Duhatscheck

While most of this manual is about improving performance and getting the most from a player in terms of off-ice development it is essential to slow things down and mention that I firmly believe in the principals of long term athlete development (LTAD). Today we are seeing National hockey organizations such as Canada, Finland, Sweden and the United States implement variations of the Long Term Athlete Development model where athletes are developed over time based on when the player is physiologically, psychologically and socially ready. This differs wildly from the previous ideas that have been employed by hockey associations and countries for many years and is a **VERY** good thing for the great sport of hockey.

LTAD Suggested Guidelines for Minor Hockey

In this section I am not going to talk about on-ice drills or practices because this manual is about dryland training for hockey. Plenty of drills and skills can be learned in an off-ice setting which is cost effective, fun and challenging for all players. Here are my guidelines for implementing LTAD off-ice programs:

- *Have fun. Nothing is more important for the kids who play this great game or for the game itself.*

- *Think about the player first. Winning at the minor hockey league level is NOT important... it really isn't. Players need this time (under-16 for sure) to develop and learn player development skills both on and off the ice.*

- *For the most part, get in lots of repetitions of drills, exercises, skills... however, tailor this to the age, level and development of the player.*

- *Realize that minor hockey is about making better people and better citizens. It's really not about the hockey. If the player grows up and never plays at the NCAA or NHL level that's fine. Hopefully that player will have had a coach that makes the game fun, challenges them and helps them become a better person, while encouraging lifelong participation in the sport. This side of hockey CANNOT be overstated.*

- *Young athletes are NOT all equal. In fact, an athlete can be measured and placed in a more appropriate training environment based on seven different perspectives: Chronological Age, Relative Age, Biological Age, Skeletal Age, Developmental Age, Training Age and Sport Specific Training Age. For example, a biologically & chronologically young athlete with a higher developmental age and training age will most likely be able to perform more and do more at a younger age than an older, less developed child.*

Dryland Training for Minor Hockey

In this section I will talk about each phase of the LTAD model (as it pertains to hockey which is a late specialization sport) and then provide my training recommendations (in bullet points). By no means is this a complete list or detailed program but a general guideline on what kinds of training should be implemented at various minor hockey ages. With all training it is essential to consult a strength and conditioning expert familiar with LTAD or a certified hockey coach currently using LTAD models. For the most part I will use the guideline ages and phases detailed by Canadian Sport for Life; http://canadiansportforlife.ca/resources/sport-parents-guide, as I prefer how they have divided the developmental ages and timelines.

The diagram below (courtesy of Istevan Bayli from the Pacific Sport Canadian Sport Centre Vancouver) details the windows of optimal trainability in males and females. It outlines how <u>typical</u> children develop and when to focus on sport specific skills such as speed, flexibility, skill development, conditioning and strength. USA Hockey uses this same graph for its American Developmental Model (ADM) of training hockey players of all ages.

Sensitive Periods of Accelerated Adaptation to Training

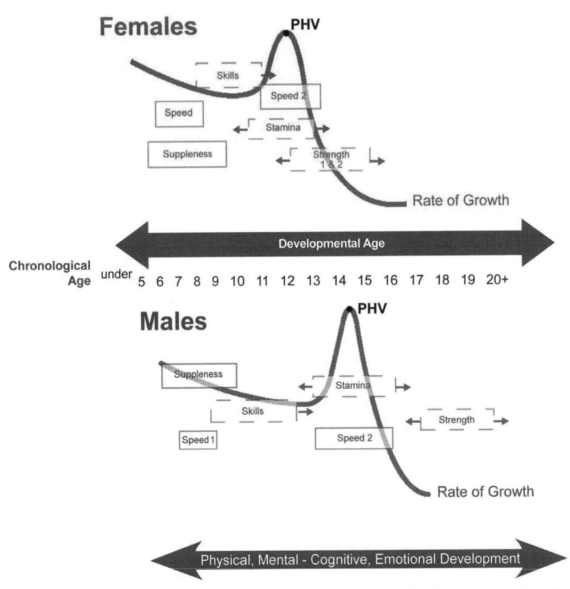

Diagram-2 – Sensitive Periods of Acceleration Adaptation to Training (Pacific Sport, Balyi et Way, 2005-2011)

NOTE: on the graph you will notice "PHV" which stands for "peak height velocity", also known as the "growth spurt" that children have during puberty.

Phase 1 (Active Start), girls & boys (0-6)

In the active start phase children show a rapid growth period and start to learn the foundational movements which all sport activities are based. Toddlers are recommended to have at least 30-minutes of organized activity (at least an hour of non-structured play), while older preschoolers should have 60-minutes of organized activity plus several hours of unstructured play. During this phase of development the parents will become very important role models with activity for children (they will want to do what you do and imitate this behavior). It is important that children perform activities regardless of the weather outside and every day, while parents should stress the importance of fun and inclusion of everyone in the activities.

- Organized activities could include learning to walk, throwing objects, kicking objects, climbing, climbing on stairs, running, pushing objects (like a wagon or cart), pulling objects (like a wagon or cart), rolling, tumbling, swimming, skating, gliding, learning to ride a bike, etc. With my young son Ethan, I have him climb up the stairs in our house several times, run through the yard as I chase him and play ball (throw, catch and hit) on a daily basis. He also has a hockey stick and we regularly pass a tennis ball back and forth in the family room or play "tackle me" with the football. All of these activities are geared for fun but we do them on a regular basis so Ethan gets in lots of "reps" of basic movement activities. For an older child including a bike ride with the family, a game of tag at the park or a day at the local pool will offer lots of other options for movement and activity.

- Unstructured play might include playing games with other children, playing with toys, building forts, imitating parental physical activities (like swimming or bike riding).

- Very basic and fun dryland training can begin at this age such as learning to squat down, a basic lunge, bear crawls, pushing up from the floor, running drills around cones, etc.. These workouts can be very short in length and really just focus on the movement (of course using NO WEIGHTS). A 5 to 10 minute session done while mom or dad workout out in the family room or garage is often all the child needs to participate and learn.

Phase 2 (FUNdamentals), girls (6-8) & boys (6-9)

This phase of development builds on the previous phase as children should learn more skills relating to agility, balance and coordination during activities. Fun, inclusion and fair player are critical to teach during this period as "future stars" may develop. For parents it's the age to turn off the TV, video games and computers in order to encourage playful activities outside (we used to play street hockey for hours at this age until our feet would freeze). Make sure all coaches working with your children are certified and follow LTAD principals as it is important not to send mixed messages to children (coach saying one thing while parents say another).

- Agility, balance and coordination can be improved upon with very basic drills such as stepping over hurdles, lunging under objects, moving around objects (cones, tires, etc.), climbing objects, playing on the local park jungle-gym, or general games and with active play.

- During this age range girls enter their first "speed window" from 6-8 years of age, and boys from 7-9 years of age (see diagram 7 above). Coaches and parents should encourage low volume sprinting type movements such as 5 to 15 meter sprints, short sprints with a change of direction, backwards to forwards sprinting (pivot in the middle), sprinting from laying on the ground, etc. If possible make it into a game such as hitting baseballs in the park and repeatedly sprinting to a cone (rather than running all the way to first base), or skating on the ice from face-off dot to face-off dot. Be creative with sprinting drills during this period of development.

- Focus on exposing your children to a wide variety of physical activities designed to foster athleticism such as gymnastics, martial arts, soccer, baseball, swimming, etc. Children should ideally be in several sports throughout the year (one summer and one winter sport at least).

15

- Parents should work on helping children learn and develop flexibility training in a learn-by-doing environment. If possible several times per week sit down with your child while watching television or after school to stretch for 15 to 20 minutes. Use the exercises and suggestions in this book to promote good form and explain why you are stretching. This is particularly important for boys at this age.

- Parents should begin to teach children about proper nutrition during this age range. Teaching healthy nutrition habits and then cementing these habits with the family committed to following these principals on a daily basis set the stage for a lifetime of healthy eating.

- During dryland training players can build on Phase 1 movement and strength principals with more involved versions of squats, lunges, step-ups, x-over deads, sit-ups, planks, push-ups, pull-ups, jumps, jumping jack type movements, jump rope, climbing trees, pushing a light sled, etc.

- Coaches can work on off-ice skill development during this phase by using ball hockey or floor hockey as a good teaching example. This takes the skating out of the equation, and allows a player to learn how to stick-handle, pass, shoot, and move with the ball. If possible spend some of the practice time working on skill development drills like moving around cones, stick-handling with the head up, shooting while moving, passing and catching passes, etc., and the other time with small area games or 3-on3 type mini-games with development being the end goal rather than winning.

- Off-ice training should be comprised of two 30-minute sessions per week (after practice if possible so parents do not have to drive to another training session each week). Include 15 to 20 minutes of dryland "training", with another 10 to 15 minutes of play type games or off-ice drills (such as ball hockey or soccer).

Phase 3 (Learning to Train), girls (8-11) & boys (6-12)
In phase three children are ready to begin training according to more formalized methods but the priority should still be general sport skills with a wide range of activities rather than single sport specialization. Let the children choose the sports they wish to participate (narrow the focus to 3-sport throughout the year) so they learn a wide variety of skills and improve upon the agility, balance and coordination focus of phase-2. All training should be fun with fairness and inclusion stressed.

For hockey coaches it is important to realize that hockey is a "late specialization sport" and coaches must monitor the training of these players to make sure they are not over-training, over-competing or specializing too early. It can be tempting for coaches to put players into certain roles on the team (forwards, defense or goaltender), but this often can be very detrimental to later development stages as this strategy promotes the likelihood of injury and burnout. As a rule of thumb training should make up at least 70% of a child's sport time while competition should occupy no more than 30% of scheduled sport time.

- Most players will see the greatest improvement in hockey skills during this phase as they naturally experience an accelerated adaptation to motor coordination. During dryland training all players should focus on the same skills and drills without position specific specialization. Coaches are encouraged to continue off-ice skill development with hockey related games (ball hockey, floor hockey, soccer, etc.) that focus on building a wide variety of skills (**as the window for skill development is highest in this phase**).

- Parents should continue teaching proper nutrition with children and encourage them to try a great many different foods as part of a balanced and well-rounded diet.

- Flexibility work should still continue so that solid habits are cemented. Progressions up to 3 - 5 sessions per week of 10 to 20 minutes will go a long way towards building and maintaining good muscle flexibility necessary for the sport of hockey as the child develops.

- With strength training children can start to use light dumbbells or light barbells (they make 15lbs barbells) to learn more advanced movements such as deadlifts, squats (most kinds), lunges, step-ups, x-over deads, presses (of all kinds), chin-ups, etc. Olympic lifting can also begin at this stage with only a PVC pipe (buy a ¾ inch pipe 7-feet long and mark out the "knurling rings") to teach lifts. Plyometric training should be limited to ground based agility work (the 12' agility drill for instance) and basic jumping movements (like jumping jacks, long jumps, vertical jumps, etc.). Organized plyometrics are NOT recommended. The most important thing to focus on during this stage is lots of variety and correct movement form.

- Speed training can continue although the child is most likely finished with the "speed zone" where rapid improvements will occur... speed can be maintained during this period.

- Off-ice training sessions should involve three 30-minute sessions per week that can include both general strength training and fun game type drills and activities (again, after practice if possible). These are great team building sessions and players can perform dryland at the rink in their under-gear, or with a track suit).

Phase 4 (Training to Train), girls (11-15) & boys (12-16)

This phase is a critical stage in athlete development as both boys and girls begin and end the growth spurt during this time (as shown by the "peak height velocity" in the diagram 7 above). In hockey it is fine for coaches to begin identifying and encouraging "talent" for phase 5 (training to compete). The ratio of skill development and training should be 60% of all sport time while competition makes up the remaining 40% of total sport time. While coaches and players can start to think about winning and maximizing performance it is advised that premature specialization in one sport or position may still lead to burnout or excessive pressure from coaches (or parents). Many young hockey players drop out of hockey during this time so it is important to provide a good experience and lots of emphasis on fun, fairness and respect.

With respect to dryland training, players should start to look at developing muscular strength 12-18 months **after** the PHV (growth spurt). At this time a periodized, appropriate strength training protocol is not only advised but necessary to enhance performance and protect players from injuries. Again, with all LTAD training it is essential to tailor all training to the developmental level of each athlete rather than by age groups or hockey division.

- In this phase players have two aspects of performance that need to be developed: speed and endurance. Before and during the PHV phase these two areas show an optimal training window. Therefore dryland should work on both of these elements at least until the child is through the PHV when the window for strength training development opens up (12-18 months post PHV). Coaches therefore have a tremendous responsibility during this phase to recognize and implement training regiments that are developmentally appropriate.

- In this phase players can start to look at performance visual testing and training to aid in physical performance in hockey. I suggest players start about 14-years of age and continue this development throughout their hockey careers.

- As flexibility declines sharply during the PHV, it is recommended to not only continue with regular flexibility training but general mobility drills for the hips and shoulders. Exercises such as walking over high hurdles, crouching to move under a hurdle, hip development exercises, etc. are very valuable for players at this age when the reduced range of motion for joints and the speed of the game contribute to a rapid rise in hockey related injuries.

- Off-ice training can start moving to an individualized plan for each player based on when they enter and exit the PHV. Players should be monitored by an LTAD qualified coach/strength coach to ensure that correct off-ice training is being implemented for each player's developmental level.

Phase 5 (Training to Compete), females (15-21+) & males (16-23+)
During the training to compete phase athletes need the most qualified and skilled coaches (preferably with lots of contacts in the hockey world) to help them develop into world class players. Competition is KEY to development in this phase as the ratio of training to competition should be 50% to 50%. Coaches are advised to bring on board a qualified strength and conditioning coach, mental performance coach and hockey/academic advisor to aid in the decision making process (regarding schools, leagues of play, etc.). Parents while move into a supporting role for their child as they help them seek better training situations from coaches who are looking out for the best interests of the player (especially in terms of LTAD).

- Hockey specialization occurs during this phase as year-round high volume and high intensity training is necessary to move the player from minor hockey into the elite levels of the game.

- Players move completely into custom designed off-ice training programs that seek to re-balance the hockey specific muscles, prevent injury, improve hockey conditioning, enhance strength for increased performance and maximize all training. These factors all become critical at this age for players as off-ice training plays a HUGE role in their ability to improve on the ice and make it to a higher level in hockey.

- Hiring a hockey skills coach at this level (and even earlier) can pay tremendous dividends for the player as they get more one-on-one attention and development away from practice or a coach.

Phase 6 (Training to Win), females (17+) & males (18+)
At this point in hockey we have moved into the elite areas of high performance hockey (for which this manual was primarily written). Much time and preparation has gone into athletes at this level and now it is time to maximize performance (ie: mental preparation, elite strength & conditioning, refining on-ice skills at full speed, fine tuning multiple tactical and technical game systems, and preparing to win at major competitions). The training to competition ratio has switched to a 25% training, 75% competition range (which includes competition-specific training such as partner workouts, strength training for set goals, sprinting against team-mates, battle drills, and small area games, etc.). Top coaching, equipment, facilities and playing at the highest level possible are key factors for high performance development so it is critical to look at options early and develop a plan best suited to play at the elite level.

- Most all of the drills and exercises within this book are geared towards the high performance hockey player...use this book as your guide. If you need/or want tried and tested hockey training programs consult my upcoming book Just Hockey Programs at **www.dphockey.com**.

- Older professional players will most likely (and should) look at injury prevention as a key aspect of playing pro hockey for a long time. Chances are that after they have been in the pro ranks for any length of time strength, conditioning and skills are not holding them back...but lack of preparation for battling during a hockey game (ie: injury prevention) will catch up to all players at some point.

- At the NCAA level and above, strength training plays a larger role than most other off-ice training as it is the platform for which all training is based. Strong players will be able to skate faster, out battle opponents and not wear down over a long season compared to weaker players. Colorado College (NCAA D1) Assistant Coach Jon Bonnett (among many others) singles out strength development as the key reason a player performs well at the highest levels in hockey.

- Mobility and flexibility become essential to the elite ice hockey player. Part of all dryland training should include methods to develop these qualities with stretching, Yoga, and mobility drills. This cannot be overlooked in program development.

- Recovery methods are of tremendous importance for the elite hockey players. With the amount of training volume, length of the season, travel for games, the overspeed methods of all training and the contact at the elite level, players must learn and integrate solid recovery methods into daily life. Consult the recovery methods chapter of this book for more information.

- Nutrition plays a huge role in high performance hockey as the fuel necessary to train and compete at the highest level is not like beer league players who can get away with pounding a burger before a game. Correct nutrition and nutritional supplementation (not performance enhancing drugs) is critical to perform at the highest level. Consult my upcoming hockey nutrition manual (fall of 2013) for more information on this subject at www.dphockey.com.

- At the elite level every player/team has an off-ice training program (or should) to compliment what is happening on the ice. Custom designed programs are ESSENTIAL for progress and maintenance at this stage of development.

- Ideally players should train (both on and off the ice) with other elite professional players during the off-season as it is important to get exposure to other forms of training, different ideas, and elite level competition during training (sprinting or dryland drills for example). Pro-style training camps are also effective to bring a group of professionals into a setting where they compete and push each other during training.

Phase 7 (Active for Life), females & males (any age)

Ideally the message of this phase should be promoted throughout all the phases so that players remain active in the sport of hockey or fitness for life. This is where for the hockey player rec-league (aka: beer league) hockey is such an important tool for fun as players finish with competitive hockey. Sometimes elite players have a tough time adjusting to life as a non-athlete but with the quality of some leagues in rec-hockey it should not be a problem to stay involved at a decent level. The most important thing in this stage is that the player is having fun, staying healthy and giving back (if possible as a coach, official or sport administrator) to the sport.

Factors Affecting LTAD

The latest research points to 10-key factors that affect LTAD. When preparing training protocols it is essential that coaches work within this framework and also adhere to the above 7-Phases outlined for development. This approach is geared towards maximal athlete develop and lifelong activity.

1. FUNdamentals.

Basic movement and sport skills taught through fun games and activities that encourage children and motivate them to continue activity are what the FUNdamentals are all about. These skills serve as the platform for all future training and sport development. Activities like gymnastics, swimming, dancing, skipping, jumping, throwing, catching, hitting, moving objects (like dragging a wagon), riding a bike, climbing and even basic martial arts are all part of these skills learned at an early age.

FUNdamentals also address each child's physical literacy (which is their ability to read and react to what is happening on the ice). An example might include when a young hockey player develops confidence in their ability to carry the puck up the ice without simply passing it away when the puck comes to them, but also that they consider passing to an open teammate in a better position on the ice. Individual skills and drills in small areas (aka: small area games) both on and off the ice can be very valuable during the first 5 to 8 years of a players career to improve physical literacy.

2. Specialization

Hockey is a late specialization sport and as such can be mastered at the elite level if specialization begins between 12 and 15 years of age (although for these players it is essential they have a wide variety of physical literacy skills prior to specializing in hockey). What this means is that players DO NOT HAVE to play hockey from an early age to become an elite player (contrary to what many coaches and parents believe). It is important that children develop as athletes before they become specialized as a player. Make sure coaches are not pushing for early specialization of an athlete (that might get them a few extra wins) as opposed to what is ultimately best for the development of the child.

3. Developmental Age

All athletes develop at different rates. This is a central factor that should permeate all training that every coach, trainer, strength coach, etc. does with each player. Many factors go into determining the development of an athlete such as their physical growth (size, weight, % body fat, etc.), maturation (amount of cartilage changing to bone for example), and the social, emotional, intellectual and motor abilities of the child.

We can also classify the training needs of a child based on their chronological age (days since birth), compared to their developmental age (the degree they are physically, mentally, cognitively and emotionally mature). In my experience I throw another variable into this equation which is training age (the amount of time a particular athlete has been training), as this plays a large role on whether or not a player is able to move to the next level in training.

For parents, keep in mind the various aspects of growth and maturation to help determine if your child is an early, average or late developer. In hockey we often stress about the birth date of the child as this has an impact on where and what level they play. But the truth is that provided the child has good coaching, the sport of hockey is a late specialization sport. What is important in the minor hockey level doesn't really matter as players mature into the elite levels. Read point-8 in this section for more information on maturing into an elite player.

4. Physical, Mental, Cognitive, Ethical, and Emotional Development

Slightly different from point-3, this section of LTAD deals with ethics, fair play and character building. In late childhood (prior to puberty), training should focus on really learning the basics of hockey skill development (both on and off the ice) and creating as many opportunities for success and recognition as possible. Self-esteem and confidence (which are so important in hockey) come from getting in lots of positive repetitions from a wide variety of skills and drills so that players evolve naturally into skilled players. During all training and competition at this age it is important to not only build into, but also demonstrate (from a coach or parents standpoint) ethical and character building values.

During early adolescence, children undergo remarkable physical, mental and emotional changes. Many players lose flexibility during this time and as the speed of the game changes these two factors increase the number of injuries in this age group. Mentally, children are certainly more coachable as they make better decisions about training and during games. Socially relationships in the sport become very important so team building exercises and outings can do wonders for a team. Children at this age still need to taste success often, but realize that due to many factors, the developmental age for each child will be wildly different and therefore coaches need to recognize and address issues as they arise. For example, one child who matures early might breeze through drills while a later maturing player may have to wait for success until enough quality practice or skill development has occurred. Many times these late developers outperform early developers in the long term.

In late adolescence, teenagers have matured in their hockey career (both physically and skill wise), but the rate at which they develop new skills decreases during this stage. Mentally players are ready to understand the game and do so with ever increasing abilities both on and off the ice. Emotionally the social interaction is still very important and self-expression now immerges (that must be respected). Ideally coaches become experts in the age group they are working with so they have a firm grasp of the challenges and skills necessary to improve at one level.

5. Trainability

This refers to the ability of the player to respond to specific training stimuli and adapt to it. Each player will certainly be different and will develop at different rates as stated earlier. Another word used with trainability is "Coachability", or the idea that a player can over time take what the coach is teaching and really learn it through practice, dryland training, reading about hockey, watching hockey, etc. Every coach loves to work with highly coachable players as they seem to soak up knowledge and apply it (even if it's not perfect at first). Parents can work with their children from a young age to help develop a more coachable nature (which every coach will thank them for later).

6. Periodization
Periodization is the training approach best used by all athletes as it sets out a plan for how much and how often a player should train, and presents this in a sequence of sessions over weeks, months and a competition year. Breaking down the year into "micro" cycles (weeks) and "meso" cycles (months) is a very efficient way to maximize training time and provides the most scientifically valid plan for training hockey players. More information is presented on periodization in the "Putting it All Together" chapter of this manual. As parents I recommend you consult with your child's coach and/or minor hockey association to determine what periodization plan is being implemented.

7. Competition Calendar
With each phase of development a LTAD model presents solid ratios with regard to training and competition. In the early years of development training (learning skills, improving motor abilities, developing speed and fitness, etc.) is critical to success later on and therefore a higher training ratio is required. As players advance to higher and higher levels in hockey, the need to compete and be evaluated at the elite level becomes more and more important. Here are the appropriate ratios for each phase of development:

- Phase 1 – No competition (just learn motor skills and have fun)

- Phase 2 – 80% training, 20% competition

- Phase 3 – 70% training, 30% competition

- Phase 4 – 60% training, 40% competition

- Phase 5 – 50% training, 50% competition

- Phase 6 – 25% training, 75% competition (which includes competition-specific training).

- Phase 7 – 100% competition (let's be honest, nobody plays rec-league hockey to practice... but they should)

8. The 10-Year Rule
Sports science research has shown that it takes a minimum of 10-years and 10,000 hours of training for gifted athletes to achieve the highest levels of competition. Many experts believe this number is just a minimum number for expertise. If you look at this another way, it would take three hours of training or competition DAILY for 10-years with athletes identified as having a "talent" for the game to develop into elite players. This can be a daunting number for most players (and parents). As a parent, if you sense that the coach or minor hockey association is emphasizing winning at the expense of fun and development it is important to talk with them about LTAD to prevent player burnout and potential damage to long-term performance.

As an example of how much practice it takes to be an elite player Wayne Gretzky was once asked by reporter Peter Gzowski (detailed in **_A Peter Gzowski Reader_**, 2001) about his hockey skills and proposed that "what we take to be creative genius is in fact a reaction to a situation that has been stored in his brain as deeply and firmly as his own phone number". Gretzky responded by saying;

> "Absolutely. That's a hundred percent right. It's all practice. I got it from my dad. Nine out of ten people think its instinct, and it isn't. Nobody would ever say a doctor had learned his profession by instinct; yet in my own way I've put in almost as much time studying hockey as a medical student puts in studying medicine."

In terms of hockey development a significant number of players in the National Hockey League were never drafted which shows how our sport is such a late development sport. Often times a good player at 16 or 17 will not have what it takes to transition into the professional ranks, while an average 17-year old can play major junior hockey followed by college, or go the college route of NCAA and end up becoming a better hockey player at a later age when they have put together all the pieces of their game. This is evidenced in studies that show hockey players don't reach their potential until their early to mid-twenties (which is right after college). Think about this when a coach or team tries to recruit your child at an early age as this may in fact not be the best course of action for LTAD.

9. System Alignment

While some countries such as the United States, Canada, Finland, Sweden and England use a variation of the LTAD model, the idea of long term athlete development is relatively new on the world stage and will take time to be fully accepted and implemented in most sports (especially hockey). In the United States for example, USA Hockey has made great strides in becoming a world leader in LTAD with their American Developmental Model (ADM at **www.admkids.com**). The key factor to why LTAD is so powerful is that it is always thinking of what's best for the children who play this great sport of ours and how we as educators/coaches/parents/officials can make it better. Let's take the politics and winning at all cost approach out of the sport, and return the game of hockey to our kids with a long term athlete development model that encourages participation and positive experiences throughout a lifetime.

10. Continuous Improvement

As the concept of LTAD is new, it is important to note that research on this topic is in continual flux as new information and training techniques develop. This idea of LTAD is a sound, researched and viable strategy that will only get better after time. You as a player, coach, trainer, minor hockey administrator and/or official can impact the use and influence of LTAD within your association as it truly is what is best for children and our great game of hockey.

My son Ethan pulling his Radio Flyer wagon (part of his play time Active Start Phase),
13-year old Kayla Nielsen (now 17) performing a set of kettlebell squat pulls at the gym (strength training has enhanced Kayla's game so much in the past several years).

General Dryland LTAD Recommendations

- Developing lifting technique and form are paramount to the development of younger players. Slow, deliberate lifting of basic exercises is recommended with light weights as younger players learn the movements correctly. Often times their central nervous system is underdeveloped for strength training and stabilizer muscles are weak and uncoordinated. As a result, when they try exercises like a dumbbell bench press, barbell squat, etc., their form is terrible and the dumbbells or barbells move all over the place. This is perfectly natural and normal, but coaches must account for this and start off with light weights used with strict form.

- Gradually develop a player's strength. Focus on mastering weight lifting techniques with basic exercises before moving to heavier weights or a faster speed of lifting. As players are ready, more complex exercises such as hang cleans, barbell jerks, or power pulls can be taught. Make sure players have a solid base of training though before such exercises are implemented.

- Make sure to work the core muscles so this area around the spine is not the "weak link" in the body as this can lead to injuries. Use a wide variety of core exercises for the front, side and low back areas. Consult chapter 12 "Core Training" for more information.

- Players should have a good base of strength before they are introduced to plyometrics or fast agility work. The muscles have to be able to accelerate and decelerate the body safely in order to limit stress on joints and growth plates which can happen if plyometrics and agility work is introduced too early in a player's career. NOTE: Most coaches do not follow this rule of thumb and have players doing plyometrics just like the pro's. This is **NOT** appropriate for young athletes unless they are strong enough to handle that kind of stress.

- Bantam and Midget players should never perform a 1 repetition maximum effort in training or for testing as they simply are not strong enough and good enough in their technique to perform this safely. As players are used to weight training and use correct form with sub-maximal weights, then supervised 1RM training can be implemented. NOTE: This rule can be broken if the Bantam or Midget player has a good training age of at least 4 years and is developmentally ready for this type of stress. This of course, must be done on a case by case basis, and **only** if it is in the best interest of the player.

- Make sure that a solid warm-up is performed by all younger players prior to any dryland training as this will develop good habits for the future and prevent possible injury (as young players tend to skip the warm-up most of the time).

- Typical LTAD is a 10 to 12 year process that focuses on physical, technical and mental preparation. Planning is sometimes quadrennial in nature (which refers to the four year Olympic cycle for elite athletes), but also serves as a method of evaluating the previous 4-years and planning for the next 4-years.

- Coaches should use a variety of games, competition and different training methodologies in order to keep dryland training fun. A player who learns to hate the gym will not make the progress they should in hockey. Make it fun for everyone and keep them challenged.

Suggested LTAD Online Resources

- http://www.canadiansportforlife.ca/
- http://www.admkids.com/
- http://www.coaching.uka.org.uk/
- http://www.youtube.com/watch?v=QChhn-MYqow
- http://www.youtube.com/watch?v=Im-qSEU9tOI
- http://birmingham.academia.edu/MartinToms/Papers/
  441355/Participant_Development_In_Sport_An_Academic_Review

Chapter 3 - Yearly Training Plan "Putting It All Together"

"Fight to Win; Train to Fight"

~ motto of the US Navy SEAL's

When planning the training for an entire year it is important to have a systemized plan for working hard and then backing off in order to recover and grow stronger. If planned correctly, this ebb and flow of training volume, intensity and recovery (weekly, monthly and yearly) will lead to higher performance levels in hockey. This is called Periodization. Entire books have been written on the concept of periodization and in this chapter my goal is to boil all the important information down into one easy (relative term) to understand section. Learning and maximizing periodization as well as LTAD learned earlier will go a long way in producing highly educated and correctly trained hockey players.

Periodization Definition of Terms

- **Phases** – within each hockey season (start to finish) a typical program is made up of 5-phases (or periods of time) specific to the age/level/player. These phases are as follows: General Preparation Phase, Specific Preparation Phase, Pre-Competition Phase, Competition Phase and the Recovery Phase (off-season). In older athletes additional phases are included to address points in the season where specific training may be necessary (such as prior to training camp, or muscle/power building in the off-season). The two main hockey season models (the 5-Phase model), and the (8-Phase model) are outlined below.

- **Macrocycle** – is a year-long period of time (12-months), or 1-full hockey season which outlines all the steps necessary to bring an athlete from the beginning of the season through to the end of the competition year.

- **Mesocycle** – a period of time from 3 weeks to 6 weeks in which specific training objectives are the focus of training (example: speed training prior to tryouts in the Specific Preparation Phase or GPP training in the off-season General Preparation Phase).

- **Microcycle** – week-long periods of time that detail the volume, intensity, frequency, duration and sequence for all training. Basically this is a one-week training plan.

- **Introduction** – when talking about periodization, this means introducing the players to various aspects of training early on in the macrocycle. For example, a coach would spend 3 to 4 weeks introducing flexibility before either increasing the volume, intensity or simply maintaining this skill.

- **Volume** – The amount of training performed (in hours) during a period of time (example: microcycle, mesocycle, macrocycle)

- **Intensity** – The level of difficulty or challenge to complete training or periods of training. Intensity generally refers to adding higher "voltage" type activities to training such as speed training, plyometrics, Olympic lifting, etc.

- **Develop** – to improve upon gradually over the time of the cycle or phase.

- **Maintain** – to maintain the level attained in the previous cycle (example: maintaining flexibility during the playoff that it took the entire season to build is important as you cannot focus "development time" on flexibility at this point as this is not needed…rather it should be maintained).

Yearly Hockey Season Models

Upon planning for the year, most seasons are broken up into the 5-phase model (for younger players) and a more complex 8-phase model (for junior age+ players). This allows the planner a lot of freedom in terms of adding or subtracting training variables, competition dates, age specific development, etc. I've also included a basic macrocycle for two age groups as an example of how I might structure the year with various forms of training. They are as follows:

Atom/Squirt (9-10) 7-month Hockey Season 5-Phase Model

General Preparation Phase	*9 weeks (September 1 to November 2)*
Specific Preparation Phase	*7 weeks (November 3 to December 21)*
Pre-Competition Phase	*5 weeks (December 22 to January 26)*
Competition/Playoff Phase	*7 weeks (January 27 to March 16)*
Recovery Phase /Another Sport	*24 weeks (March 16 to start of next season)*

NOTE: *Much variability can be built into this general yearly plan depending on the level of play, age, LTAD plan, etc. Coaches need to take this basic framework and develop a plan for their team and a more specific plan with each player (if possible) in order to maximize LTAD performance.*

Example of a 9-10 Year Old (Atom/Squirt)
General Periodization Marcocycle (7-Months) for Hockey

Off-season Or another sport					General Preparation Phase		Special Preparation Phase		Pre-Comp. Phase	Comp. Phase	PO
April	**May**	**June**	**July**	**August**	**Sept**	**Oct**	**Nov**	**Dec**	**Jan**	**Feb**	**March**
Off-season					Introduce Strength	Develop Strength				Maintain	
Off-season					Fitness Eval	Limited Evaluation		Fitness Eval	Limited Evaluation		
Off-season					Intro Speed	Develop Speed Technique		Volume Speed	Intensity Speed	Maintain Speed	
Off-season					GPP Volume Conditioning	Sport Specific Conditioning				Maintain Conditioning	
Off-season					Introduce Flexibility	Develop Flexibility				Maintain Flexibility	

Diagram 3 – Schedule used from Rimby Renegades Atom (9-10) Hockey Team, Rimby, Alberta

Age Specific Goals

General Preparation Phase

- Improve overall strength.
- General physical preparation (GPP), increase volume of conditioning throughout phase.
- Learn basics of flexibility (or Yoga), warm-ups, cool-downs.
- Complete a fitness evaluation (pre-training, for records).
- Learn the basics of speed development.

Specific Preparation Phase

- Continue overall strength development, but add in hockey specific training.
- Specific Physical Preparation (SPP), keep volume of conditioning work medium/high.
- Develop flexibility.
- Develop speed technique and move to high levels of training volume for speed.

Pre-Competition Phase
- Continue to develop strength & hockey specific strength training.
- Specific Physical Preparation (SPP), lower volume of conditioning but raise intensity.
- Add hockey skills to dryland training (ball hockey, stick-handling) for more exposure.
- Maintain flexibility.
- Increase volume of speed training and then back off volume but add intensity prior to playoffs.

Competition/Playoff Phase
- Maintain strength, flexibility, and conditioning during this phase.
- Keep intensity high for speed training but volume low.
- Recovery methods and time off is important during the playoffs to keep players fresh.

Recovery Phase /Another Sport
- Kids will transition into another sport (ideally) or take the summer off.

Junior-A Year-Long Hockey Season 8-Phase Model

The Hypertrophy Phase	8 weeks (April 22 to June 16)
The Power Phase	6 weeks (June 17 to July 28)
The Tryout Preparation Phase	4 weeks (July 29 to August 18)
Tryouts Phase	2 weeks (August 19 to September 1)
In-Season Phase	18 weeks (September 2 to January 3)
Pre-Competition Phase	8 weeks (January 4 to February 28)
Playoff Phase	2 to 6 weeks (depending on your team)
The Recovery Phase	4 weeks (April 1 to April 21)

NOTE: *Again a lot of flexibility can be added into this type of macrocycle. For instance, if your team is in last place and won't make the playoffs it would be pointless to go through a playoff cycle (you can end the season and start the recovery cycle early). On the other side of things your team may go far into the playoffs and you need a longer break from training in the recovery cycle.*

Example of a Junior-A General Periodization Marcocycle (12-Months) for Hockey

General Preparation Phase		Special Preparation Phase		Pre-Competition Phase				Competition Phase		PO	Rest
April	**May**	**June**	**July**	**August**	**Sept**	**Oct**	**Nov**	**Dec**	**Jan**	**Feb**	**March**
Build Muscle Mass/Strength		Build Strength/Power			Maintain Strength/ Slowly Build Strength				Reduce for Peak	Maintain	
Fitness Eval	Limited Evaluation			Fitness Eval	Limited Evaluation			Fitness Eval	Limited Evaluation		
No Speed	Volume Speed		Intensity Speed	Maintain Speed					Intensity Speed	Limited Speed	
Limited Conditioning	Maintenance		Volume	Inten.	Maintenance				Volume	Inten.	off
Introduce Flexibility	Develop Flexibility				Maintain Flexibility						

Age Specific Goals
The Hypertrophy Phase
- Low volume GPP (1-3 conditioning workouts per week) is recommended.
- Limited speed, or skating is recommended so the body can recover from intense strength training.

- Most players at the Junior level need to add muscle mass with hypertrophy strength training but a full fitness evaluation is necessary first to determine weak areas or muscle imbalances. Specific add-on strength training may be necessary to correct issues that come up in physical testing.
- Develop flexibility with direct stretching or Yoga.

The Power Phase
- Switch strength training to more strength and power development by adding Olympic lifting, low level plyometrics (box jumps, etc), and more sport specific strength training.
- Increase the volume of speed training to prepare for the tryout prep phase.
- Increase volume of GPP (2-4 conditioning workouts per week).
- Add 1-2 skating sessions per week to the program (skill sessions not just skating around).

The Tryout Preparation Phase
- Strength training moves to higher intensity strength and power development. Less overall hours of strength training, but high intensity.
- Limit off-ice conditioning and flexibility to maintenance levels so as to focus on quality strength training and on-ice sessions.
- Include 2-on-ice speed/conditioning sessions per week.
- Include 2-skill sessions or 3-on-3 type small area games to get lots of puck touches before tryouts.

Tryouts Phase
- Just make the team!

In-Season Phase
- During the hockey season I plan up to three strength training workouts for elite players (junior and above) as they need to maintain and improve if possible on the gains they made in the weight room during the season. NOTHING is worse than a player who stops lifting during the hockey season as they start all over again the next summer. These workouts will be 45 to 60-minutes in length and focus on 1-upper body lift, and 1-lower body lift, with lots of assistance exercises, Olympic lifting and plyometrics added in to complement the program.
- Conditioning during the season happens mostly on the ice but it is strongly recommend coaches and players implement sled dragging during the season in order to recover faster and to add GPP workouts to the program for increasing work capacity.
- Speed training happens mostly on the ice, with specific focused speed training happening in the next phase (pre-competition phase). Speed & agility drills can be run during dryland sessions if necessary for some members of the team.
- Hockey specific skill sessions (during dryland) can/should be run during the season to work on tactics related issues or player skill development.
- Flexibility is maintained throughout the season.

Pre-Competition Phase
- This phase is also known as the "peaking" phase. The goal of this phase is to focus on speed & agility development, and bring up the intensity level on the ice (during practices and games).
- Add more power training (Olympic lifting, plyometrics, etc.) into strength training.
- Maintain overall strength, conditioning and flexibility.

Playoff Phase
- Maintain strength, flexibility, power training, conditioning and speed to focus on hockey performance (quality practices and games).

The Recovery Phase
- *At this level a 3-4 week recovery phase of little to no training is advised to heal injuries, take a physical break from training and mentally refresh from the long season.*

Basics of Periodization

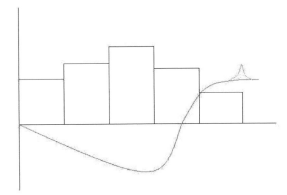

You cannot simply keep increasing the amount of hours and intensity you train each week (referred to as a micro-cycle) as the body needs to adjust and adapt to new levels of training. This is where the planning of a season for each athlete is CRITICAL because not every athlete will respond to the training load the same way. The goal of all training is to get players to a higher level than before they started training and this is outlined with a periodized approach as shown in the graph to the left.

Diagram 5 – Outlining the relationship between hours (in blocks) to recovery (the line)

In the above diagram we see how as the hours go up in blocks of time each week (or even within a week), the level of the player recovery drops (they are starting to get worn down from training). As the hours drop off and are reduced to lower values than at the start of training, the athlete is able to recover stronger than before (thus increasing performance). This is a fine relationship that must be developed over time and monitored with great care as overtraining, sickness or less than optimal training are all possible and affect performance if not implemented correctly.

Similarly when planning the yearly program it is important to note the relationships between volume of training, intensity, and recovery periods as this has a tremendous impact on how players develop. The chart below demonstrates the various phases (of a 5-phase training model) and how these three training qualities are developed during the year.

	General Preparation Phase	Specific Preparation Phase	Pre-Competition Phase	Competition Phase	Recovery Phase
Intensity	Low	Low	Medium/High	High	Low
Volume	High	High	Medium	Low	Low
Recovery	Low	Low	Medium	High	High

Diagram 6 – General relationship between Intensity of Training, Volume of Training
and Recovery Time Allowed within a hockey season.

Mesocycle Periodization

Typically I employ two types of mesocycle periodization schemes within training cycles for 80% of my training programs I design for hockey players. I use either a 4-week mesocycle, or a 3-week mesocycle. I agree with noted Canadian Strength Coach Charles Poliquin when he states "your program is only as good as the time it takes to adapt to it". It is with this statement I like to plan a lot of variety into training protocols, and therefore my programs will change based on a number of situations and data from the athlete (and coach). Both types of mesocycle programs are outlined below in bar graph form.

4-Week Mesocycle

With this type of loading, a player increases the amount of volume (hours) trained each week for three straight weeks, and then the volume is dropped in the fourth week to slightly less than week-1 training. This is repeated with another similar mesocycle only at a higher level. Most players tolerate this type of training very well and make solid progress on this type of plan.

Of course all mesocycle preparation has to take into consideration what time of year it is, what the goal of training is and what type of athlete we are training.

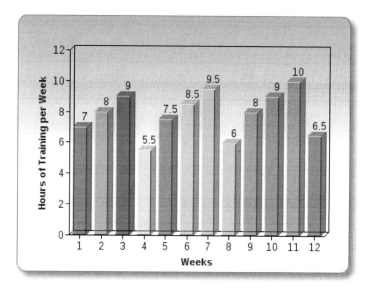

3-Week Macrocycle

The 3-week mesocycle is a more aggressive type of volume loading, and should be used for higher level athletes such as junior, college and pro players. The goal is to load for three straight weeks, and then slightly increase the numbers for the next three weeks. This type of loading will go on for up to 3 mesocycles (of 3-weeks), before I prescribe a de-loading week. Ideally I like to push players until they are near the breaking point (when the resting heart-rate is elevated and the athlete shows signs of over-training), before I de-load the player so they can recover and rebuild. This is a tricky method of training, but highly effective if done correctly.

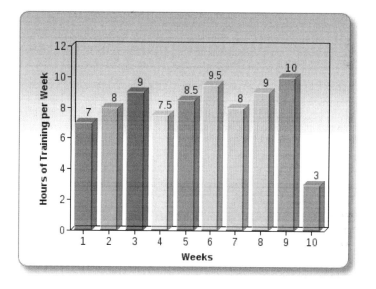

NOTES:

- *Strength training hours are determined based on the need of the player and therefore should be planned first in the training process.*

- *These are only two examples of what I use to periodize the volume of a players training program, but are very effective as long as you monitor the athletes and make sure they do not dip into an over-training state.*

Suggested Yearly Training Hours

When figuring out what number of hours to train for the age/level/development of each player, refer to the suggested guide below. This list is complied with information from USA Hockey, Hockey Canada, other developmental models and my own experience in this industry training hockey players of all ages. I have used the USA Hockey age categories to break down the number of hours I would suggest for players, but understand that many factors go into figuring out the correct number of hours (and the type of hours in terms of quality) that is best for each player. Consultation with a qualified LTAD hockey coach or strength coach will be very valuable in zoning in on what numbers **you** should be shooting for and how to get more quality training out of each hockey macrocycle.

- Under 8   50 to 80 hours (4-month training & competition season)
- Under 10   120 to 130 hours (7-month training & competition season)
- Under 12   140 to 165 hours (7-month training & competition season)
- Under 14   170 to 270 hours (7-8 month training & competition season)
- Under 16   250 to 330 hours (year-round hockey training & competition season)
- Under 18   350 to 420 hours (year round hockey training & competition season)
- Over 18   450+ hours (year round hockey training & competition season)

A sample table that outlines the maximum number of recommended training hours per year is listed below as a quick reference. As with all training remember that it is very person specific and these numbers will vary based on many factors.

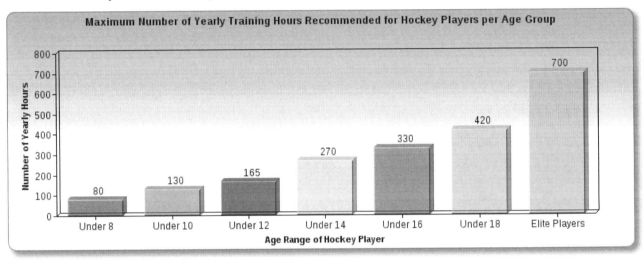

Yearly Periodization Hours

In the section below I will outline (in table format) how I might plan a macrocycle (in this case a 7-month hockey season) for a 9-10 year old Atom/Squirt age player. Notice how the weekly hours are structured using the 4-week mesocycle as shown earlier.

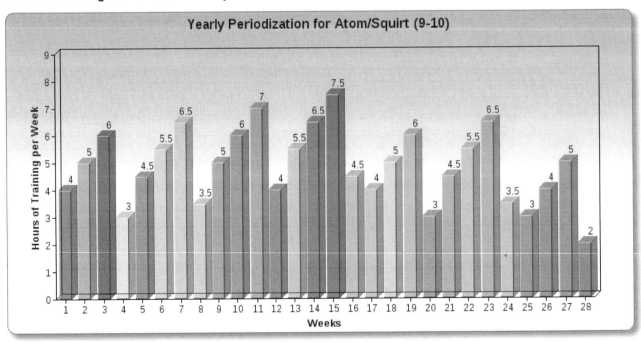

NOTE: *The above graph is set for 136-hours of training.*

Periodizing Strength Training

In order to prevent confusion, I must mention how one provides periodization to strength training. Strength training hours are determined based on the need of the player and therefore should be planned first in the training process as strength makes up the platform for most all hockey dryland training. Do not periodize weight training (hours), as all weight-room programs require certain hours and cannot be altered without affecting the desired outcome. Strength training is periodized by loading (weight), reps, sets, rest, and specificity. Rather, you should adjust the amount of conditioning work, speed, agility, ice, hill work, or hockey specific training to hit your target hours for a certain training cycle.

An example of this might be a weight-room training program requiring three 45-minute training sessions during a week. These "hours" will not be periodized, rather just counted into the total amount. So if a player was training 6-hours one week in the General Preparation Phase the strength training would account for 2¼ hours of training, and the rest would be made up of GPP, on-ice training, speed work, etc.

In reality strength training tends to periodize itself because younger players will not be in the weight room 5-days per week, and older players train a lot more hours and can accommodate the higher volume of weight training. Similarly during the season the strength training programs will usually be maintenance programs 2 to 3 times per week for less than 1-hour, compared to the off-season when more weight room training is appropriate.

Periodization NOTES & Suggestions:

- *It is **ESSENTIAL** to note that all players should start off with the least training that helps them improve, and then work up from that amount of volume. It is ALWAYS important to keep making progress in your training. If this does not happen, most likely you are doing too much and not allowing the body to recover properly. More is not always better... better is better.*

- *Along the lines of the above point, **NEVER** train if you are really sore (muscle soreness) as you will not be fully recovered and the likelihood of making progress is minimal. As you progress you will know when this "law" can be broken, but in the beginning if you are very sore, don't work out.*

- *Planning a good training program for one athlete takes years of skill development, education and experience to get the best results. In the first few programs, a player or coach using this program will have setbacks and problems that can only be hammered out by trial and error. Don't worry about this, you can learn to develop your own programs over time. I tell players that my job is as much a science as it is an art.*

- *Always plan your strength training first (as in hockey it should make up the backbone of all training) and then add in all the other forms of training with correct periodization.*

- *As soon as possible find out the date your team has training camp and work backwards in the summer from that date. You will need to adjust various training phases based on when you go to camp. For instance, if you play junior hockey, camps are in late August, while if you play in the East Coast Hockey League (ECHL), tryouts won't be until early October.*

- *It is **CRITICAL** to keep a training log or notes on your training. The more information you have, the better future decisions you can make based on what works and what doesn't work for your specific training. I have notes on every client I work with and all the teams I have worked with, so my "tool box" is enormous. Build your own "tool box" of information by keeping notes and learning from past successes and failures.*

31

- *Remember the amount of recovery methods you use will impact the level and intensity of the training you can perform each week without overtraining, injury or illness. Consult the "recovery methods" chapter for more information on this important aspect of training.*

- *I have included two sample in-season and off-season complete training programs in this book to help you understand and see how I progress players through a mesocycle of training.*

- *For those who want pre-made hockey specific training programs that have been tried and tested by thousands of hockey players I suggest you look into my upcoming book Just Hockey Programs (scheduled to be released in the fall of 2013. Find out more information at www.dphockey.com. Using this type of systems takes the guess work out of your strength training and now allows you to periodize the rest of the training program specifically for your goals.*

- *Ideally if the sport of hockey wants to get serious about LTAD then each player, coach and hockey association should have a copy of every physical test each hockey player ever does, performance reviews (during camps and a season review), a periodization plan drawn out for each year in the sport, and all the training logs (and records) to document all training. This would be INVALUABLE to an association or hockey coaching body for informational purposes, and for each player as now they know what they have done throughout the years to become a skilled player.*

Setting up Your Own Training Plan

In order to design your own program, you will need to address the following areas and then play around with what works and doesn't work for your specific goals. As part of the online videos that accompany this book I have included a section on hockey to develop your own training plan that goes into much more depth than this written section.

Step 1 – Determine the length of the hockey year for the age/level. (Example: the Atom/Squirt age group will have a 7-month hockey season where a junior player will definitely train all year).

Step 2 – Determine the number of hours that are appropriate for the age/level of play (see graph on the previous pages).

Step 3 – Start building the season with a general preparation phase, specific preparation phase, pre-competition phase and competition phase. The length of each should be is determined by a LOT of factors (which is why it's best to employ a qualified coach to help with this step).

Step 4 - Pick your focus/goals (testing helps you determine weak areas). Are you strong but lack conditioning or are you weak but very skilful as a player? This determines what you need to work on in dryland and strength training.

Step 5 – With the strength training portion of the program, select the exercises, sets, reps, load, rest, and tempo to accomplish your goals (see the "Strength Training Methodology" chapter).

Step 6 – After the strength training is planned, add in all the other areas of the program (in what amounts, when in the week, the intensity, etc.). For example, if you are planning on 7-hours of training during the General Preparatory Phase and strength training accounts for 3-hours, you will have 4-hours left over. Based on the goals of each phase you will want to perform some GPP exercises, perhaps one session on the ice and two speed sessions (these hours will make up the rest of the week's training of 4-hours.

Step 7 – Plan the first 3 to 4-week training program, evaluate it with physical testing (before and after) and record it in a log-book (in the appendix section). Now look at the results and plan the next program. It takes time to learn how your body responds to training.

Step 8 – Look at training as a long-term investment and if possible, plan year to year rather than just thinking short term. Mistakes can be made as long as the long term plan is in place.

Chapter 4 - Sample Off-season Training Program

"Take the shortest route to the puck carrier and arrive in ill humor."

~ Fred Shero (Head Coach of the Philadelphia Flyers, NHL, 1971 to 1979)

Ideally every player should have their own customized training program, but often that is not possible. Rather than taking an existing program from a college or junior team, or reading a book with one basic program it is important to have many training options and be able to determine what your specific needs are and how to remedy weak areas while building strong areas. This is why I offer custom programs to players, and why I also wrote an entire book on training programs for hockey players.

In the following section I am showing an actual program that American Hockey League player Stephen Margeson (shown above on the right) used in the 2007 off-season. I wanted to demonstrate how I set up a program for an elite type of player in the middle of summer. Naturally your program will be very different from Stephen's, but you can use this as an example of how to set up a base program. As YOU determine what your weak and strong areas are, you can add or subtract training from this type of program to produce results just for you. Remember, IT IS NOT THE TRAINING YOU DO THAT IS IMPORTANT, BUT THE TRAINING YOU DO, RECOVER FROM AND IMPROVE that is important. Therefore, don't start adding all kinds of training to your program if you are not improving…this leads to overtraining and potential injury.

Program Goals

In this program my goal for Stephen was to prepare him for the upcoming training camp in mid-September, to start speed and agility work and to improve maximum strength. During this phase Stephen was to participate in two skates a week with his former junior team (The Canmore Eagles), and other junior/pro players in the Banff/Canmore area. Recovery methods in this phase became very important as Stephen was participating in a lot of training each week (training frequency), at a higher altitude than he was used to (4800 ft), and at a higher than normal intensity level that had been building all summer long. Stephen was able to make use of the natural hot springs in Banff for many of his recovery sessions which allowed for a higher than normal training volume.

Strength Training

In this off-season portion I will separate workouts into Maximal Effort (for both lower body and upper body), Dynamic Effort and Repetition Days. A Max Effort day means you will try to load barbells or dumbbells with a very heavy weight for low repetitions (as outlined in the program). Dynamic effort means you will try to move weights or your body weight as fast as possible, and repetition days mean you will try to perform sets of higher repetitions to aid the development of both the max effort and dynamic effort workouts.

Also in this section I use terminology such as RM behind exercises. This mean that for a given repetition range you will seek to do the heaviest weight possible to only complete those repetitions. For example if I put down a 5RM, that means you would do those 5 reps with the heaviest weight you could so you can only get out 5-reps. Therefore to "work up to a 5RM" might mean I do 4 to 6-sets to get to a point where I max out at 5RM.

In addition I will also state that I will want you to "work up to a _RM". What this means is if I want a final 5RM you will perform at least 4 to 5-sets with a lighter submaximal weight (for 5-reps) and build up until you max out with the heaviest weight you can for those 5-reps.

July 16th to August 26th (6-weeks), Summer of 2007

Week 1
Monday – Max Effort Upper Body
1. Dips, work up to a 6RM
2. 1-Arm rows, 3x8 reps/arm
3. Barbell Shoulder Press, 4x8 reps
4. Hungarian Press, 3x12 reps
5. Side Shoulder Raises, 3x8 reps/side

Wednesday – Max Effort Lower Body
1. Squats (wide stance), work up to a 6RM
2. Step-ups (with barbell), 3x8reps/side
3. Cross-overs, 4 sets of 8 reps (with added weight)
4. Seated Calf Raises, work up to a 8RM
5. Plate Drags, 3x8 reps

Friday – Repetition Day
1. Push-ups, 5 sets of max reps (60 seconds rest between sets)
2. Pull-ups, 5 sets of max reps (60 seconds rest between sets)
3. Bar External Rotations, 3x12 reps
4. Plate Raises, 4x8 reps
5. Barbell Shrugs, 3x6 reps

Saturday – Dynamic Effort Lower body
1. Box Jumps, 6x8 reps (jump onto a box that is as high as possible)
2. Jump Lunges, 3x12/leg (with added weight)
3. DB/KB Power Cleans, 4x5 reps/side (as heavy a weight as possible)
4. Speed Skater Jumps, 3x8 reps (holding added weight)
5. Squat Pulls, 4x6reps

Week 2
Monday – Max Effort Upper Body
1. Dips, work up to a 4RM
2. 1-Arm rows, 4x6 reps/arm
3. Barbell Shoulder Press, 4x6 reps
4. Hungarian Press, 3x10 reps
5. Side Shoulder Raises, 3x6 reps/side

Wednesday – Max Effort Lower Body
1. Squats (wide stance), work up to a 5RM
2. Step-ups (with barbell), 4x8reps/side
3. Cross-overs, 4 sets of 6 reps/side (with added weight)
4. Seated Calf Raises, work up to a 6RM
5. Plate Drags, 3x6 reps

Friday – Repetition Day
1. Push-ups, 5 sets of max reps (60 seconds rest between sets)
2. Pull-ups, 5 sets of max reps (60 seconds rest between sets)
3. Bar External Rotations, 3x10 reps
4. Plate Raises, 4x6 reps
5. Barbell Shrugs, 4x5 reps

Saturday – Dynamic Effort Lower body
1. Box Jumps, 8x6 reps (jump onto a box that is as high as possible)
2. Jump Lunges, 3x12/leg (with added weight)
3. DB/KB Power Cleans, 4x5 reps/side (as heavy a weight as possible)
4. Speed Skater Jumps, 3x8 reps (holding added weight)
5. Squat Pulls, 4x5reps

Week 3
Monday – Max Effort Upper Body
1. Dips, work up to a 3RM
2. 1-Arm rows, 4x5 reps/arm
3. Barbell Shoulder Press, 4x5 reps
4. Hungarian Press, 3x8 reps
5. Side Shoulder Raises, 3x5 reps/side

Wednesday – Max Effort Lower Body
1. Squats (wide stance), work up to a 4RM
2. Step-ups (with barbell), 4x8reps
3. Cross-overs, 4 sets of 5 reps/side (with added weight)
4. Seated Calf Raises, work up to a 5RM
5. Plate Drags, 3x5 reps

Friday – Repetition Day
1. Push-ups, 6 sets of max reps (60 seconds rest between sets)
2. Pull-ups, 6 sets of max reps (60 seconds rest between sets)
3. Bar External Rotations, 3x8 reps
4. Plate Raises, 4x6 reps
5. Barbell Shrugs, 5x5 reps

Saturday – Dynamic Effort Lower body
1. Box Jumps, 8x6 reps (jump onto a box that is as high as possible)
2. Jump Lunges, 3x12/leg (with added weight)
3. DB/KB Power Cleans, 5x4 reps/side (as heavy a weight as possible)
4. Speed Skater Jumps, 3x8 reps (holding added weight)
5. Squat Pulls, 4x5reps

Week 4
Monday – Max Effort Upper Body
1. Close Grip Bench Press, work up to a 6RM
2. Chest Supported Rows, 4x8 reps
3. Externals on knee, 3x12 reps/side
4. 1-Arm Hungarian Press, 3x10 reps
5. Biceps Curls, 3x6 reps/side

Wednesday – Max Effort Lower Body
1. Squats (close stance), work up to a 6RM
2. Cross-over Step-ups (with barbell), 4x10reps/side
3. Hang Cleans, 3x6 reps
4. RDL, work up to a 6RM
5. Hockey Lunges, 3x8 reps/side

Friday – Repetition Day
1. Push-ups with feet up on a bench, 4 sets of max reps (45 seconds rest between sets)
2. Chin-ups, 4 sets of max reps (45 seconds rest between sets)
3. Side External Rotations, 3x12 reps/side
4. Dips, 3x10 reps
5. Barbell Jerks, 4x12 reps

Saturday – Dynamic Effort Lower body
1. Leg Box Jumps, 4x6 reps (jump onto a box that is as high as possible)
2. Jump Hockey Lunges, 3x12/leg (with added weight)
3. KB Swings, 3x5 reps/side (as heavy a weight as possible)
4. Standing Long Jump, 3x8 reps
5. Power Pulls, 3x5reps

Week 5
Monday – Max Effort Upper Body
1. Close Grip Bench Press, work up to a 5RM
2. Chest Supported Rows, 4x6 reps
3. Externals on knee, 3x10 reps/side
4. 1-Arm Hungarian Press, 3x8 reps
5. Biceps Curls, 3x5 reps/side

Wednesday – Max Effort Lower Body
1. Squats (close stance), work up to a 5RM
2. Cross-over Step-ups (with barbell), 4x8reps/side
3. Hang Cleans, 3x6 reps
4. RDL, work up to a 5RM
5. Hockey Lunges, 3x8 reps/side

Friday – Repetition Day
1. Push-ups with feet up on a bench, 5 sets of max reps (45 seconds rest between sets)
2. Chin-ups, 5 sets of max reps (45 seconds rest between sets)
3. Side External Rotations, 3x10 reps/side
4. Dips, 4x8 reps
5. Barbell Jerks, 4x10 reps

Saturday – Dynamic Effort Lower body
1. 1 Leg Box Jumps, 5x5 reps/side (jump onto a box that is as high as possible)
2. Jump Hockey Lunges, 3x10/leg (with added weight)
3. KB Swings, 3x4 reps/side (as heavy a weight as possible)
4. Standing Long Jump, 3x10 reps
5. Power Pulls, 3x4 reps

Week 6
Monday – Max Effort Upper Body
1. Close Grip Bench Press, work up to a 4RM
2. Chest Supported Rows, 4x8 reps
3. Externals on knee, 3x12 reps/side
4. 1-Arm Hungarian Press, 3x10 reps
5. Biceps Curls, 3x4 reps/side

Wednesday – Max Effort Lower Body
1. Squats (close stance), work up to a 4RM
2. Cross-over Step-ups (with barbell), 5x4reps/side
3. Hang Cleans, 3x5 reps
4. RDL, work up to a 4RM
5. Hockey Lunges, 3x8 reps/side

Friday – Repetition Day
1. Push-ups with feet up on a bench, 6 sets of max reps (45 seconds rest between sets)
2. Chin-ups, 6 sets of max reps (45 seconds rest between sets)
3. Side External Rotations, 3x8 reps/side
4. Dips, 3x6 reps
5. Barbell Jerks, 4x8 reps

Saturday – Dynamic Effort Lower body
1. 1 Leg Box Jumps, 6x5 reps/side (jump onto a box that is as high as possible)
2. Jump Hockey Lunges, 3x8/leg (with added weight)
3. KB Swings, 3x3 reps/side (as heavy a weight as possible)
4. Standing Long Jump, 3x12 reps
5. Power Pulls, 3x3reps

Core Training

Choose three exercises each day from the list of abdominal exercises (the "core training" chapter), and perform between 8 and 50-reps for 3-sets of each exercise as we have discussed before. Make sure to always choose different exercises and vary the repetitions ranges for maximal benefit. Log this information with your strength training and send this to me each week.

Conditioning

The following is your conditioning workouts:

Monday & Friday
Interval Runs – 400 meter runs.
After a good warm-up (light jogging and stretching) perform 1 – 400 meter run and then follow that up with 90 seconds of rest. Complete the required sets at maximum effort.

Weeks 1 & 2 = 8 intervals of 400 meters
Weeks 2 & 3 = 10 intervals of 400 meters
Week 4 = 6 intervals of 400 meters
Weeks 5 & 6 = 12 intervals of 400 meters

Tuesday & Thursday
Skate with Junior players/pros in Canmore, Alberta.

Wednesday & Saturdays
Sprints –
On sprinting days, go to the rec grounds (a large recreation facility, track, field, etc. in Banff), warm-up with some light jogging, easy stretching, and perform the standard hockey warm-up (see Warm-up chapter). After this, start off with some light sprinting. The first sprint I want you to run at 75% of your maximum speed so as not to pull anything. Walk back to the starting line, then sprint again, this time at 85% of max speed, and then walk back to start line. The third sprint you can work up to 90-95% of max speed, then walk back. The fourth sprint through the 10th sprint I want you to go all out and run like hell. THIS IS JUST THE WARM-UP! Now do the work portion of the workout, as follows:

- 25 meter sprints (run the sprint, walk back, sprint again)
- 50 meter sprints (run the sprint, walk back, sprint again)
- 25 meter grapevine crossovers (run the sprint, walk back, sprint again)
- 25 meter side shuffle sprints (do 5 side sprint on each side)
- 25 meter backwards sprints (run the sprint, walk back, sprint again)
- 25 meter repeated 2-leg standing long jumps (keep jumping with both feet for 25m, walk back, repeat).

Weeks 1 & 2 = 4-sets of each drill
Weeks 2 & 3 = 6-sets of each drill
Week 4 & 5 = 8-sets of each drill
Weeks 6 = 3-sets of each drill

Recovery

The following recovery methods are <u>required</u> each day:

→ Pre-workout shake (50 grams of carbohydrate powder + 25 grams of whey protein).

→ Adequate dryland warm-up before any training (on or off-ice).

→ Foam roll, (10 minutes AM, 10 minutes PM, 10 minutes after workouts before stretching).

→ Stretching or Yoga, (10 minutes AM, 10 minutes PM, 10 minutes after workouts after foam rolling).

→ Post Workout Shake, (100 grams of carbohydrate powder + 50 grams of whey protein powder).

→ Adequate hydration (4000ml or 120 ounces of water per day), more if necessary. See the Recovery Methods chapter for more information on hydration.

→ At least 8-hours of sleep per night, plus a 1-hour nap each afternoon.

→ Use the hot springs (Stephen lived in Banff back then during the off-season) several times per week (daily if possible), during your summer training (evening after dinner is best option).

→ At least one day OFF (Sunday in this case) is planned each week.

NOTES:

Remember, it's not the amount of training you do that matters... it's the amount of training you can do that you recover from and improve that matters! Write down your workouts, your nutrition schedule and any comments so you can email me each week.

Stephen Margeson playing for the Mississippi Riverskings (CHL) 2006

Chapter 5 - Sample In-Season Training Program

"Half the game is mental, the other half is being mental".

~ Jim McKenny (retired NHL defencemen & sports reporter)

In this section I provide an In-Season training program prepared for professional hockey player Justin Todd during the 2008/09 season where he played in Germany for the ERC 99 Sonthofen Bulls.

This program was designed to allow Justin a great deal of flexibility in his training so he could accommodate his hockey schedule with the limited dryland training options the team had available, while maintaining and improving his level of fitness during the hockey season. It is so important for players to at least hold their level of conditioning during the season so that the next season they can make gains right away.

The basic idea of this program is a form of the Russian Conjugate Method, only simplified and condensed into 45 to 60 minute workouts, 2 times per week. The goal is to keep Justin strong and in shape, not slow his progress on the ice by making him sore with dryland workouts.

Far too often in-season training programs either neglect weight training and dryland conditioning, or even worse, it over-train athletes which ultimately has a negative effect on their performance.

As Justin is an advanced trainee (425lb for a 3RM squat for instance), and since I have worked with him for over 8-years, I trust his decision-making process on when to schedule his assigned workouts and when to back off and rest. We talk on the phone once per week or via email so that I know what he is doing and can provide feedback on his training.

Strength Training

In order to keep your fitness level high and accommodate your hockey schedule I have prepared two main workouts per week with the goal of maintaining strength and explosiveness. Use them during the week starting with the Max Effort Day early in the week (Monday or Tuesday), and the Dynamic Effort Day later in the week (many games are during the weekends). Make sure to schedule the Dynamic workout with one day rest between game day. If you have multiple games it's okay to schedule two Dynamic workouts (say on Thursday, and then on Saturday after a game).

As usual, I use terminology such as RM behind exercises. This mean that for a given repetition range you will seek to do the heaviest weight possible to only complete those repetitions. For example if I put down a 5RM that means you would do those 5-reps with the heaviest weight you could so you only can get out 5-reps. Therefore to "work up to a 5RM" might mean I do 4 to 6-sets to get to a point where I max out at 5RM.

In addition I will also state that I will want you to "work up to a _RM". What this means is if I want a final 5RM you will perform at least 4 to 5-sets with a lighter submaximal weight (for 5-reps) and build up until you max out with the heaviest weight you can for those 5 reps.

November 3rd to December 14th (6-weeks), 2008

Week 1
Training Session 1 - Max Effort Day

A1	Barbell Squats	Work up to a 3RM
B1	Bench Press	3x5 reps
B2	Supported Horizontal Rows	3x5 reps
C1	Power Pulls	2x12 reps
C2	External Rotations on knee	2x12 reps/side
C3	Plate Drags	2x12/side
D1	RDL	3x5 reps
D1	Cable Skating Abduction	3x15 reps/side

Training Session 2 - Dynamic Effort Lower body

A1	Box Squat into Box Jump	3x10 reps
A2	Hang Cleans	3x5 reps
B1	Plyometric Push-ups	3x maximum reps
B2	Pull-ups with band assistance	3x maximum reps
C1	Modified Russian Box Jumps	2x15 reps/side
C2	Bench Band Pull-ins	2x15 reps
D1	KB Snatches	2x15 reps/side
D2	KB Jerks	2x15 reps/side
E1	Slideboard Intervals	10x30 seconds with 30 seconds rest between

Week 2
Training Session 1 - Max Effort Day

A1	Barbell Squats	Work up to a 3RM
B1	Bench Press	3x5 reps
B2	Supported Horizontal Rows	3x5 reps
C1	Power Pulls	2x12 reps
C2	External Rotations on knee	2x12 reps/side
C3	Plate Drags	2x12/side
D1	RDL	3x5 reps
D1	Cable Skating Abduction	3x15 reps/side

Training Session 2 - Dynamic Effort Lower body

A1	Box Squat into Box Jump	3x10 reps
A2	Hang Cleans	3x5 reps
B1	Plyometric Push-ups	3x maximum reps
B2	Pull-ups with band assistance	3x maximum reps
C1	Modified Russian Box Jumps	2x15 reps/side
C2	Bench Band Pull-ins	2x15 reps
D1	KB Snatches	2x15 reps/side
D2	KB Jerks	2x15 reps/side
E1	Slideboard Intervals	10x30 seconds with 30 seconds rest between

Week 3
Training Session 1 - Max Effort Day

A1	Barbell Squats	Work up to a 3RM
B1	Bench Press	3x5 reps
B2	Supported Horizontal Rows	3x5 reps
C1	Power Pulls	2x12 reps
C2	External Rotations on knee	2x12 reps/side
C3	Plate Drags	2x12/side
D1	RDL	3x5 reps
D1	Cable Skating Abduction	3x15 reps/side

Training Session 2 - Dynamic Effort Lower body

A1	Box Squat into Box Jump	3x10 reps
A2	Hang Cleans	3x5 reps
B1	Plyometric Push-ups	3x maximum reps
B2	Pull-ups with band assistance	3x maximum reps
C1	Modified Russian Box Jumps	2x15 reps/side
C2	Bench Band Pull-ins	2x15 reps
D1	KB Snatches	2x15 reps/side
D2	KB Jerks	2x15 reps/side
E1	Slideboard Intervals	10x30 seconds with 30 seconds rest between

Week 4
Training Session 1 - Max Effort Day

A1	Barbell Squats	Work up to a 3RM
B1	Bench Press	3x5 reps
B2	Supported Horizontal Rows	3x5 reps
C1	Power Pulls	2x12 reps
C2	External Rotations on knee	2x12 reps/side
C3	Plate Drags	2x12/side
D1	RDL	3x5 reps
D1	Cable Skating Abduction	3x15 reps/side

Training Session 2 - Dynamic Effort Lower body

A1	Box Squat into Box Jump	3x10 reps
A2	Hang Cleans	3x5 reps
B1	Plyometric Push-ups	3x maximum reps
B2	Pull-ups with band assistance	3x maximum reps
C1	Modified Russian Box Jumps	2x15 reps/side
C2	Bench Band Pull-ins	2x15 reps
D1	KB Snatches	2x15 reps/side
D2	KB Jerks	2x15 reps/side
E1	Slideboard Intervals	10x30 seconds with 30 seconds rest between

Week 5
Training Session 1 - Max Effort Day
A1	Barbell Squats	Work up to a 3RM
B1	Bench Press	3x5 reps
B2	Supported Horizontal Rows	3x5 reps
C1	Power Pulls	2x12 reps
C2	External Rotations on knee	2x12 reps/side
C3	Plate Drags	2x12/side
D1	RDL	3x5 reps
D1	Cable Skating Abduction	3x15 reps/side

Training Session 2 - Dynamic Effort Lower body
A1	Box Squat into Box Jump	3x10 reps
A2	Hang Cleans	3x5 reps
B1	Plyometric Push-ups	3x maximum reps
B2	Pull-ups with band assistance	3x maximum reps
C1	Modified Russian Box Jumps	2x15 reps/side
C2	Bench Band Pull-ins	2x15 reps
D1	KB Snatches	2x15 reps/side
D2	KB Jerks	2x15 reps/side
E1	Slideboard Intervals	10x30 seconds with 30 seconds rest between

Week 6
Training Session 1 - Max Effort Day
A1	Barbell Squats	Work up to a 3RM
B1	Bench Press	3x5 reps
B2	Supported Horizontal Rows	3x5 reps
C1	Power Pulls	2x12 reps
C2	External Rotations on knee	2x12 reps/side
C3	Plate Drags	2x12/side
D1	RDL	3x5 reps
D1	Cable Skating Abduction	3x15 reps/side

Training Session 2 - Dynamic Effort Lower body
A1	Box Squat into Box Jump	3x10 reps
A2	Hang Cleans	3x5 reps
B1	Plyometric Push-ups	3x maximum reps
B2	Pull-ups with band assistance	3x maximum reps
C1	Modified Russian Box Jumps	2x15 reps/side
C2	Bench Band Pull-ins	2x15 reps
D1	KB Snatches	2x15 reps/side
D2	KB Jerks	2x15 reps/side
E1	Slideboard Intervals	10x30 seconds with 30 seconds rest between

Core Training

Choose three exercises each day from the list of abdominal exercises (the "core training" chapter), and perform between 8 and 50-reps for 3-sets of each exercise as we have discussed before. Make sure to always choose different exercises and vary the repetitions ranges for maximal benefit. Log this information with your strength training and send this to me each week.

Conditioning

During the season I hesitate to schedule any conditioning work for players as I usually am not around to monitor what they are doing on the ice (for practices and games) and I find that most coaches frown on extra conditioning work that might take away from performance on the ice. I agree, but it also depends on the demands of the player in question. If we are talking about a junior player who is on the 4th line and gets 8-minutes of ice time per game then we can add in conditioning work. If it's an AHL pro who is one of the top 2-defencemen and plays 25-minutes a night they most likely need more recovery than extra conditioning sessions. Only you will know what is necessary. In the case of Justin he did not need any additional conditioning work while in Germany as he practiced 4 to 5-days per week on the larger Olympic ice surface and played at least 2-games per week (on the first line).

Recovery

The following recovery methods are <u>required</u> each day:

- → Pre-workout shake (50 grams of carbohydrate powder + 25 grams of whey protein). Use this pre-workout shake before games.

- → Between periods use either diluted orange juice or Gatorade Recover drink to help recovery.

- → Adequate dryland warm-up before any training (on or off-ice).

- → Foam roll, (10 minutes AM, 10 minutes PM, 10 minutes after workouts or games before stretching).

- → Stretching or Yoga, (10 minutes AM, 10 minutes PM, 10 minutes after workouts or games after foam rolling).

- → Post Workout Shake, (100 grams of carbohydrate powder + 50 grams of whey protein powder). Use this type of shake after games and practices as well.

- → Use the cool-water tub following games for faster recovery if necessary, and at night when required.

- → Adequate hydration (4000ml or 120 ounces of water per day), more if necessary. See the Recovery Methods chapter for more information on hydration.

- → At least 8 hours of sleep per night, plus a 1-hour nap each afternoon (especially on game days).

- → Limit drinking alcohol 1-day before games and on game day to stay hydrated and limit the negative effects. If traveling by plane also avoid alcohol. Post-game alcohol is not the best recovery solution, but not as bad if you make sure to drink equal parts water. *(NOTE: Justin is 28 and plays in Germany so the team WILL go out for beers following a game).*

NOTES:

- *The periodization for in-season programming is always dictated by the hockey program (and coach). How much you practice/play, on what days, and for how long are often not under your control. Therefore I plan strength training with most programs twice a week in-season so as not to disturb the periodization plan of the coach too much.*

- *Remember, it's not the amount of training you do that matters... it's the amount of training you can do that you recover from and improve that matters! Record workouts, nutrition schedule, practice schedules, ice time, game stats and any other information that will be useful when evaluating the training program effectiveness following the season.*

Chapter 6 - Physical Testing

"The important thing is this: to be able to sacrifice at any moment what we are, for what we could become."

~ **Chinese Proverb**

Ok, so now we have an overall idea of what the year is going to look like and we've seen some sample programs. Now it's time to find out some physical readiness information. With every player or team I work with I always insist on testing physical abilities both on and off the ice with a variety of methods to determine a player's ability. How can a program be set up for an athlete if I don't know where they started, or later if they have made any progress with training?

It is essential to test players in a manner that replicates the demands seen on the ice as much as possible. Standardized tests such as the 1-mile run or the MVO2 bike test do not correlate well for hockey as this is an interval based sport rather than a steady state activity as those tests focus on. You cannot test or train a hockey player by having them run for a long distance or ride a bike as this never happens on the ice. Testing has to focus on what makes a great hockey player. Test for those qualities and then develop those skills with a sound physical training program both on and off the ice.

Due to these guidelines for testing athletes I have modified existing testing protocols or created entirely new testing procedures so that players, coaches and trainers can determine real hockey abilities from physical testing. As I am developing a data base on all of these numbers you can send testing data from any of the physical tests in this book to me through the website at **www.dphockey.com**, and I will log this into my data for future standardization. I have provided a blank testing data form (APPENDIX A), that players can photo copy and use for testing purposes throughout the year.

Testing however, should not dominate your season as the focus should be on playing hockey. While I have included all of my preferred tests for hockey, coaches are advised to only use some of these tests each year with players. These tests require a minimal amount of equipment and set up time so that coaches can focus on building hockey players. Under most circumstances, I usually do full testing **only 3 (often less) times per year**: early offseason, training camp and midseason. This way I find out important information to improve the training stimulus but do not over-stress athletes with testing. However, I do schedule monthly testing of one or two certain skills (such as the 300-yard shuttle run, bench press & deadlift) to see where a team or player is at, rather than a full battery of tests.

Base Testing

Before physical testing starts I always perform dryland evaluations that include many useful tests where I can learn more information about a player. I start with a traditional 4 page questionnaire that lists things like nutritional habits, training issues, previous injuries, current injuries, and future goals.

From this point I move into testing resting heart-rate, resting blood pressure, weight, height, and girth measurements. After I have that base line data, I move to body-fat testing. Body fat testing is much more important than weight for instance, as the more fat a player carries the more this negatively impacts on-ice performance. In regards to body-fat testing my goal is for all hockey players to be in the 8 to 12% body-fat percent range to maximize the strength to body weight ratio on the ice. Outside this range and a player will carry too much fat to maximize agility and power on the ice. In my evaluations of players over the years I have found these ranges to be of value:

→8-12% Body Fat (optimal)

→13-16% Body Fat (borderline)

→17-20% Body Fat (needs improvement)

→20%+ Body Fat (lots of work to do)

NOTE: In the NHL entry draft the evaluator's state in their pre-evaluation report "In order to perform optimally a hockey player should aim for 9.5% or less body fat (determined by the Yuhasz equation)."

All of this information is used as a baseline so that throughout the season I can monitor these numbers and stay on top of an athlete's progress. For example, if I know the baseline resting heart-rate and weight of an athlete, and have them monitor this throughout the season I can find out when overtraining may start to occur based on an increased average resting heart rate and decreased average body weight. Coaches who do not monitor these factors may never know if an athlete has fully recovered from training or is burning out during a season. In my mind I agree with noted strength and conditioning coach Istvan Javorek when he mentions that "daily pulse and bodyweight checks can be a very effective mirror of an athlete's level of preparation, and this should be considered one of the most important duties for every strength and conditioning or hockey coach".

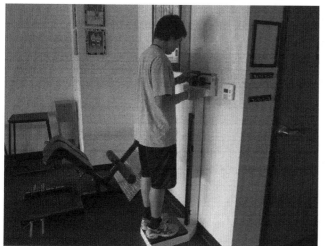 

WHL prospect Bryan Hodges checking his weight prior to a training session (picture 1), and being evaluated with the Functional Movement Screen step-over test (picture 2) prior to testing.

Following the standard testing I move on to the Functional Movement Screening. Developed by physical therapy expert Gray Cook, this evaluation helps coaches determine players who may be at risk for injury based on their movement patterns, flexibility and body coordination. When evaluated with other physical testing, experienced coaches can look at the data and start to plan appropriate training programs and conditioning regiments for each hockey player, rather than "cookie cutter programs" that many teams still use year after year.

It is important to note that players, coaches and trainers should attempt to make each and every test as safe as possible so that injuries **DO NOT HAPPEN**. The goal for testing is to set the standard for all future evaluations and to assist the hockey coaches with information for on-ice practices and performance. Some testing such as 1RM (repetition maximum) testing can be very useful but also very dangerous for the novice lifter or for teams that rush through testing. Injuries should **NEVER** occur from dryland testing or training.

Strength Testing

If players want to be fast on the ice they must also have a high strength to body weight ratio. Testing in this area should be a true measure of performance and not expose the athlete to possible injury that can happen with certain tests. In younger players (less than 16 years of age), I generally stay away from the heavy deadlift or squat tests as I do not believe the risk to reward value of this test is worth it, especially in these younger athletes who often do not have the necessary experience to perform these tests correctly. Carolina Hurricane's Strength Coach Peter Friesen backs this up as he mentioned to me that he does not use exercises that can stress the lumbar spine and discs during physical testing such as the back squat. Having said that, older players with more lifting experience such as juniors, college and pros should do <u>at least</u> 3 or 5 repetition maximum testing (the highest load that can be used in correct form for either 3 repetitions or 5 repetitions), to evaluate players strength. When I'm able I like to use a 1RM test for certain exercises as outlined later in this chapter.

Basic Strength Testing

In this section below I have picked out my favorite field tests that are easy to implement in a short period of time (so a team can get through basic dryland testing in a morning if needed).

Maximum Push-ups in 2-Minutes

Performing the maximum push-up test in 2-minutes requires a great deal of upper body strength and endurance. Unlike the bench press that isolates the upper body musculature, the push-up test engages the core muscles into the test along with the upper body to create a highly effective test.

To perform this test players will start flat on the ground, face down with hands under them and with a flat, board like body push themselves up to lock out. Lower yourself down to the starting position without flexing or dipping the middle part of the body. When the player cannot perform any more repetitions, rests on the ground for <u>more than a second</u>, or their form deviates from the correct technique on three consecutive repetitions (that do not count), the test is finished.

Start flat on the ground and push up to full extension...repeat. DO NOT REST on the ground.

For this test the following standards are recognized:

→68 Repetitions = 100%   →44 Repetitions = 70%
→60 Repetitions = 90%   →36 Repetitions = 60%
→52 Repetitions = 80%   →28 Repetitions = 50%

NOTE: For all players I consider a passing grade in push-ups to be over 80% (52 reps), and most players should be able to work up to 68+ repetitions.

Maximum Sit-ups in 2-Minutes

The sit-up test is a good overall field test of the abdominal and hip flexor musculature. To perform this test correctly lay down on your back with the knees bent at 90 degrees. The legs are held either by an object or by another person. Hold the hands on the head (without ever letting go of the head during the test). Curl up so the elbows go over the knees and then return back to the starting position so your shoulder blades contact the ground. If you stop to rest during the test your test is finished. If you raise the hips to perform a repetition, remove your hands from your head or fail to curl up so your elbows go over your knees that repetition will not count towards your total for the test.

When testing set the timer at 2-minutes and perform as many sit-ups as possible within that time allowed with perfect form. If you need a high number to shoot for in testing try beating the top Navy SEAL (in BUDS class 228), LtJG Bill Gallagher who completed 158 perfect sit-ups in 2-minutes.

For this test the following standards are recognized:

→78 Repetitions = 100%   →59 Repetitions = 70%
→72 Repetitions = 90%   →53 Repetitions = 60%
→66 Repetitions = 80%   →47 Repetitions = 50%

NOTE: For all players I consider a passing grade in sit-ups to be over 80% (66 reps), and over time some players should be able to crank out 90+ sit-ups in 2-minutes.

NCAA division I basketball player Julie Young (Arizona State) performs sit-ups for testing

Maximum Pull-up Repetitions

College player Cody Kreger performs pull-ups as part of his off-season testing

Pull-ups are a good overall measure of upper body strength, muscular endurance and body balance between pushing and pulling muscles. To start the test jump up and grab the bar with an over-handed grip, 10 to 16 inches apart and hang so the body doesn't move around with the arms straight (see below).

From the starting position, lift yourself up and bring your chin over the bar (see above) without moving your legs all over the place. Lower yourself back down to a straight arm hang and repeat this action.

When you can't do another repetition or your technique deteriorates by any curling up of the legs the test is done. Have someone watch that you do this test correctly (it's easy to cheat).

A good starting number for this test is 15+ repetitions for players less than 160lbs, 10+ repetitions for players between 160 to 200lbs, and 7+ for players over 200lbs.

Standing Long Jump

The standing long jump is a good field test to measure a player's ability to generate leg power in a horizontal movement. An added benefit of this test is it is very easy to implement with an entire team in a very short period of time and will not require any external loading of the spine. To perform this test a player stands on a line (no pre-movement), squats down and jumps forward as far as possible. The distance from the line to the heels of the players feet are measured to determine the distance jumped. Each player is allowed three attempts and the longest distance is recorded.

For this test the following standards are recognized:

→ >250cm (100in) = **excellent**
→ 230cm (92in) = **average**
→ <190cm (76in) = **poor**

1-Leg Lateral Standing Long Jump

This tests a player's ability to generate one leg power in a similar plane of action as on the ice. Players are scored from the inside of the jumping foot to the inside of the landing foot (test both sides 2x each). Scoring is as follows:

Men
→ >195cm (78in) = **excellent**
→ 160cm (64in) = **average**
→ <125cm (50in) = **poor**

Women
→ >170cm (68in) = **excellent**
→ 135cm (54in) = **average**
→ <100cm (40in) = **poor**

Grip Test

Bryan performs the grip test (picture 1), and shows the result (62kgs, or 137lbs of force), (picture 2)

The grip test is completed with a specialized piece of equipment called a Grip Dynamometer made by a company called Jamar. It tests general upper body strength, and more specifically grip strength through the ability to grip an object maximally. To perform the test you grip the dynamometer, hold it with a straight arm to the side and grip the handle as hard as possible for 3 to 5 seconds. Record the number on the dial (the red hand, see above), and try the other hand. Perform a total of 2-tests on each hand and take the best number as your testing result.

In terms of results, I like to see women with grip strength in the 40 to 50+ kg range, and men in the 52 to 65kg range. Pro players should aim for a grip strength of greater than 70kg (>155lbs). If these numbers are less than the suggested range please consult chapter 13, "Grip Training" on ways of developing your grip.

Weighted Sled Pull

Using the weighted sled pull is a great way for an entire team to evaluate leg strength and conditioning in a safe and controlled manner. As roughly 85% of all skating is done on one leg, it stands to reason that testing should try to mimic this performance condition.

To perform the test I load up a standard 28lb sled with 2-45lb weight plates, (118lbs total) and set a course of 40 meters (the same as the sprint test distance). Players are fitted with a shoulder harness attached to the weighted sled and then step forward to tighten the chain as they stand on the starting line.

On the signal from the coach the player attempts to maximally accelerate the heavy sled over the same 40 meter course, while the coach starts the stopwatch. When the player reaches the finish line the stopwatch is stopped and the time is recorded. Players get 2 attempts to record the best possible time. A good time for the weighted sled pull is anything less than 8 seconds.

Advanced Strength Testing

In order to properly evaluate elite level athletes it becomes necessary to use more technically advanced lifts with greater loads for 1 repetition lifts (1 rep max or 1RM). These tests are only mentioned for elite players with at least 2 years of weight training experience and who are at least 15 years of age. In addition, it is critical that the player have good form when completing these lifts under the supervision of a qualified strength coach and with spotters present.

1RM Power Snatch
The power snatch is a complex and dynamic version of the Snatch Olympic lift. In terms of evaluating athletes I use the power snatch to measure the power production capabilities of the posterior chain muscles (the hamstrings, glutes and low back). As a lighter weight is used for this lift compared to the power clean, this enables the player to move the barbell faster and provides a good assessment of the velocity side of the force-velocity curve in the lower body. This exercise also involves the hamstrings more than the quadriceps such as during the skating stride and due to the wide hand placement requires the player to bend their knees more which works these muscles through a greater range of motion.

Pro hockey player Kevin Flather performing a basic power snatch during training in Vancouver, BC

When testing the power snatch it should be performed as a maximum single (1RM) rather than with multiple reps. Lift the barbell from the floor (as shown in picture 1 above) to overhead (picture 3) all in one explosive motion. Consult the "Olympic Lifting" chapter in this book for more information on this lift and watch this exercise in the online video section. It is <u>very important</u> that a lifter know how to perform the power snatch and have experience with this lift before a 1RM lift is performed.

1-RM Front Squat

Kevin demonstrates the full range of motion seen in the front squat

When testing advanced hockey players the number one test I use to determine leg strength is the front squat. Numerous strength and conditioning coaches have moved to the front squat as a safer and more "back friendly" exercise but I like this test as it effectively evaluates the force side of the force-velocity curve in the lower body. While players can often find ways to cheat during the traditional back squat it is very difficult to cheat with the front squat. Good form must be maintained or the lifter will lose the lift (fail to complete the repetition). Additionally the front squat helps a coach assess the flexibility in ankles, knees, and hips very quickly as all of these are key to performing this lift properly. I find that players with high front squat numbers are the ones who put time in the gym over the summer.

This test is **NOT** recommended for players younger than 18-years of age and/or for players with less than 12-months of training under their belt. Players must exhibit good form with lighter weights before they should ever be allowed to use heavy or maximal weights.

Start the front squat by stepping under the bar so the bar is in front of the body under the chin with the hands shoulder width apart (see picture 1 above). When in this basic position, pull the shoulder blades tightly together and arch your back to lock the back into a good position, and then push outwards with the abdominal muscles, and generally hold the body tight throughout the lift. Set the feet shoulder width apart and make sure your <u>knees track over the toes</u>. Descend by breaking at the hips, and then the knees as you lower downwards. Use a 40X tempo (4 seconds down, 0 seconds rest at the bottom, and then rise up as fast as possible). Remember to keep the trunk upright throughout the lift (as seen in picture 2). At the bottom position (when the hamstrings touch the upper calf muscles), start to rise upward with the legs. On the ascent make sure your hips and shoulders come up at the **SAME TIME** to prevent the back from losing its angle and stressing the low back.

To perform the test, players should start out with lighter weights and perform progressively heavier sets of 3 repetitions. As you get closer to your 1-RM, reduce the repetitions to 1 rep. It should take you 5 to 6 sets to reach your max weight. For example, if I wanted to find the 1-RM of a pro-player like Kevin Flather (whose 1-rep max is currently 315lbs), his front squat warm-up would go like this:

→135lbs x 5 reps
→185lbs x 3 reps
→225lbs x 3 reps
→285lbs x 1 rep
→305lbs x 1 rep
→320lbs x 1 rep (trying for a new personal best 1-RM squat)

As you can see, I structured this testing session so that Kevin does not actually do a lot of reps to hit his maximum weight, but is enough to fully warm-up the squatting muscles and mentally prepare him for the heavy load of the 1-RM front squat. This type of formula should be used with **EVERY** type of 1-RM lift.

NOTE: I also test players with 3RM or 5RM lifts (front squat, squat, deadlift, RDL, bench and pull-ups) throughout the year. In fact, I believe that most players should not go for a true 1RM test more than 4 times a year. Therefore, lighter tests in the 3RM or 5RM range are perfect to keep up with regular testing to see if the program is on track, but are less stressful than a 1RM test.

1RM Incline Barbell Bench Press

Justin grinds out 20 repetitions with 55lbs in the incline DB bench press

While many players, coaches and teams use the bench press as the "gold standard" for evaluations the incline bench press actually has a much more practical application as it more closely simulates many of the actions used in hockey (from punching to battling for a puck). This exercise also helps to determine the overall balance from the chest to the shoulders at this intermediate pressing angle. As an additional caveat it demands that a player spend time on this lift as opposed to just performing rep after rep of the standard bench press (which can over time create all kinds of shoulder imbalance issues).

To perform this exercise, lie back on a bench that is set to 45 degrees, hold the barbell (shown with dumbbells in the picture above), with a shoulder width grip. Lower the barbell to the upper chest and then push straight up (as shown above). Make sure to have a spotter (or two) in place before performing this 1RM lift.

Evaluating the Results

Elite strength & conditioning coach Charles Poliquin has developed a system of evaluating the above three lifts against each other to determine general weak areas and potential spots for muscle or training imbalances. I have used this system of evaluation for a while as one of my methods of assessing a hockey player while also helping me to correct physical preparation issues.

→**Front Squat: 100%**
→**Incline Bench Press: 73%**
→**Power Snatch: 65%**

When applying this information into your specific results the ratio's for each lift is based off of the front squat load. Therefore a player with a 315lb front squat should have a 230lb incline bench press number and a 205lb power snatch. Here are some general guidelines with regard to these ratios:

Front Squat
- >100% (work on more speed development and/or reduce the lower body workouts)
- <100% (increase strength in the lower body immediately)

Incline Bench Press
- >73% (then focus on more lower body strength and/or speed development)
- <73% (work on developing the upper body in relation to the stronger legs)

Power Snatch
- >65% (then the focus should be on strength training the lower body)
- <65% (focus on more speed development in the lower body)

NOTE: *You can find out more about Charles Poliquin online at* www.charlespoliquin.com

1-RM Deadlift

NCAA division III player Justin Anonas (Wentworth) starting the deadlift (picture 1) and near lockout (picture 2)

The deadlift is an easy to perform test of maximal strength. Start with your shoulders over the bar (critical), back flat, head up and with an alternating grip (one hand with palms facing forward and the other facing backwards). Rise up from the start (the head and shoulders must rise the SAME TIME as the hips). Continue to a full lockout with the legs, back and arms straight (not shown in these pictures). Return to the start position (under control), by lowering the bar in the same manner as you pulled it from the floor.

For testing, players should warm-up with lighter deadlifts in sets of 3-repetitions until you approach your maximum weight and then reduce the final warm-up sets to 1-repetition only. It should take you at least 5-6 sets to get to the point where you can try for a maximum lift (see the example shown above with 1RM squats). At this point pick a weight you think you can do once, try it and see. If you make the weight then take a 3 to 5 minute break and add weight to the bar. You should only try for a maximum lift 3-times with the deadlift and no more. If after three tries you cannot break your personal best, then use the last weight lifted as your testing number.

As the deadlift is a 1RM strength test I only allow experienced lifters (8-months of training at the minimum) to complete this test. Younger players (less than 16) should be able to pull 225lbs from the floor while older junior and college age players should pull at least 365lbs for a 1RM. Currently my best junior aged player for the 1RM deadlift is Justin Anonas, who pulled 485lbs at 18-years of age before playing 4-years at Wentworth (NCAA DIII).

Speed & Agility Testing

Hockey players need to be fast, agile and very powerful to compete at the highest level. The following are some of the speed and agility tests I use with hockey players:

40-Yard Sprint

While this test doesn't really tell me how fast you will be on the ice (skating technique does play a large role in on-ice testing performance), it gives a pretty good indication of your potential ability to accelerate. I prefer the 40-yard test as hockey players should just be hitting a full stride by the end of the test as opposed to an 80 or 100 meter test which opens the hips too much in the full stride and actually can cause injury. This test is more effective in the off-season (as there is not as much snow on the ground), but you can always find a gym or university track that is indoors and you can use for testing. Use a stopwatch (preferably with someone else timing).

When marking off your 40-yards note that it converts to 36.57 meters or 120 feet. Use a rolling measuring tape or a tape measure with a buddy prior to running the test to ensure accuracy. Make sure you do a good warm-up of 5 to 10 minutes of easy jogging and then several short sprints before the 40-yard test. Have a friend/coach/teammate time you with a reliable stopwatch. Perform 3 sprints, (with 2-5 minutes between sprints as a rest) to get the best time possible. A very good time for the 40-yard test is anything under 4.5 seconds, and players should aim for less than 5.3 seconds.

12' Agility Test

Justin Todd runs through the 12' agility drill/test at Revolution Athletics in Orange, California

The 12-foot agility drill is one of my favourite tests of a player's ability to move side to side, accelerate and decelerate, and change directions quickly. To start, place two hockey sticks 12 feet apart with one cone in the middle. The player starts at the cone in the middle and runs to the right, touching one foot over the hockey stick, and then running left to the other hockey stick and crossing over that stick. This side to side running continues for 10 total repetitions (5-each way as shown in diagram 2). Make sure that the player faces forward during the entire drill and holds a hockey stick in one hand to simulate an on-ice situation (see pictures above). The clock stops when the player returns to the middle cone after 10-repetitions. The best time to date with this test is 10.68 seconds, but a good time is anything close to 12-seconds. Players who are heavier or do not possess adequate strength to body weight ratios will have times in the 13 to 15 second range. I use this drill as both a test and a agility training drill as it combines many different skills in an easy to perform test.

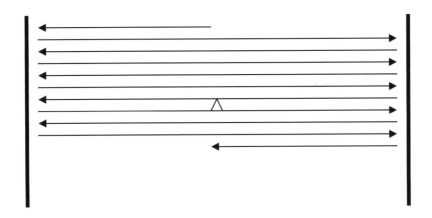

Diagram 10 – The 12' Lateral Agility Test

Conditioning Tests

Testing a player's conditioning is important to know if they have been training hard in the off-season and to find out possible deficiencies or potential areas of injury. At training camps for junior, major junior, college and professional teams they use a variety of testing methods that usually include some form of bike MVO2 test, 1.5 mile run or even repeated line drills on the ice with little rest which is hardly game specific.

The following are some of my favorite conditioning tests to determine cardiovascular fitness levels and general physical abilities for hockey players. Choose-1 of the following tests for your hockey player or team and use that for the entire season, rather than performing all three tests each time. Adjust the tests as needed for different ages and abilities, and make sure that testing is done for a purpose, not just for the sake of testing.

20-Meter Beep Test

The Beep test is a simple to use test of your VO²Max (the maximum amount of oxygen you can take and use at the cellular level), as well as your mental focus and ability to withstand pain. Many NHL teams such as the Florida Panthers and Phoenix Coyotes use this test at training camp to determine a player's conditioning and mental ability to keep going when the legs and lungs are burning.

To set up the course you mark out 2-lines 20-meters apart (on cement), and then start the beep test on your portable stereo. It requires a special audio CD that will give a series of beeps. You only have a certain amount of time to run from one line to the next before the CD signals a "beep", and players must be at the line when the "beep" sounds. If a player misses two consecutive "beeps" they are done with the test and the level they made it is recorded.

I suggest that coaches or athletes buy the 20-Meter Beep online at Amazon. The best part of the Beep test is that it is pretty accurate in determining a players conditioning and coaches are able to test the entire hockey team in a short period of time (about 25-minutes).

Shuttle Run Test

The shuttle run test was designed to evaluate a player's ability to accelerate, decelerate, and change directions over and over again. This drill consists of repeated 100-meter line sprints starting every 60 seconds.

A player (or team) starts on a line or cone, and on the "start" command from the coach who begins a timer, the player sprints to the first line or cone that is 5-meters away. The player touches the line and sprints back to touch the starting line. Now the player sprints to the second cone or line, touches it, and sprints back to touch the starting line. Repeat this out and back process to the third line and then the forth line. Sprinting to all 4-lines (or cones) and back is considered one set (100-meters), and should take players roughly 25 to 30-seconds to complete (when fresh).

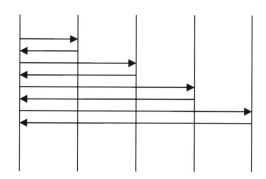

Diagram 11 – Shuttle Run Test

When an athlete cannot complete a set in the 60-seconds allowed, the test is finished for that player and the level they achieved is recorded (along with the time it took to finish the last set). For example a player might have the following times and rest intervals:

Set 1 = 25 seconds sprinting, 35 seconds rest
Set 2 = 29 seconds sprinting, 31 seconds rest
Set 3 = 35 seconds sprinting, 25 seconds rest
Set 4 = 39 seconds sprinting, 21 seconds rest
Set 5 = 45 seconds sprinting, 15 seconds rest
Set 6 = 52 seconds sprinting, 8 seconds rest
Set 7 = 56 seconds sprinting, 4 seconds rest
Set 8 = 69 seconds sprinting – TEST STOPPED (484 seconds recorded)

The coach would record that the player completed 8-sets of the test and the time (in seconds) it took to finish the test. Players are then ranked according to the level (number of sets) they achieved and the time it took to complete the levels (therefore a player who finished level-8 in 489 seconds would be ranked ahead of a player finishing level-8 in 493 seconds). The entire test should take about 10-minutes to complete. Make sure you have an assistant to record times and levels.

I like to use this test much more than a 1-mile run or bike test because it works a player's ability to accelerate and decelerate many times within a short period of time, and more closely simulates what happens on the ice, only with <u>much less</u> overall recovery. This test is also a very good evaluation of an athlete's mental fortitude and grit as it's very challenging. If possible I try to have two or more players race each other during testing so I get the best possible performance out of each player.

300-Yard Shuttle Run Test
This standard field test is a favorite of the Boston Bruins and Anaheim Ducks (among other NHL and NCAA programs) as it quickly measures what is most in need for hockey players (either more sprint based work or more recovery work). The test is very simple to perform and takes less than 10-minutes to complete. Personally I like this test for hockey players as it provides me some good information on who has been training hard in the off-season (or during the season) and who needs more work. I can also determine whether or not a player is over-training or burning out during the season based on off-season and in-season numbers.

To perform the test, set up two cones (or lines) 25-yards apart. The player will sprint from the first cone to the second and back (50-yards for each sprint & back) without rest for 6-repetitions (50 x 6 = 300-yards). After each 300-yard set the player will get 3-minutes of rest. A total of 3-sets will be performed (3-sets of 300-yards). Therefore a typical test will go like this:

- Set 1 = 300 yard set
- Rest = 3-minutes
- Set 2 = 300-yard set
- Rest = 3-minutes
- Set 3 = 300-yard set

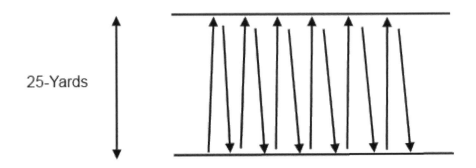

25-Yards

Diagram 12 – 300-Yard Shuttle Run Test

Evaluating the 300-Yard Shuttle Run
Upon completion of this test a coach can record the data and see where a player may need further training to bring up fitness or speed levels. Ideally players at the college and pro levels should be able to complete all three sets in under 60-seconds (< 65-seconds for midgets & junior players). If wide variations occur (such as a performance drop-off) or the player is simply slower than the required time allowed then coaches can make corrections in each players training protocols that will help to re-balance their performance. Consider the following examples:

Player 1			Player 2			Player 3		
60-secs	60-secs	60-secs	58-secs	66-secs	77-secs	75-secs	75-secs	75-secs

In the example above player one has met the criteria for an elite level player (3-sets in 60-seconds or less). This is the type of result I would expect from a 1st or 2nd line forward, a top-four defensemen or a starting goaltender.

With player two they certainly are able to run the test in allotted time (as shown by their first sprint), but they lack the ability to recover fully from set to set, which causes a drop-off in performance with each sprint. Ideally the drop-off of performance should be no more than 3-seconds with each set. This athlete should perform more recovery based conditioning drills with 1:1 or 1:2 work/rest ratio. Drills for this player should be in the 60-second to 3-minute range. Therefore a player might perform 4 to 10 sets of 90-seconds work with 90-seconds rest. This would be altered and changed depending on the time of year, the athlete and the level, but the idea would be improve overall conditioning of this player as quickly as possible.

In the third example (player-3) this player lacks the speed to perform the test at the required level and therefore drills should focus on the 1:3 to 1:5 work/rest ratio. With this type of protocol the athlete will build more intensity into the workouts and therefore improve speed. When this athlete is re-tested this might solve the problem, or it might be evident that this player now requires more conditioning work to recover quickly (like player-2).

5-Minute Kettlebell Snatch Test **(<u>Advanced Level Test ONLY</u>)**

Kettlebells are one of the finest training methods around and the snatch is the premier exercise of all kettlebell movements. A kettlebell snatch works most muscles in the body and especially the low back, hamstrings, core and glutes.

To perform the 5-minute KB snatch test you take a 53lb kettlebell and try to complete as many snatch repetitions as possible within a 5-minute time period. Have someone count your repetitions and make sure that all of them are done correctly. Check the section of this book on the proper methods of performing the KB Snatch and consult with a certified strength coach if you have questions about this movement. Here are the rules for this test:

- *If you set the kettlebell down on the ground or rest it on any body part your test is finished.*

- *The free hand should not provide assistance to the KB or stabilize any body part or the test is done.*

- *All repetitions must be locked out overhead for one full second.*

- *You may switch hands as often as necessary provided the KB does not touch the ground.*

- *To perform this test you need at least 1-year of training experience with kettlebells on a regular basis as this is a pretty brutal test. I include it in this section only because it is also a great test for elite players and coaches looking to determine high end conditioning of players. Players under 18-years of age are not advised to perform this test.*

- *Players should try to achieve 100+ repetitions in 5-minutes.*

<u>On-Ice Testing</u>

I have never been a big fan of using on-ice skating tests to test a players conditioning. Agility, speed and quickness can (and should) all be tested for on the ice, but not conditioning. Why? A player who continually skates up and down the ice during a test of conditioning will undoubtedly be using flawed technique for at least 50% of the test (as correct skating technique deteriorates after 20-seconds). Hockey is a game of 2-second accelerations, gliding, change of directions, stick-handling, passing, shooting, checking, and battling for a loose puck. How does skating a team into the ground test any of these abilities that are seen during a routine shift?

With on-ice testing the goal of every coach should be to design tests that measure the qualities of a hockey shift as close as possible, while ensuring that the test can be duplicated by other players, coaches or teams throughout the world. This way a standardized measure of a player's ability can be compared to everyone else (provided the rink dimensions are the same). As with the conditioning tests I recommend you <u>choose only 1 of these tests</u> and use that for the entire season, rather than having athletes perform all three tests each testing cycle.

In the following section I describe the three tests I use to test a players speed, agility, quickness, skating skills, and in some cases, puck-handling. Each of these tests is done for a short period of time rather than for a conditioning affect. Coaches are advised to use each drill listed below (done in both directions in some cases) so that a true measure of performance can be achieved.

T-Skating Test/Drill

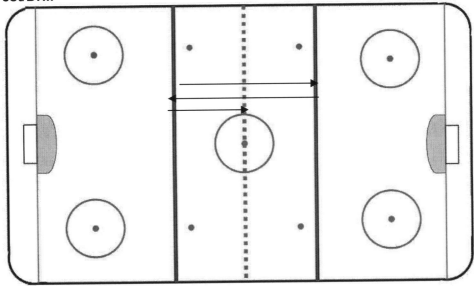

Diagram 13 – Blue to Blue to Red Skating Test

A standard test that all coaches should implement is the T-Test. This easy to perform test (with a stop watch or laser time if possible) provides a good measure of a player's ability to accelerate, decelerate, stop and then re-start (just like skills that would be used in hockey). Players start on one side of the blue line and skate towards the opposite blue line. Players have to stop with both feet on the blue line, and then accelerate to the starting blue line. Upon touching the skates to the line the player now skates to the red line where the test is stopped. The stop watch is stopped when the player reaches the red line and the time is recorded.

Banff Agility Skating Test/Drill

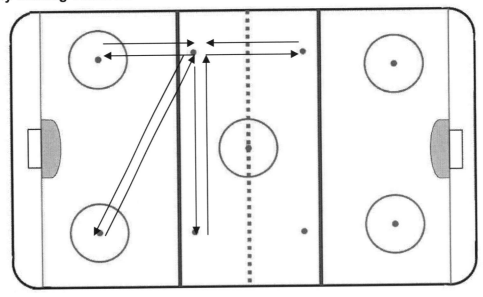

Diagram 14 – Banff Agility Skating Test

The Banff agility skating test first started when I was the strength & conditioning coach at the Banff Hockey Academy. I wanted to create a test that demonstrated various abilities of the hockey player such as starting, stopping, change of direction and skating technique (both forwards and backwards).

Starting at one of the off-side circles, a player skates to the upper right face off dot and back to the start position, to the far face-off dot and back, to the opposite off-side circle and back, and finally to the other off-side dot and back (as shown in diagram 2). **Please note that players should skate forwards towards each cone, and then skate backwards back to the starting cone.** A cone should be set up at each of the face-off dots so the player has to skate around it.

I suggest that coaches run through this drill once as is, and then another time with a puck so that players can get used to performing all of these stopping, starting, turning and backwards skating with a puck. Record both times and use the information to design future drills or practices.

MA Skating Test/Drill

The MA skating test uses standard distances found on every hockey rink (the face-off dots), so this type of testing can be duplicated everywhere a standard hockey rink is found. When the coach signals go and starts the stop watch, the player takes off from the starting triangle (lower left hand corner of the diagram 3), and skates back and forth as shown on the diagram through the entire course stopping at each dot. At the end of the course when the player touches the last face-off circle the timer is stopped and the player's time recorded. To add another challenge to this drill I recommend that coaches have player's stick-handle a puck through this course and record this time as well to get another good piece of data.

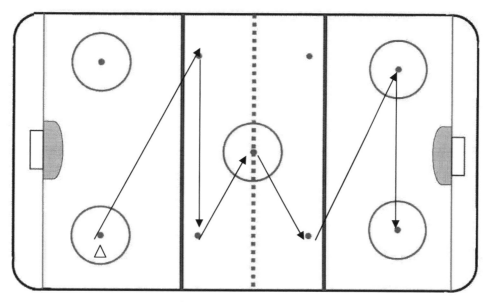

Diagram 15 - MA Skating Test

Vision Testing & Training

After looking at the research done at the United States Air Force Academy in Colorado Springs and seeing the vast improvement that visual training can have for a player I am totally sold on the practice. Some specialized equipment does need to be purchased and the coach needs to have a solid grasp of what, how, and why they are conducting visual training for the player. I find that vision training works extremely well at developing a hockey players peripheral vision, tracking abilities, and identifying important targets. I highly recommend it to any player or team looking for that extra edge in performance.

Additionally, it may prove valuable to have your eyes checked by a qualified sports vision doctor. While the general public may be happy with 20/20 vision, more and more research is finding that elite athletes often have 20/16 or even 20/12.5 vision which allows them to "see" the play happening much better than normal. Corrective measures can be taken to improve vision if this is necessary.

NHL Entry Draft Combine Testing Protocols

While very few hockey players will ever participate in the NHL entry draft physical testing evaluations I think it's important to note the various tests (and the results) that the NHL uses to assess players prior to the draft. Here are the tests:

Body Composition

- Standing Height (feet & inches)
- Wingspan (measurement of arm width from finger tips to finger tips)
- Body Weight (pounds)
- Skinfold Fat Measurement

Strength, Power & Muscular Endurance

- Grip Strength (using a grip Dynamometer testing both hands in pounds of force)
- Push/Pull Test (stand and push & pull on handles to determine maximal force)
- Bench Press Repetitions with 150lbs (done at 25 reps/minute speed using a metronome)
- Sit-up Repetitions (done at 25 reps/minute speed using a metronome), 100 reps is max score.
- Push-up Repetitions (done at 25 reps/minute speed using a metronome)
- Seated Medicine Ball Throw (use a 4kg ball to throw while seated with legs straight)
- Standing Long Jump (inches)
- Vertical Jump (inches)
- Jump Timing Mat (tests leg power in foot pounds per second)

Flexibility

- Sit & Reach Test (measures trunk flexibility using a flexometer inches)

Anaerobic Fitness

- Wingate Bike Test for 30 seconds (measures the peak power output, mean power output, minimum power output, fatigue index and overall RPM's)

Aerobic Fitness

- VO2 Max Testing (done on bicycle ergometer to test the ability to take in and use oxygen at the cellular level and reported in ml/kg/min)

NHL Draft Combine Physical Testing Results

MEASUREMENT	2004 Average	2005 Average
Body Composition		
Height (ft:in)	6:1.4	6:1.3
Weight (lbs)	192	192
Yuhasz % Body Fat	9.4	9.9
Musculoskeletal Fitness		
Grip Strength (lbs), right/left	129/125	129/126
Push Test (in lbs)	233	229
Pull Test (in lbs)	258	258
Bench Press Reps (150lbs)	10	8
Sit-up Repetitions	24	25

Push-up Repetitions	24	24
Seated Medicine Ball Throw (in)	200	182
Standing Long Jump (in)	100	97
Vertical Jump (in)	25	24
Jump Timing Mat (ft-lb/sec)	1045	1043
Sit & Reach Flexibility (in)	38	38
Anaerobic Fitness		
Peak Power Output (Watts)	1044	949
Mean Power Output (Watts)	822	796
Fatigue Index (% drop from peak)	39.6	35.7
Overall RPM	399	387
Aerobic Fitness		
VO2 Max (millilitres/kg/min)	57.8	53.4

NOTES:

1. Medical testing is performed prior to any fitness testing and looks at the following areas: health questionnaire, examination by doctors, photographs of players, an eye test, two hand/eye coordination tests and an echocardiogram test. It is important that teams looking to select a player have a complete picture of their physical health prior to selection.

2. A psychological evaluation test was introduced in 2007 in response to the teams' request for a mental assessment of the potential draftees. While most of the psychological testing is administered prior to the Combine, a neuro-cognitive test is administered immediately after players complete Wingate and VO2 max testing.

3. After all of the physical, medical and psychological testing is complete teams are then allowed to conduct a 20-minute face-to-face interview with players. While the people who make up the interview panel vary from team to team, most teams include their own sports psychologist as part of the panel to evaluate players fully.

4. As of 2008 the NHL was looking at adding skill testing into the draft to make it more hockey specific but as of yet have not included an on-ice portion to the Combine.

5. Sources for this portion of this book come from an un-copyrighted journal article labeled as such:

Gledhill, N. and Jamnik, V. Detailed Assessment Protocols For NHL Entry Draft Players, York University, Toronto 2007. http://centralscouting.nhl.com/link3/sections/cs/public/combine/protocol.pdf

Chapter 7 - Strength Training Methodology

"The legs feed the wolf."

~ Herb Brooks, Head Coach of the gold medal winning 1980 Olympic Hockey Team

It is important to go over and learn all the various aspects of strength training from the basic principles to the design and implementation of a workout as these form the basis of a hockey players training program. A poorly designed strength program will surely hold back a player from developing correctly and all of the following principals should be factored into each and every training program.

Principals of Strength Training

Strength training and the principals behind them are an entire science that must be learned with skill over a great deal of time. In the following section I have included the basic principles of strength training and the various terminologies:

Training Age: The amount of time spent working out with weights. If a 19 year old player has only been training with weights for 2 years, his training age would be 2 years of age. The older the training age, the more volume of training that player will need as they have developed a good level of work capacity. For example, a beginner with less than a year of training might see good results with 12 sets and less than 30 minutes of training per workout. A more advanced athlete needs up to 28+ sets and 45-75 minutes to stimulate growth and results.

Frequency: The amount of strength training (and total training) done over a week long period of time. Frequency is expressed in the number of sessions per week (4 hours per week or 2 hours per week).

Goal: The goal of a workout should be determined before ever planning the sets, reps, load, etc. of a workout. If you do not have a goal, then you are simply doing some weight training in hopes that it will make you better. Determine a specific goal or focus for each and every workout so as to make each training session count. From this point, you can now plan the volume, sets, reps, etc.

Volume: The volume of a training session is the total amount of sets done for the workout. In the beginning of an athlete's training the volume should be less than 15 total sets. As players develop their training age they can perform between 22 and 28 total sets. Not many athletes can handle repeated high volume of 28+ sets per workout without increasing the risk of injury or over-training.

Number of Exercises: The lower the training age of a player, the more exercises should be prescribed during each workout. Generally I like to have players with less than 2 years of training perform 8 to 14 exercises. With this strategy a player works many body parts from multiple angles so they develop quickly. As a player gets older less variety is necessary and more volume on certain exercises is important to properly develop the athlete.

Order: Also called the Training System, this is the placement of the exercises within a workout. Generally the big exercises such as squats, deadlifts, bench press, chin-ups, etc. should be performed **first** in the workout so you are the most fresh for the hardest part of the workout. This rule however, can be broken depending on the order of the exercises and the goal of the workout. Think carefully when selecting the order of a workout as you must know that in the first 20 minutes of the workout a player is most able to perform at a maximum level, and as the workout drags on, the player will get tired and less focused which results in decreased performance.

Sets: A set is a specific number of repetitions of one exercise, followed by a rest period. Beginning players with a low training age should complete less than 12 sets per workout. More advanced players can work up to 28-sets depending on training age, time of year, work capacity and their level of recovery.

Repetitions (Reps): One repetition is the completion of one exercise, one time. A repetition is comprised of two actions: the concentric action (lifting the weight against gravity), and the eccentric action (lowering the weight against gravity). When a person does a bench press for example, they would lower the weight to the chest (eccentric) and then raise the weight back to the starting position (concentric). Repetitions are usually determined by the load that is chosen. Heavy loads should be lifted 1 to 5 times, moderate loads 6-12 times, light loads 13-30 repetitions and light loads done quickly should be done 5 to 15 times (explosively).

Load: The load is the weight (either classified in pounds or kilograms) that is lifted by the player. A load is always expressed as a value of the 1RM, and this greatly determines the amount of repetitions that a person will be able to perform in the set. For example, a player might have a 1RM of 300lbs, but only be able to lift 245lbs 5 times (or 5RM).

Supra-maximal loads are expressed as (100-125%) of the 1RM and should only be performed as negatives (eccentric only actions) with spotters and a coach present. An example of supra-maximal loads might be a player wanting to work the bench press with heavy weights and doing 325lbs for 3 reps when their 1RM is only 300lbs. Too much supra-maximal work will lead quickly to overtraining as this is very intensive exercise.

Intensity: The intensity is how hard it is to lift a load (barbell, dumbbell, keg, kettlebell, etc.). Intensity is dependent upon either load or tempo (lifting speed). A heavy load lifted slowly will have a high intensity. A lighter load (50-60% of 1RM) will have a low intensity level. That same light load (50-60% of 1RM) lifted explosively such as with Olympic lifting or jumps drastically increase the intensity of the exercise. These factors need to be looked at when designing a workout.

Tempo: The speed at which each repetition is performed. Olympic lifts are done as explosively as possible for instance, while traditional training has a moderate tempo of 2 to 5 seconds to lift the weight (concentric muscle action), and 2 to 10 seconds to lower the weight (eccentric action).

Tempo is expressed as follows: 4020. The first number is the length of time (in seconds) it takes to lift the weight. The second is the pause in the bottom position of a lift (usually this number is zero seconds). The third number is the time (in seconds) it takes to lift the weight (concentric action). The final number indicates a pause in the top position (usually zero seconds). As tempo is a very advanced lifting technique I recommend that players use a 3020 tempo for most lifting, and a 20X0 tempo (the X represents a lifting speed as fast as possible), for explosive lifts, plyometrics or jumps.

Rest: The rest internal is normally expressed as the time between sets a player will get to rest before performing another set of exercises. When lifting heavy weights or when the exercise is done explosively I want players to take as much rest as they need (3 to 5 minutes) to get the most performance out of these lifts. With most other training I recommend a 2 minute rest between supersets. When conditioning is the primary concern for the workout, the rest interval should be dropped to 45 seconds to 1 minute.

Supersets: Performing an exercise and then resting is a waste of time and prolongs a workout to a great extent. When training I usually use supersets which are the combination of two exercises done one right after the other. These exercises will usually be exercises that are the opposite of each other. For example, if I work a player's quad with one exercise (such as with hack squats, or close stance squats, I will superset this with a hamstring exercise such as x-over deads or slide board hamstring curls. The reason for super-setting antagonist muscles groups (the opposite) is because it will not affect performance and allow more work to be done in a shorter period of time. Super-setting agonist muscles groups (the same area) are done to fully exhaust a muscle group or muscle action.

Giant Sets: A giant set is the combination of 3 or more exercises in a row (done back to back with little to no rest between exercises). Giant sets can work the same area for all three exercises (like only the core area or legs for instance), or can be a collection of three different exercises for different areas (like squats, bench press and core). For instance, if you do a set of abdominal crunches, then do overhead abdominal raises and then add the abdominal roller this is a giant set of core exercises.

Muscle Actions: For the purposes of this book I will talk only about isotonic muscle contractions. There are two types of isotonic contractions: (1) concentric and (2) eccentric. In a concentric contraction, the muscle tension rises to meet the resistance, then remains the same as the muscle shortens (like the biceps muscles in the lifting portion of a barbell biceps curl). In the eccentric contraction, the muscle lengthens due to the load being greater than the force the muscle is producing (an example might be the slow lowering of the barbell during a biceps curl). Players will usually be 10+% stronger in the eccentric phase of a muscle contraction compared to the lifting portion of an exercise (the concentric action). Therefore, in elite trainees, I can use training techniques such as "negative repetitions" where a spotter or coach helps the player lift a maximal weight to full extension and then the player slowly lowers the heavy load (as they are stronger in this action).

It is important to note that a good deal of muscle soreness comes from the eccentric action of a muscle and not the concentric action...therefore training techniques such as sled dragging or concentric only training (like deadlift lift and drops) are amazing techniques to add volume into a training program without producing soreness from eccentric actions.

Muscle Balance: The relationship between the Agonist and Antagonist muscle pairings. For example if you were doing a barbell biceps curl the biceps muscles would be the agonist in the action and the triceps muscles would be the antagonist muscles. If the action was a triceps dip or skull crusher exercise the triceps would be the agonist muscle while the biceps would be the antagonist muscle. It is important to have muscle balance in all parts of the body between agonist and antagonist muscles to prevent injury. If the agonist is much stronger than the antagonist is, the agonist can overpower and injure the antagonist. In my training facility I spend a great deal of time evaluating players to make sure muscle balance is correct...something very few trainers or programs address. Also realize that with all muscle actions there will exist stabilizer muscles that help to keep everything working smoothly and prevent injury. For example, the deltoid muscles of the shoulder (along with numerous other muscles) help to stabilize the shoulder joint so a trainee can perform a biceps curl or a triceps dip properly.

Specificity: Some exercises are general exercises that build overall strength but not sport specific strength (like squats, deadlifts, bench press), while others are specific to the skating motion or hockey action (like plate drags, cable skating abduction, or cross-over step-ups). Generally the non-specific exercises will be the heavy duty type of movements and the sport specific exercises will focus on refining muscles to the specific demands of the sport.

General Training Methodology

The central form of off-ice training for hockey should revolve around strength training as this helps to develop strength and power, prevent injuries and generally armour the athlete with muscle mass for the gruelling hockey season. Hockey players must adapt the same type of strength training philosophy as a Navy SEAL or Special Forces soldier as they must have a high strength to body weight ratio, in combination with amazing agility, speed and endurance. As strength training workouts are very physically taxing on the body I plan these first and then integrate all other forms of dryland training such as speed, agility, conditioning, balance, core work and injury prevention around the basic strength training program.

Strength Training Methodology

The base strength training program that I develop for many hockey players is one made from a type of training periodization called the Russian Conjugate Method. What this means is that we take several different training abilities (such as maximal strength, power development, hypertrophy, speed/agility, etc.), couple them together and train them at that same time throughout the year. Over the years I have adapted this model of training from Louie Simmons (of Westside Barbell fame) and Joe Defranco who have revamped strength training over the past 15-years.

This approach to strength is different than what many other hockey training programs look like as they base their systems on a concept called Linear Periodization. Popularized by Dr. Tudor Bompa in the 1960's, this method of training sets out specific training phases or block of time (such as hypertrophy, maximal strength or power development), and trains these qualities to the exclusion of all other components of training. The central problem with this type of Linear Periodization is that as you move on to your next training phase you neglect what you did in the previous phase and end up losing some of what you worked hard to gain during that phase. For example if a player took 4-weeks to put on muscle mass at the beginning of the off-season in April, they will definitely loose some muscle size as they move into other phases of training in the summer that focus on conditioning, maximal strength and more ice.

With the Russian Conjugated Method of Periodization my athletes never run into these same problems as they train all the various components of a complete athlete (max strength, power, hypertrophy, speed, agility, conditioning and flexibility) throughout the year. If athletes follow this program they can expect to not only make dryland gains in all of those training components, but keep them throughout the season so that starting the next year they are much further ahead compared with other hockey players who lose a lot of strength, muscle mass and body balance during the season.

When talking about the types of dryland strength training we use various methods of training, specifically, the maximal effort method, the dynamic effort method and the repetition effort method (as indicated below). With each day of training I typically choose 1 or 2 main exercises that I want to focus on, and then use 4 to 6 exercises to supplement the training for that particular day. A sample schedule is listed below.

Please note that the Russian Conjugated Method is certainly **NOT** the only way to train hockey players and I often must create a specialized training program for each player based on their testing data, age, level of play, time of season, ability, etc. This is why I offer training programs on my website **www.dphockey.com**, or in my upcoming book _Just Hockey Programs_ so players can have customized programs made for what they need both in-season and off-season.

Maximal Effort Method

The maximal effort method is included so that players increase maximal muscle strength. I have never come across a hockey player that was strong enough (at any level), and couldn't improve some aspect of their training. You can only get stronger by trying to lift heavier and heavier weights for repetitions of 1 to 5, which constitutes 90%+ of a person's 1 Repetition Maximum (1RM). With this kind of training it will stimulate the central nervous system and greatly improve inter & intra muscular coordination (which results in the development of maximal strength through adaptation to these demands). If players fail to lift heavy weights throughout the year they continually loose what they gained in the off-season and start off the following year at roughly the same level each year.

The problem with training with heavy weights is that the body can only lift heavy weights for a short time before progress will decline. The key to successfully implementing the max effort method is to rotate the exercises chosen for maximal lifts (ex: bench, or squat), every few weeks to stimulate further adaptation. For advanced players with a long history of training I rotate these max effort exercises every 3 weeks, and with beginner and intermediate lifters I change max lifts every 4 weeks.

The other key ingredient for making progress is that lifters must always try to go for a new personal best in the max effort lift. For example if in week 1 you were able to bench press 225 for 3 repetitions, in week 2 you would shoot for 230lbs for 3-repetitions and 235lbs for 3-repetitions in week 3. Athletes should **ALWAYS** try to break a record in their max effort lifts to make continual progress. Here are some of the exercises that should be used with the max effort method:

Legs
-Squat (BB, DB, & KB)
-Chain or Band Squats (BB)
-Box Squats (BB)
-Box Squats with Chains or Bands (BB)
-Lockout Squats (BB)
-Deadlifts (BB, DB, & KB)
-Sumo Deadlifts (BB)
-Snatch Grip Deadlifts (BB)
-Rack Pull Deadlifts below knee (BB)
-Trap Bar Deadlifts (BB)
-Trap Bar Deadlifts off a Box (BB)
-Front Squats (BB, DB & KB)
-Heavy Tire Flipping

Upper Body
-Bench Press (BB, DB)
-Chain or Band Bench Press (BB)
-Floor Press (BB, DB)
-Rack Bench Press Lock-outs (BB)
-Incline Bench Press (BB, DB)
-Close Grip Bench Press (BB)
-Board Press (BB)
-Bent over Rows/Horizontal Rows (BB, DB)
-Chest Supported/Machine Rows
-Pull-ups/Chin-ups (Weighted if possible)
-Suspended Horizontal Rows
-Military Press (BB, DB)
-Dips

Dynamic Effort Method
With the dynamic effort method players are asked to lift lighter weights (40-60% of a person's 1RM), and move the weight as fast as possible. This works to develop great power and explosive ability. The benefit to dynamic effort training is that if you only lift heavy weights you can become bigger and stronger, but slower as an athlete. Using dynamic effort training in conjunction with maximal effort lifts will produce a much more complete athlete.

Olympic lifts such as the snatch, the clean & jerk, and many of these variations are unmatched in the development of power but take time and a good strength coach to teach proper form. If players only have a limited amount of training time for lifting weights then that time should be used training, rather than learning more complex Olympic lifts. In fact, any exercise that is performed with sub-maximal weight can develop explosive force (such as box jumps). Recommended exercises for Dynamic Effort training might include the following:

Legs
-Box Jumps
-Single Leg Box Jumps
-Single Leg Side Box Jumps
-Russian Box Jumps (for distance & height)
-Box Squats into Box Jumps
-Depth Jumps onto a Box
-1-Leg Depth Jump onto a Box
-Box Squats (BB or with Chains or Bands)
-Side Jumps onto Bosu
-1-Leg Front Jump onto Bosu
-Broad Jump
-Vertical Jump
-Tire Flipping (lighter tire)

Upper Body
-Bench Press (BB, DB)
-Chain & Band Bench Press (BB)
-Plyo Push-ups onto Boxes
-Jerks (BB, DB, KB)
-Power Pulls (BB)
-Push Press (BB, DB, KB)
-Med-Ball Chest Throws, for distance (MB)
-Med-Ball Chest Pass + Plyo Push-up (MB)
-Med-Ball Chest Pass, for speed (MB)
-Sledge Hammer Hits
-Seated DB Powerclean
-Ballistic 1-Arm Rows (DB, KB)
-Med-Ball Squat Throws

Olympic Lifts
-Hang Cleans (BB, DB)
-Power Pulls (BB)
-Hang Snatch (BB, DB)
-Squat Press (BB, DB, KB)

-KB Squat Pulls (KB)
-KB Snatch (KB)
-KB Swings (one & two arm with KB)
-Power Clean (KB, BB, DB)

Repeated Effort Method

The goal with using the repeated effort method is to increase muscle size and endurance. A larger muscle has more potential to develop maximal strength and therefore it should be the job of every hockey player to gain as much useable muscle mass as possible. The term "useable" refers to your ability to increase muscular size while also improving other attributes such as speed, agility, and power. This is not like bodybuilding where the goal is just to get as big as possible...as this will have a negative impact on the ice.

Another side benefit with the repeated effort method is that if done properly it helps to balance the musculature of the body (ex: between pushing and pulling or between the hamstrings and quads). As much effort will be put towards making certain qualities strong and explosive the body balance must be maintained with repeated effort type of lifts that promote full range of motion, functionality of the joints and general body "armour" to protect against injuries.

When performing the repetition effort method the idea is to always lift more repetitions in a given exercise, rather than simply increasing the weight. By this I mean that athletes should choose one weight for an exercise and stick with that weight for the 2 to 4 weeks of the program they are on, and always try to improve the number of total repetitions they perform with that weight. An example of this would be:

Week 1 – DB Bench Press on Swiss Ball, Set 1= 23 reps, Set 2=19 reps, Set 3=16 reps, 58 reps total
Week 2 – DB Bench Press on Swiss Ball, Set 1=25 reps, Set 2=20 reps, Set 3=17 reps, 62 reps total
Week 3 – DB Bench Press on Swiss Ball, Set 1=26 reps, Set 2=22 reps, Set 3=17 reps, 65 reps total

NOTE: Notice that the athlete used the same weight in all three weeks, but tried to get more total repetitions each week. At the end of the cycle, another exercise and weight would be chosen and in the new cycle starts all over trying to get more and more repetitions out of the exercise and weight chosen.

It is also important to note that for the repetition effort method athletes should rest between 2 to 3 minutes between sets, so as to recover, but not fully recover from the previous set. Examples of some repeated effort method training exercises include:

Legs
<u>Quadriceps Dominant Exercise</u>
-Split Squats
-Elevated Split Squats
-1¼ Split Squats
-Overhead Keg Split Squats

-Bosu Split Squats
-Bosu Lunges
-Lunges (all varieties)
-Hockey Lunges
-Barbell Reverse Lunges
-Elevated Barbell Reverse Lunges
-Side Lunges
-Cross-Over Lunges
-Cross-Behind Lunges

Upper Body

-Bench Press & all variations (BB, DB, KB)
-Chain & Band Bench Press (BB)
-Close Grip Press
-Reverse Grip Bench Press

-Push-ups & all varieties
-T-Bar Rows
-Suspended Horizontal Rows
-Lying DB Rows
-1-arm Rows
-Face Pulls
-Chin-ups & Pull-downs
-Shoulder Press & all varieties
-Shoulder Press Lockout

-Step-ups
-Step-ups + Hockey Knee Lift
-Side Step-ups

Posterior Chain Dominant Exercises
-Deadlift
-RDL
-Good Mornings
-Glute-Ham Raises
-45 Degree Back Extensions
-Pull-Throughs
-Swiss Ball Hamstring Curls
-Slide-Board Hamstring Curls
-X-Over Deads

-Bradford Press
-Upright Rows
-Shoulder Flys
-Trap Bar Shrugs (BB)
-Dips
-Skull Crushers
-Band Tricep Pressdowns
-Barbell Curls

General Rules of Russian Conjugate Method Training

The Russian Conjugate Method has a lot of flexibility built into the program so that players, coaches and teams can craft workouts based on their specific season or situation. There are however several rules that should always be followed when developing training programs so that quality of workouts and integrity of the strength training plan can be maintained.

- This method of training must have consistency for 3 weeks followed by changing the exercises and especially the maximum effort exercises so that burn-out does not happen. Players simply cannot lift heavy all the time using the same exercise and expect to make progress...it doesn't work that way. But, by changing the exercise from say bench press to bench press lockout or to floor press, and then to another exercise there is enough variation that heavy maximum effort sessions can be carried out year round.

- During maximum effort day you always try to lift heavier and heavier weights for a record. Some weeks it might be a 1 repetition maximum, while other weeks it might be for a 2, 3, 4 up to 5 repetitions maximum. Always record the weights you used during any max effort days to compare to future training.

- Lifting heavy weights is as much a mental thing as it is a physical test. Visualize how the lift will go, get prepared for the weight, make sure you have spotters handy in case you miss the lift and do your absolute best every time you lift heavy.

- When using the dynamic effort method it is essential to lift or move the weight as fast as possible each time. This builds consistency with the central nervous system and improves the response time and power output that can happen by moving lighter weights very quickly.

- During the season only two sessions of weight training will be possible with all of the other conditioning exercises (such as sled dragging, band work, speed & agility, etc.) that needs to be continued. These two sessions should be a total body maximum effort day and a total body dynamic effort day. All other training should be supplementary to build, fix or change various physical attributes.

- For most players it is **ESSENTIAL** to keep lifting hard with weights throughout the season (as long as you don't over-do-it and hurt your performance on the ice). If a player can maintain or even improve strength training numbers through the season they will be in a much better overall position in the off-season so that real progress can be made from season to season. This is where many hockey players make mistakes and actually start over each off-season with basically the same weight they used the previous summer.

- Players must really put a lot of effort into the recovery portion of training as this is essential to long term improvement and injury prevention. Following training, athletes should ice the various tendons, ligaments and muscles that were used in the workout. As discussed in the "Recovery Methods" chapter, an ice bath/tub works best to apply ice uniformly.

Setting Up a Strength Training Workout

When I design a workout I make sure to plan exactly what I am looking for in a training session so that my players know what to expect. Most workouts start with a 5-minute cardiovascular warm-up such as a light jog or bike to get the blood flowing. Immediately following this a dryland warm-up is performed (see the chapter on Warm-Ups), for 10-minutes. The strength training portion of the workout follows for the next 45-minutes or so. Right after the strength training I usually do muscle/area specific conditioning (such as jump squats, shuttle runs, kettlebell work, etc.) for the last 15-minutes of the workout. The last portion of the workout is the cool-down segment that involves some light cardio and foam rolling the muscles trained. Adjust these numbers for your own workout needs and time constraints. A typical workout is portioned out in the following pie graph.

Example of a Strength Training Workout

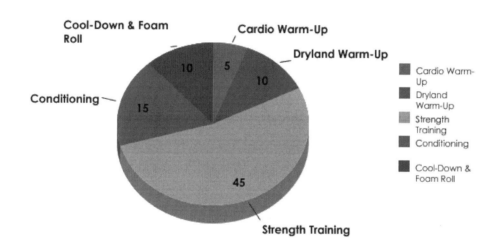

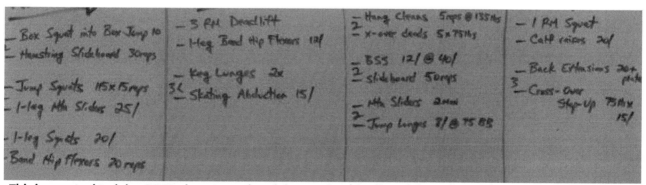

This is an actual training DP Hockey strength training session (the first of three that day) from the summer of 2011. Notice how each player has a different workout as there are junior players mixed with pros and each have a different goal & training camp date.

Scheduling Strength Training

In order to have a proper plan the strength training portion of your dryland training needs to have a regular schedule. In this section I will discuss the various forms of setting up a strength training program for hockey.

Off-Season

During the off-season the goal is to improve muscle hypertrophy, strength, power, speed and general athletic abilities. Most players will not spend more than 2 days on the ice each week so this allows strength training and conditioning to take more of a role in the daily schedule.

Monday	Tuesday	Wednesday	Thursday	Friday	Saturday	Sunday
Max Effort Legs	Upper Repetition	off	Dynamic Effort Legs	off	Max Effort Upper	off

Table 1 – Sample off-season weekly training schedule

A sample week during this time might look like this:

Monday
Max Effort Lower Body

A1 Pick a primary lower body movement	work up to a 3-5RM
B1 One-leg repetition training	3 sets of 15 reps
C1 Hamstring Movement	2 sets of 8 reps
C2 Hamstring Movement	2 sets of 12-15 reps
D1 Grip Work	4 sets of 5 to 20 reps (depending on exercise)
E1 Slide board or Russian Box	10 sets of 20 seconds (40 seconds rest)
F1 Squats	2 sets of 20 reps

Tuesday
Upper Repetition

A1. Horizontal Pushing	3 sets of Max reps
B1. Vertical Pulling	3 sets of 8-12 reps
B2. Horizontal Pulling	3 sets of 8-12 reps
C1. Vertical Pushing	4 sets of 20 reps
D1. Traps	3 sets of 8-12 reps
D2. Dips	3 sets of 8 reps*
E1. Plate Drags	2 sets of 12 reps
F1. Slide Board	5-10 sets of 30 seconds work, 30 seconds rest

Thursday
Dynamic Effort Lower Body

A1. Box Jumps	8 sets of 3 jumps
B1. Olympic Modified Lift	5 sets of 3 reps
C1. KB Work	3 sets of 10reps/side
D1. 45 Degree Back/Glute Ham/RDL	3 sets of 15reps
E1. Russian Box	5 sets of 20 seconds (un-weighted)
F1. Squats	2 sets of 20 reps

Saturday
Max Effort Upper Body

A1 Horizontal Push	work up to 3-5RM
B1. Assistant Horizontal Push	2 sets of 20 reps
C1. Horizontal Pull	3 sets of 12/side
C2. Horizontal Pull	3 sets of 15 reps
D1. Triceps Exercise	4 sets of 5 reps
E1. Explosive Modified Olympic lift	2 sets of 3 reps
F1. Conditioning Work Legs	5 sets of 20-60 seconds
F2. Conditioning Work Legs	5 sets of 20-60 seconds

In-Season

In order to keep all of the strength and conditioning gains made in the off-season it is **critical** to work hard in the weight room during the season. By keeping the gains you made in the gym throughout the off-season you will start the next year at a much higher level of strength and performance, rather than if you stopped or greatly reduced the training load in season. The important part of training at this time is to make sure that the training does not affect the performance on the ice or the general body recovery that is needed during the season. For this reason I tend to schedule only 2 strength training sessions per week that work the whole body. When combined with several conditioning workouts each week, hockey practices and games this will be more than enough training for players.

Monday	Tuesday	Wednesday	Thursday	Friday	Saturday	Sunday
Max Effort	off	off	Dynamic Effort	off	off	off

Table 2 – Sample in-season weekly training schedule

In some cases a player may need more or less strength training or conditioning work during the season for a variety of reasons. If this is the case make sure to monitor your morning heart-rate, body-weight and body-fat percentage to make sure that you are recovering from any training that is performed. **Remember it is not the amount of training you can do, but the amount of training you can recover from and still make progress that is important.**

A sample workout during this time will look like this:

Monday
Max Effort Lower Body
A1	Pick a primary lower body movement	work up to a 3-5RM
B1	Pick a primary upper body movement	work up to a 3-5RM
C1	Hamstring Movement	2 sets of 8 reps
C2	Chin-ups	3 sets of max reps
D1	Mulit-hip Machine	2 sets of 10 reps/side
D2	Band Pull-ins	2 sets of 15 reps
E1	Horizontal Rows	3 sets of 8 reps
F1	Squats	2 sets of 20 reps

Thursday
Dynamic Effort Lower Body
A1.	Box Jumps	8 sets of 3 jumps
B1.	Olympic Modified Lift	5 sets of 3 reps
C1.	Jump Lunges	3 sets of 5 reps/side
C2	Explosive Rowing Action (DB rows, etc.)	3 sets of 5 reps/side
D1.	Plyometric Push-ups or bench press	3 sets of 10 reps
D2.	Medicine Ball Squat Throws	3 sets of 10 reps
E1.	Kettlebell exercise (snatches, swings, etc.)	5 sets of 5 reps/side (heavy weight)
F1.	Squats	2 sets of 20 reps

Chapter 8 - Strength Training Rules

"There's a difference between knowing the path, and walking the path"

~ actor Lawrence Fishborne in the movie, "The Matrix"

Most people workout wrong. I've seen so many instances of poor lifting form, too much weight loaded onto the bar, unsafe situations (like no spotters on a max lift), guys fooling around, wrestling matches (in the weight room) and even guys slapping each other to get pumped up for a lift. I could fill a book with the stupid things I have seen in a weight room. It's no wonder some hockey coaches don't send players to strength train at the gym.

This is exactly the reason that strength and conditioning coaches have become an essential part of every hockey team in the world. Hockey is one of the most difficult sports to train for, and every team, player, coach and owner wants to be the best. In order to see the results you want, and to prevent injury you must train correctly, with good form and with the following moto running through your brain at all times: **"NEVER HURT YOURSELF DURING DRYLAND TRAINING... EVER"**!

In this chapter I present to you the most important basic rules of lifting weights that MUST be followed so that you prevent injuries and get the most out of your time in the gym.

Warm-ups

You never go into a hockey game without a warm-up and you should never weight train without a warm-up, period. The purpose of the warm-up is to get the blood moving, stretch the muscles, warm-up the lifting muscles, increase core body temperature and to mentally prepare for this increased physical exertion. Consult the warm-ups and flexibility chapters (#28 & #29) for more information.

In the picture to the left players from the Banff Hockey Academy warm-up prior to dryland training with Coach Pollitt (2009).

Correct Lifting Technique

Correct lifting is something that should be taught early on in a players career (Peewee or Bantam if possible), and developed over a players training lifetime. Correct form is ESSENTIAL to making the progress you want and preventing injuries in the gym. All exercises, training programs and drills should be taught by a qualified strength and conditioning coach (not a personal trainer or some guy who works out at the gym twice a week). Learn the movements, and know why you are performing a lift in a certain way to get the most out of your dryland time.

With all weights you want to keep them close to the body, as this keeps the load near your body's center of gravity. This will not only reduce your potential for risk, but it will greatly improve your strength. The two major areas that people screw this up is with overhead lifting (they let the arms and elbows fly out to the side) and when pulling from the ground (they let the kettlebell or DB go too far away from the legs, which puts more force on your low back).

Establish a Stable Position

Unless otherwise noted, always try to set up a stable base of support when lifting a weight. Spread your feet to at least shoulder width apart (sometimes further apart for increased support) and bend your knees while standing. Make sure your feet are firmly on the floor throughout the exercise and keep your head up to avoid rounding your back.

The next thing is to focus on squeezing your butt together (like your holding a $100 bill between your butt checks), and simultaneously push out your abdominal muscles as if you were bracing for a punch or going to the bathroom. This is your body's natural method of stabilizing the spine and preventing back pain during training. The best method is to take a deep breath and hold that while you use that air to push your abdominal muscles outwards (think of it like pushing against your belt). Complete the lift and then take in more air between lifts. By using this trick you effectively anchor your core area which provides critical stabilization for your spine. At first this may seem difficult, but doing this on a regular basis will certainly pay off with better results and much less chance of injury.

Finally, try to create maximal tension throughout the body by squeezing all of the muscle you can before you lift your chosen weight (regardless of the load). When gripping a weight you should squeeze your hands around that bar so tightly that your knuckles turn white. Next you tighten your calfs, hamstrings, upper body and neck as hard as possible. The reason for using maximal tension is similar to contracting the core area during a lift, in that it is harder to hurt yourself during a lift with everything held tight.

Eastern Washington University defencemen Nick Kooiker shows a good solid base of support, as he full squats 225lbs for 12-reps. In this picture however, Nick is only 15 years of age!

Use a full range of motion

The most important thing in training is using a full range of motion with any action. If you do only half the action it is like paying only half of your taxes. At first it may seem easier, but in the end it will come back to kick you in the butt. With a shortened range of motion it can lead to injuries, a shortened functional range for that particular joint and even poor posture. Take a look at the picture of Nick Kooiker above for an idea on full range of motion for a proper squat.

Momentum

If you look carefully you will see many people lifting weights that are too heavy for them and therefore using momentum to get the weight up. They may use a jerking motion like a hip twist or shoulder push which creates momentum that helps get the weight up. Now if you really know what you're doing this may be all right in certain situations, but generally this is not advisable. It looks ridiculous and you are just cheating yourself into thinking you are stronger than you really are.

Under most circumstances try to move the weight under control (1-5 seconds to lift a weight, and 1-5 seconds to lower the weight). Tighten the body and focus on your breathing. You will find you get a lot more out of the exercise if you perform it properly.

NOTE: The exceptions to this rule are of course explosive lifts, Olympic lifts, plyometrics and speed work, where the weights should be lifted explosively. This however does NOT mean that exercise form is sacrificed for moving a weight quickly... in fact, it's quite the opposite. I have all my players learn movements slowly, with good form, before they speed up the movement or lift heavier weights. Use good judgement and a good coach for feedback if in doubt about your lifting form or abilities.

Never bounce weights

This is pretty obvious, but you would be surprised at the people who do weird things with weights in the gym. Bouncing the weights can injure muscles and more specifically harm joints with the shock of bouncing. Also try not to clank weights together or drop them on the floor between repetitions.

Proper breathing

When you lift any weight it is best to control your breathing by pushing your tongue against the roof of your mouth tightly, and then exhale against this resistance. You will make a hissing sound if this is done properly. What this does (without a conscious effort) is it forces the entire core area to push out and tighten up to force the air out of your lungs. This anchors and supports the spine (which is good). You may not want to do this at first due to the sound you make, but you can find a way to hide the sound (and besides, it will help you protect yourself against injuries). As you lower a weight or when you are at the bottom of a movement you can then inhale and load up your lungs full of air.

Training System (Order)

Notice that in many workouts I use the A1, B1, C1 type system, or order of the workout. What this means is that I ask athletes to perform all the A category exercises first, then do all the B exercises, C exercises, etc. So if the workout calls for A1, A2, B1, B2, B3, C1, C2, then you would do exercise A1, followed immediately by exercise A2, rest for 1 to 2 minutes, and then repeat exercises A1 and A2 until all the required sets in the "A" group are finished. At this point you move on to the "B" exercises, and then the "C", "D", etc. exercise groups until the workout is finished.

Loading Parameters

At first the most important thing in weight training is adopting correct lifting form. During this period it is not important to lift a maximal weight (or anything even close). As you get stronger and more comfortable with your abilities you need to crank up the weight to build a solid base of strength (that will lay the foundation for your entire training). As long as you're doing the exercise correctly and you have spotters than using a heavy weight should not be a problem. Also it is important to test yourself from time to time and occasionally go for a 1 repetition maximum in the bench press, the squat and the deadlift. Just remember when other players are fooling around during the summer you will be taking that next step to perform at your best during the hockey season.

Lifting straps

 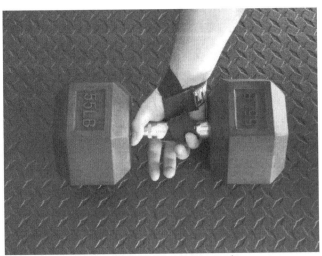

The right way to put on a lifting strap (picture 1), wrapping the lifting strap (picture 2)

When the weights get heavy, sometimes the use of straps are necessary to help you grip the bar or dumbbell, so that the grip doesn't fail before the body part being worked is trained appropriately. Use these only when the weight is really heavy. If your grip is pathetic, than get to work training this area (it will help in all aspects of your game). Your grip will improve in time just by handling the various dumbbells, barbells or kettlebells, as well as with all of the grip training information later in this book.

Weight lifting belt

Generally it is not advisable to use a lifting belt with your training because you won't get to use a lifting belt on the ice so why use one in training. Having said that in certain situations it is perfectly fine to use one (such as when you are lifting a heavy deadlift, squat, RDL or exercises that involve the low back). During max effort day for the legs it is usually acceptable to use a weight belt if the weight you are moving is close to your maximum. Using a belt helps the athlete contract the stomach against the belt and really works to anchor the core area while using a heavy weight.

Weight Collars

I have seen way too many weight room accidents that involved people not securing a weight collar to the outside of the barbell. Using collars help to prevent the plates from shifting during an type of lifting motion and therefore works to keep everyone safe. It is also a chance for lifters to make sure that the weight plates used is equal on both sides (just about everyone at some point in time loads the barbell differently on both sides) which creates a potential for injury during the lift.

Spotters

Whenever you use a heavy weight, or are unsure about the proper lifting mechanics of an exercise it is very important you have a friend or team-mate to assist you while performing the exercise. Having that person hold your wrists, support your elbows or simply offer encouragement during the exercise is invaluable. Make sure that person has their hands close to the weight, on the bar, wrists, or body-part that is being used, and is ready to offer assistance with a difficult lift. Often times the person just needs a little assistance to lift the weight, while in other circumstances may need the weight lifted by the spotter.

Injury Prevention Exercises

Injury prevention exercises such as drills for the adduction and abduction of the hip, neck work, shoulder training (the external rotators mostly), and ankle development can be done virtually every day. The thought behind this concept is that these muscles are more supportive, small muscles that need to be strong to prevent injuries. Often times these are neglected or under-trained in most people, especially hockey players.

Start off slowly with light loads for high repetitions (15-30) and vary this with higher loads and lower repetitions (8 to 15). Always look at this as injury prevention work rather than how much weight can be used (READ don't go too heavy).

Bryce Nielsen (#20) with the Nelson Leafs of the KIJHL

75

Chapter 9 - Olympic & Kettlebell Lifting

"There are some people, who live in a dream world, and there are some who face reality; and then there are those who turn one into the other."

~ Doug Everett (member of 1932 USA Olympic Ice Hockey Team)

Olympic lifting is a key piece of the puzzle for dryland training that should be incorporated into every player's off-ice training. Used correctly it can function as a primary method in power development and learning to coordinate the body during complex movements. I also believe that every exercise has a time and place in any type of training program, just as a screw driver has a place inside of a tool box. The important thing to note is you don't always need, nor should you use a screw driver for every job. Similarly, Olympic lifting should comprise a certain role in your hockey training.

My primary issue with Olympic lifting for non-weightlifting sports is that it takes a good deal of time, and practice for hockey players (or any athletes) to become proficient in these lifts. Often, a player will come to a strength & conditioning coach for a limited amount of time (say the summer for example), and it's my job to prepare them for the following season. If this is the case, then Olympic lifting is lower on my priority list (depending on the player) as there is too little time to develop and learn these lifts correctly (unless with a kettlebell) while getting in all the other dryland training they need. If however, I get to work with that player for an extended period of time then Olympic lifting will become a staple in their dryland development as a hockey player.

Players who use Olympic lifting movements should have prior training on the various techniques from a qualified Olympic Weightlifting Coach. A personal trainer, athletic trainer or hockey coach is not a qualified instructor for Olympic lifting as it takes a good deal of skill to demonstrate, teach and correct Olympic lifting movements. As the goal for Olympic lifting is to accelerate a heavy weight quickly, you need to learn how to do it right and avoid possible injuries. Instructional video of all the lifts in this section (the swing, snatch, C&J, etc.) will soon be available to watch online at **www.dphockey.com**.

As a note on equipment it is important that teams/players/coaches that do use Olympic lifting as part of their program have rubber bumper plates for their barbells. The standard iron plates will not do, and will only lead to injury. Players need to be able to drop barbells if they miss a lift, and this ONLY works if you use rubber bumper plates. Also it is important to use a quality Olympic lifting bar that will flex correctly under load, compared to the standard gym Olympic bar. There is a HUGE difference in performance and standard bars typically do not stand up to long term use with Olympic lifting.

The following are some of the Olympic lifts I use when working with hockey players as they are easier to learn, can be performed with lighter weights for speed type actions and provide the biggest bang for the training buck.

Barbell Power Pulls
The barbell power pull is an awesome exercise for both players and goaltenders. A player starts holding the barbell with a palms down grip, in front of the body just above the knees while keeping the back flat (picture 1). From this position forcefully extend with the legs (as if you were going to jump), while pulling the elbows to the ceiling (like you are trying to elbow someone standing behind you in the face). The barbell should travel up towards the chin (picture 2), as you keep the elbows high. I tell my hockey players to think of this exercise like you are battling an opponent in the corner for the puck and you try to elbow them in the face (it's the same type of movement). Oddly enough, every hockey player I know gets this exercise very quickly!

Power pulls done in Richmond, BC

Hang Cleans

Clint shows one of the best Olympic lifts I use to develop hockey players

A hang clean is a good way to improve explosive power and the ability to transfer energy between the legs, core and upper body. From a hang position (bar just above your knees while keeping a straight back posture, picture 1) explode up with the legs, shrug the shoulders and try to rack the weight as if you were performing a power clean. Push the weight forward slightly and let it lower to your knees to repeat the movement. Really try to explode from the knees as much as possible and quickly move the elbows under and around the barbell in order to get to the "rack" position (picture 2).

Hang Snatch
The hang snatch (not shown in pictures) is perhaps the most difficult to learn exercise I use at DP Hockey. A variant of the Olympic Snatch lift, the hang snatch starts with a wide, overhand grip on the barbell. Pick the barbell up to just above the knees while keeping the back straight. Explode upward with the legs, shrug the weight with the shoulders and lift with the weight to a lockout position above the head. This lift can be a very complicated and tough to learn so it is best to have a professional strength coach teach and correct this lift until you develop good form and start to use heavier weights. Consult the upcoming online videos for more information and details of this lift.

Barbell Power Clean
Start in the typical deadlift position with your back flat, shoulders over the bar and feet shoulder width apart. With the clean and jerk your hands will be facing your body (overhand grip). From this start

you try to explosively pull the barbell from the floor, engaging your back and legs first (in the low pull position), then include the traps, and then finally sink under the bar as your hands clean the weight up under your chin (the catch position). This is a typical power clean (or clean).

Only perform power cleans if you have bumper plates and an Olympic lifting bar as these are made to be dropped. Ideally once you have cleaned the weight to the shoulders you can either jerk the weight overhead (as in Olympic Weightlifting), or you lower the barbell by dropping it in front of you. When you drop the weight, keep your hands on the barbell for most of the drop so you know where the barbell will land. You don't want heavy weights crashing all over the place out of control as this poses a safety issue.

Strength Coach Clint Hazen demonstrates a proper power clean at the Canada Sport Centre Vancouver. He starts by pulling from the floor (picture 1), the violent pulling motion in the middle part of the lift (picture 2), and the "catch" portion of the lift (picture 3).

NOTE: The power clean is a <u>*great testing exercise*</u> *in more advanced hockey players who have worked with a strength coach and know how to perform the exercise with good form. If you do not know how to perform the power clean it is important to have a qualified strength and conditioning coach (not a hockey coach or personal trainer) teach you the lifts correctly.*

Power Snatch
The power snatch is a complicated explosive exercise that I usually only use with advanced athletes who I have personally worked with for a number of years. It takes a while to get the mechanics of the lift down correctly so that you can start using a decent weight on the bar to make improvements.

To start the lift approach the bar much like a power clean, only with the hands spread apart further (the index finger should be on the knurling spaces). From this position, pull from the ground like a deadlift only with more explosive power. The goal is to get the weight from the ground to overhead as quickly as possible. When catching the weight overhead there should be minimal knee bend (unlike a traditional weightlifting snatch).

Pro hockey player Kevin Flather performing a basic power snatch during training in Vancouver, BC

Jerk

From a rack position (barbell on the shoulders) take a slight dip (6 to 10 inches) with the legs (to load up like a spring) and then explode upwards with the legs and arms together to extend the barbell overhead to lockout (picture 2), with the legs spread forward and backward as you might see in Olympic Lifting. Lower the weight to the rack position for another repetition. The idea is to explode upwards as quickly as possible from the slight squat position by transferring the power of the legs through the core area and ultimately over the head. Start off with light weights (an un-loaded barbell) and progress from there using good form and explosiveness.

From the rack position dip the legs and thrust upwards to extend the barbell overhead
with legs in an Olympic style front/back position (picture 2)

Push Press

Professional hockey player Justin Todd completes a set of push-presses during a conditioning workout

Much the same as the Jerk, a push press does not involve a split leg lockout typically seen in Olympic lifting. Therefore, this style of lift is used more often with athletes as it's easier to learn and perform for non-Olympic Lifting athletes.

Start this lift with a kettlebell (dumbbells or barbells also work well) at the shoulder level and dipping the legs into a ¼ squat position (picture 1), and then explode with the legs first and then the upper body to extend the weight overhead (picture 2). The key in this exercise is to transfer the energy you produce in the lower body through the core area and continue this with the upper body to an overhead position. The more you use your legs, the easier this lift becomes.

Swings

Swings are the basic starting point for all kettlebell lifting because it is an awesome developer of the posterior chain muscles, quads, upper back and gripping muscles. Start by holding a kettlebell in one hand, squatting down while swinging the weight back between the legs (picture 1). From this position explosively come out of the squat by contracting the hamstrings and glutes, extend the hip and start the kettlebell moving with the shoulder (picture 2). At the top of the exercise with the arm extended to roughly head height the hips should have fully extended forward and the momentum of the kettlebell should have carried it up to the finish position (picture 3). Let the kettlebell swing back between the legs (without trying to slow it down) and allow the weight to stop itself as the arm acts as a brace to stop the kettlebell. Remember to keep the head up, the back straight and the core area held very tightly to prevent injury and increase performance in the swing. At first a 35lbs kettlebell will seem heavy, but in time even a bigger kettlebell such as the 72lb or 88lb weights will not be that bad.

Former UCLA assistance strength coach Todd demonstrates
the beginning, middle and finish of the one-handed swing

KB Cleans & Jerks

The clean & jerks is a kettlebell variation of the Olympic Weightlifting exercise that utilizes a barbell and rubber bumper plates. The clean portion of the lift starts by lifting the kettlebell from the ground to the shoulder (picture 1 and 2), this is called the "catch" position. From the catch position the forearm should be held close to the body (along the mid-line of the chest) with the kettlebell on the outside of the wrist. Take a brief pause in the catch position to steady the kettlebell and take a breath. From this position bend the legs while keeping the upper body tight and upright, and push the kettlebell overhead by using the legs and upper body at the same time (picture 3). Lower the weight down to the shoulder and then to the ground to start another repetition. Tips on getting the most from the clean & jerk include keeping the kettlebell as close to the mid-line of the body and using the legs as much as possible to push the weight overhead.

Many variations of this exercise can be used such as one handed clean & jerks, two handed clean & jerks, double clean & jerks (a kettlebell in each hand).

Completing the clean & jerks is a two-step process of bringing the weight to the shoulder,
and then pushing it overhead by using the legs and arms together

Kettlebell Snatches

The KB snatch must be thought of as the king of all kettlebell exercises because it works many different muscles at once and when performed in high repetitions is one of the best conditioning exercises in the world. With the snatch the gripping muscles, low back, legs, upper back, shoulders and core area are all worked to a great degree. Many well-conditioned athletes <u>suffer</u> when forced to do multiple repetitions with a heavy kettlebell.

To begin the snatch start off in a swing type position holding the kettlebell in one hand, squatting down and swinging the weight between the legs (picture 1). Much like the swing the legs extend, the back stays flat and the hips forcefully come forward to swing the kettlebell upwards (picture 2). Unlike a swing, the finish of the snatch occurs when the kettlebell continues rising upwards and flips over onto the back of the wrist with the arm extended overhead. Beginners should simply let this happen (letting the swing keep going and flipping around onto the back of the wrist). Advanced trainees will use a technique called the "cork screw" where the wrist turns outwards as the weight is swinging overhead, and rather than flipping the weight over the wrist, you spin the wrist around, catch the weight and drive the arm upwards to full extension (picture two demonstrates this technique). This is done very quickly so it is best practiced slowly and with a very light weight.

To do another repetition simply lower the arm slowly and let the kettlebell flop forward and back into the same type of motion of a typical swing. Remember this exercise is an explosive exercise so do not try and "muscle the kettlebell up" as this simply will not work. To add a challenge a second kettlebell can be added so the snatch is performed with two kettlebells (this is a very advanced exercise and does take practice, and a good deal of strength).

Todd demonstrates snatches with a 53lb kettlebell. In the first picture Todd swings the kettlebell back between the legs, then he explodes upwards swinging the weight in front, and ultimately over the head letting the kettlebell flip over and hit the back of his forearm

Squat Pulls

The beginning of the pull phase of the squat pull (above). Top portion of the pull phase (below)

Squat pulls are a great hockey exercise as it builds the explosive muscles in the lower body, the transferring power throughout the core (to transfer energy from the ground to the hands), and the shoulder and trap muscles that must finally lift the kettlebell to chin height. Try to keep the elbow high throughout the entire motion (as if you were going to elbow somebody in the face while battling for a loose puck). When lowering the kettlebell down to the floor make sure to bring it into the middle of your stance as you want to keep it away from the knee (it hurts really bad if you bash your knee with a heavy kettlebell).

It is also important to note that this is fluid and explosive exercise, which mean you do not slow down the action at all or stop at the top like many other weight training exercises...keep moving the kettlebell up and down for the required number of repetitions. With the squat pull you can use one or two hands on the kettlebell to complete the action depending on your goals for the training session.

Olympic Lifting Rules

As Olympic lifting is the pursuit of moving heavy weights as quickly as possible I always coach my players on the various rules I have for Olympic lifting outlined below:

- *Always use rubber bumper plates (such as Uesaka, Eleiko, Ivanko), and a quality Olympic lifting barbell (examples: York, Ivanko, Eleiko, Uesaka). Using a standard Olympic weight, plates will not bounce when dropped, ruin floors and break equipment in a short time. Normal (non-Olympic) lifting bars will break or warp from being dropped with weights on them.*

- *Always use collars on the side of weight plates to prevent the movement of the bumper plates during any type of Olympic lift. I have seen countless injuries and property damage due to people not using collars while lifting.*

- *Lift weights on an Olympic lifting platform. You can either buy a ready-made platform, or build one with 2 layers of ¾ inch plywood, and ½ an inch of rubber. Using a platform will help absorb the force of a loaded barbell falling to the ground and provides a safe area for lifters in a gym.*

- *Learn good Olympic lifting techniques with a light pvc pipe or hockey stick (with the blade cut off). As you gain confidence in the basics, move to just using the Olympic barbell (unloaded). At this point start out with light weights and keep developing form while under the guidance of a qualified coach. It may take a month or two of lifting to get used to the various lifts before you start using decent weight on the barbell.*

- *Once a player starts lifting on a platform they "own" the platform. Other lifters must recognize this and walk around the platform while lifters are moving around on the lifting surface.*

- *If you EVER get in trouble with a lift (failure or fall), try to DROP THE WEIGHT. As you drop the barbell, push it away from the body so you don't drop it on a body part. The bumper plates and Olympic barbells are made to be dropped without damaging the equipment. I would much rather a player drop a loaded barbell than have it fall on their head. So to repeat...if you miss a lift, drop the weight away from the body. This should be taught to beginning lifters with very light weight so when a heavy loaded barbell is used, they know what to do to stay safe.*

- *Use higher than normal sets (3 to 8) and lower repetitions (1-5) with most Olympic lifting. The idea is to lift a maximal weight quickly...and this will NOT happen with high repetitions. High repetition Olympic lifting is also a great way to get injured so avoid sets of more than 8-reps if possible.*

- *Make sure you perform a good warm-up before doing any Olympic lifting. When lifting use lighter weights for 2 to 4 sets to get the correct movements and speed of the lift, before moving to heavy maximal lifts.*

- Lots of rest should be used between Olympic lifts (as much as 5 minutes between maximal lifts). The reason for this is that the goal of all Olympic lifting is to perform QUALITY lifts with a heavy weight. This cannot be done with little rest between sets.

- Good training facilities will allow (& provide) chalk for players so they can get a better grip on the barbells during lifting. Do not use gloves when Olympic lifting, but if possible use chalk to enhance your grip.

- Generally it is a good idea to start with full body lifts (power cleans, C & J's, Hang Snatch, etc.) before moving to partial or assistance movements later in the workout. Of course under the guidance of a qualified coach these rules can certainly be altered as it may be necessary to work the partial movement first to fix lifting technique before integrating it into the full lift later in the workout.

- Olympic lifting movements should be done first in the workout (before slower movements like squats, deadlifts, bench press, lunges, chin-ups, etc.). Again, this rule can be broken if under the supervision of a qualified strength coach.

- Maximal lifts are NOT in the best interest of the younger or inexperienced hockey player as the risk to reward ratio is just too high. Players should have at least 8-months working with a qualified coach on Olympic lifting form prior to testing for a maximal lift.

- If necessary a weightlifting belt may be used for maximal lifts to help provide additional support for the low back and core area. Belts should not be used for most other lifting as players need to develop correct lifting technique and core stability without the aid of a belt.

- If possible it is best to use a pair of Olympic lifting shoes with hard wooden soles and an elevated heal to get the best results. These shoes (usually made by Adidas) will last a long time but provide a good base for the feet and transfer all of the force into lifting the weight rather than "absorbing energy" in the rubber of running shoes.

U19 Lady Ducks Kayla Nielsen (#26), on a breakaway during tournament play

Chapter 10 - Plyometrics

"Hockey is a skaters game. If you can skate and move you can defend,
and therefore you have a place in our line-up"

~ Frank Serratore (Head Hockey Coach at The United States Air Force Academy, NCAA D1)

A lot of hockey coaches talk to me about the lack of plyometrics in my training programs. While I do like plyometrics (as a training tool), I am under the opinion that few players below the age of 18-years of age (and without a considerable training history) are able to correctly perform "real" plyometrics (see my "**NOTE**" section down the page), without it impacting the player negatively. Players who are not ready for plyometrics see poor technique during jumps, improper muscle firing, lack of/or over-muscle recruitment which leads to poor motor pattern development and a much greater chance of impact related injuries. During interviews with the Hungarian National Speedskating Team strength coach Wolfgang Unsöld was asked if he used plyometrics with the elite Junior National Team athletes and his response was,

> "at this point, none of the skaters I work with are strong enough to use plyometrics and jump training optimally. At training camps I observe other coaches and their training methods, and one thing that amazes me is their emphasis on jumps, especially the volume of jumps – up to 30 jumps a set. With the athletes I train who can't pass the Klatt test, much less squat 1.5 times their bodyweight, this type of training puts the athletes at a high risk of injury and does not make them more powerful."

Plyometrics like all other methods of training are but ONE training tool to accomplish the goal of player development. Far too many coaches rush into plyometric training (at much too young an age before players are developmentally ready) as they wish to emulate what NHL teams are doing to condition players. Rather, think of plyometrics like giving a 3-year old a nail gun and expecting good things to happen. There is a time and a place for the nail gun, but not with a 3-year old. Instead, do what is BEST for the athlete...it all comes back to the LTAD model presented in chapter two.

Defining Plyometrics
In a nutshell, plyometrics are a form of physical training designed to develop the explosive power of a muscle group or muscle action. If we think of the muscles like a spring, that the spring has the ability to absorb ground forces, store that energy and then quickly spring back to the original shape. In hockey the important take away message of plyometrics is that we are training the body to absorb ground reaction forces, and then quickly perform another skating stride as quickly as possible to keep momentum. In order to achieve this training affect, plyometrics involve jump-type training that loads and requires the player to move from this loaded position quickly. Due to the high stress nature of plyometrics it is important to use teach progressions (of jumps), and to first screen players for physical readiness to perform plyometrics (both are shown below). Additionally I have included my recommendations for volume, repetition, and periodization recommendations to fully advise you of the time and place to use plyometrics as part of an overall training methodology.

NOTE: I stated earlier that I do not use plyometrics often, and that is actually untrue. I refer to levels 7 to 10 from the teaching progressions below as true plyometrics, an all of the other forms as teaching aids or "lead up exercises". With true level 7 - 10 plyometrics, I do not in fact use this with every hockey player, but only those who pass the required 4-tests as outlined below.

Readiness for Plyometrics
In order to determine which athletes are ready for plyometrics I use a system of tests that are designed to show readiness for the intense stress that plyometrics can impart. If an athlete fails a test

or is lacking in an area I work to build up that area in an effort to ready them for high stress type plyometric training in the future. Here are the tests I use:

1. Vertical Jump Test

First I measure what an athlete's vertical jump actually is (inches), with a best-of-three series of jumps. These are regular vertical jumps where the athlete stands in one spot beside a wall or testing device, squats down as far as they wish, jumps up extending the hands over head to determine the number of inches they can jump into the air.

At this point, now bring an 18-inch box over to the same position by the wall. Have the athlete stand on the box and when ready the player jumps off the box (both feet equally), lands and does a vertical jump (so a vertical jump from a depth jump). Athletes who are not ready for plyometrics are the athletes who are not able to match or exceed the level (inches) of the "normal vertical jump" with this depth jump – vertical jump test. If they are off by a little bit (and inch or two) then mild plyometric training can begin if supervised. If the player is off by several inches then they are simply not strong enough to perform plyometric training.

2. Squat Test

In order to perform plyometrics correctly there needs to be a base level of strength which every athlete should attain prior to plyometric training as the landing forces that a player will have to absorb are very high (up to 4-times the bodyweight per square inch). Therefore, the baseline that most experts agree on is a full barbell squat with 1.5 times the bodyweight. So if a player weighs 150lbs, they will need to squat 225lbs for 1RM (and these are not half squats, rather a squat through a full range of motion).

In the picture Pro-player Kevin Flather squats 315lbs (not his max), which is already more than the number he needs to begin plyometric training.

3. 1-Leg Squat Test

A big part of plyometric training is the ability to show muscle balance, flexibility, stability and maintain correct posture throughout movements. Often when a player fails at a plyometric assessment it's because a muscle or muscle group cannot stabilize the joints effectively, flex properly, or maintain balance. Strength and Conditioning expert Vern Gambetta found with his research that "for the beginner, strength in the stabilizing muscles is primary, and you can easily test for it."

The test I use is a 1-Leg Squat, which requires balance, stability, flexibility and correct posture to execute. I ask players for 3-good repetitions on each leg (this is a pass/fail exercise).

4. Modified Klatt Test

The Klatt test is a series of tests to determine how an athlete moves and what issues may need to be addressed with overall training. I use one of the tests in the Klatt test, and assign my own value to it as a method of plyometric loading suitability.

Start by having a player stand barefoot on a 6-inch box, with arms stretched out in front. Extend one leg out in front, and with the other leg hop off the box and, "stick the landing" (as in a gymnastics type landing) and hold for 10-seconds. Watch the landing closely and determine if they:

- Are able to hold the landing for 10-seconds.
- That all three joints, the ankle, knee and hip bend to absorb the force of the landing
- The knee does not "cave-in", towards the middle of the body.
- That both legs are equal in terms of reaction to the landing.
- The athlete does not loose balance with the upper body.

In part two of the test, re-test the player using a 12-inch box (same test as above). Again, look closely at the players leg as it lands to determine visual cues about performance issue.

When evaluating the results of the 6-inch and 12-inch, single-leg jump tests use the following:

- Knee "caves-in" = Weak Vastus Medialis (VMO), the tear-drop muscle on the lower medial portion of the quadriceps next to the knee. (Remedy this with front squats, hack squats, close stance squats, etc.).
- Player hops forward = Weak Hamstrings. (Fix this by RDL's, x-over deads, glute-hamstring raises, Nordic Eccentric Hamstrings, 1-leg hamstring curls, etc.)
- Bends forward at the waist = Weak Glutes. (Low full squats, lunges, RDL's, glute-ham raise, deadlifts, etc. will help solve this problem.)
- Player hops inward = Weak Adductors. (Use cable adduction exercises, plate drags, stability ball adductions, etc. to develop this area.)
- Player hops outward = Weak Abductors. Try cable adduction exercises, skating cable exercises, multi-hip machine, etc.)
- Heel rotates in = Weak Hip Rotators. (Use side lunges, standing band hip rotation with leg at 90 degrees rotating it outwards, band hip external rotations, etc. to correct this problem.)

When evaluating the Klatt test, if a player displays 2 or more of the above for either the 6-inch height, or the 12-inch height they fail this test and must then work specific areas of the body to correct imbalances before being re-tested, and allowed to participate in a plyometrics program.

Plyometric Teaching Progressions/Levels

In order to perform plyometrics correctly and with the highest degree of benefit it is important to go through the various progressions of levels involved in plyometrics. Teaching a player how to land for instance is very important before we move to higher stress movements. There is no hurry to get from one level to the next, and some athletes may never need or be ready to go all the way through level-9. As with all training it is critical to look at the athlete who is going to use this type of training and determine whether or not it is in their best interest for LTAD.

Level-1. Landings

The goal for plyometrics and this level is to teach the proper landing techniques used during jumps. Players must get used to absorbing the force of the jump with the legs in sequence (ankle/knee/hip), and in form (sticking the landing for 2-seconds, not altering the knee position, not leaning forwards or backwards after the jump, etc.). Landing should occur over the entire foot with a slight forward lean toward the balls of the feet. Start with basic two foot forward jumps where the player sticks the landing, holds for 2-seconds and then repeats the jump. Ensure the movements are performed correctly. After 20 to 30 "perfect" jumps, have the player move to using only 1-foot and repeat on each leg for another 15-30 jumps.

Level-2. Stabilization Jumps
This phase is much like the first level only the player will jump and land with correct technique while "sticking" the landing for 5-seconds. Start with forward jumps again and have the player perform a number of trials (jump, stick for 5-seconds, repeat). Move to one-foot jumps and repeat, again working on the solid landing (absorbing the force correctly). Repeat until players can perform 5-landings in a row (on each leg) while holding the landings for a count of five.

Level-3. Jumping Up
The next level in the sequence is the ability to jump up. I generally start with a vertical jump as my teaching exercise as it is the basic jump that precedes all others. Show the athlete how to sink down into a good crouch position, with hands loaded, and then forcefully extend the legs while "throwing the arms" into the sky to jump vertically as high as possible. I start out on a gym mat so the surface is cushioned. Once they have mastered the two leg vertical jump, and then try the one-leg vertical jump. Make sure with all landings that the player lands correctly (as learned in stages 1 & 2). If not, go back a level and repeat until they can perform a vertical jump properly. Sometimes it may require fixing a strength problem (as mentioned in the Klatt test).

Once the athlete has performed well on the cushioned surface, now it's time to move to a hard surface and see about reducing the time they take on the crouching down (to load the legs) and springing back up part. Ideally the athlete will want to get to a point where they can quickly drop, transition and jump back upwards as fast as possible. Coaches can determine if a player has mastered this level by how they perform the one and two-leg vertical jump, and how they land with each jump.

Level-4. Jumping Up Onto a Box
Great power develop can be achieved by learning how to perform box jumps correctly...and then doing lots of them. With very little in the way of landing force I put this next in the sequence because the player must be able to generate a great deal of power, without stressing the joints so much. I start with a low box (8 to 12 inches) and have players get used to dropping down to load the legs, bring the arms back and then explode upwards onto the box (similar to the vertical jump in stage-3). The difference is now they are having to jump slightly forward and onto a box/bench. As players get better and better at this (the jumps are going well and the landings look clean), move to an 18-inch box, then next onto a 24-inch box (this is mid-thigh for most players over the midget age). Stop at the 24-inch box, and make sure technique is solid at all box levels.

Justin warms-up for box jumps by using a 30-inch box

Level-5. High Vertical Jumping

At this level I expect players to be able to jump high off the ground onto boxes and therefore maximize their ability to produce power from the ground. High jumps take time to learn and confidence to try (boxes over 30-inches can be intimidating for many players).

Pro player Kevin Flater jumps onto a 40-inch box during training at the Canadian Sport Centre (Pacific)

Box Squat into Box Jumps

Performing box squats into box jumps

One of my favorite power development exercise for hockey players is the box squat into box jumps. Similar to the box jump, this exercise requires the athlete to overcome their own body weight from the parallel (or lower) squat position as they jump onto the box in front of them (all in one smooth movement). Start with a 14-inch box to sit on and decrease the height of this box when possible to simulate a low squat position. With the box to jump onto, start with a smaller box and increase this height as you gain confidence in jumping ability.

Level-6. Short Jumps

This is the first level of what I consider plyometrics (in which there needs to be a readiness evaluation (the 4-tests outlined later) prior to performing these jumps. Short jumps teach vertical and horizontal movements and involve more repeated and stressful jumps. I start by teaching the two foot jump (laterally, forwards, backwards, etc.). Once this is mastered then I teach the same jumps with one foot. After this I show players how to link multiple jumps together with 3 to 5 jumps (in all directions, on both legs and on one-leg). When this is finished we move to the stairs and have them jump up the stairs forwards and to the sides (two feet at a time to start, and then one-foot at a time later on). Next I teach hockey skate jumps (side to side lateral jumping that mimics that skating motion). After this I then move to a skills oriented version of the hockey skate jump where the players will stick-handle while performing the jumps (see above for pictures). All jumps in this level are relatively short (less than 24-inches in distance so the player can master the methods of jumping. This is an advanced skill at this level and will not be easy for all players to master.

Kayla uses a Smart hockey ball to stick-handle while performing lateral skate jumps

Level-7. Long Jumps & Long Repeated Jumping

This next phase involves repeated jumping where the player jumps, lands, and then jumps again. The goal is to teach quick reactions off the ground, and multiple correct landings. Learn how to repeat longer jumps and absorb the landings "without making a sound". This teaches players how to use the body to absorb forces correctly. Move to one-leg longer jumping with the same principals of quiet jumping and correct landings.

Justin performing repeated long jumps

The next movement learned should be the squat jump where the player squats way down, loading the legs, and then jumps up as forcefully as possible, and then upon landing absorbs the jump by going back into a squat position for another jump. Repeat for 3 to 5 jumps and evaluate. There should be no pause in the "action" during these jumps (just squat, jump, squat, jump, etc.).

Now teach the long multi-directional jumps (forwards, backwards, and laterally), with both legs, and then one-leg). When this is performed correctly, link consecutive multi-direction maximal jumps. Ensure a soft landing and correct form with all jumps.

After learning longer, maximal multi-directional jumps now try a knee-tuck at the top position (not shown), or jumps with a tuck to the sides or onto different levels (boxes or slight drops). This is much harder and requires quick hip flexors to bring the knees up (to the chest) before extending them to land and repeat the jump. This is a much higher stress movement then in previous levels so care must be taken when implementing this type of jump.

Kayla performing repeated lateral jumps (picture 1),
Kayla and her brother Bryce perform repeated lateral jumps (picture 2).

Level-8 Stress Jumps

This level includes jumps that involve stress jumps that require a solid base of training prior to learning. The player needs to know how to land properly as weights are often added at this point in the plyometrics to achieve a greater loading (like weight vests, plyo-tubes or dumbbells). Examples of high stress jumping are the Russian Box, Weighted Jump Lunges, West Vest Repeated Squat Jumps, Frog Jumps (multiple squat jumps moving forwards/backwards/laterally), Bulgarian Split Squat Jumps (weighted or un-weighted). These jumps due to the nature of the landing (mostly single leg) and the added weight, are referred to as high stress jumps.

Professional hockey player Justin Todd practicing hockey specific skate training on the Russian Box

Bulgarian Split Squat Jump

To develop explosive single leg power I often use the Bulgarian Split Squat Jump as part of my lower body plyometrics. Begin the exercise without weight, using the same form as a normal split squat. From the low position, explode upwards and jump off the ground with the front foot (while keeping the back leg on the bench/box). Upon landing, quickly reload the leg (like a spring) and repeat the exercise. As this exercise gets easier I have my players use a weighted vest or dumbbells to provide extra resistance. The idea isn't to overload the jumping leg too much as we are trying to develop explosive power more than anything with this exercise.

Bryan is one of the best athletes I train at the Bulgarian Split Squat jump

Weighted Jump Lunges

Clint jumps from a lunge position (picture 1), as high as possible (picture 2), then lands (picture 3)

Jump lunges are a plyometric exercise that helps develop explosive power unilaterally. Using this exercise with a weighted version develops these properties but also works a player's conditioning as they have to overcome the exercise and the additional weight of a dumbbell, plyotube or weight vest. Used as a transition exercise between conditioning drills this exercise can be a great unilateral leg conditioning tool. Note that players can also use a training tool called the plyotube which is a large 4' fabric tube filled with sand that can be hung around a player's neck to add resistance.

Level-9. Shock Jumps & High Stress Jumps

A very advanced form of plyometric training is known as shock jumps (aka drop jumps), which is also the highest level of plyometric training used only with elite athletes. The drop jump is basically a two leg jump from a box or platform that is 12 to 48" in height. When beginning to learn drop jumps the goal should be to absorb the landing force over a wide range of motion (so an athlete would land and descend into a squat to absorb the force of the jump). The problem is this does not build eccentric force production and therefore it is best to teach athletes (after the initial stages) to jump and land by bending the knees as little as possible on the landing, which forces the leg muscles to forcefully absorb the landing force over a short distance (therefore developing a higher degree of power). It is important to note that this is a very advanced method of training and something that only experienced hockey players with at least 2-years of training, and progression through the various levels of plyometric training should even try. The height of the box and how it is integrated into the program depend on a wide variety of factors and as such should only be implemented under the guidance of a qualified strength and conditioning coach.

Collegiate goaltender Dan Spence performing shock jumps at the Canadian Sport Centre (Vancouver, BC)

Weighted Squat Jumps

6th Round (2009) NHL draft pick Connor Knapp performs barbell jump squats with 95lbs.

The second form of high stress jumps involve higher loading of the body with barbells, kettlebells, dumbells or heavy weight vests. The goal is to perform movements (either vertically or horizontally) with correct form and higher loads for lower overall training volume. Players can be challenged with either a lighter load (for more explosive jumps) or heavier weights (for a greater stress). Provided the players use correct form, coaches can load athletes with higher and higher weights (up to several hundred pounds) if this fits with their particular program. Remember, these are very advanced methods of training, and not appropriate for everyone.

Suggested Plyometric Volume

There is a wide range of volume suggestions for plyometrics training and the final answer is that it all depends on the goals of the workout and the level/abilities of the player who is performing plyometrics. Here are my standard protocols measured in number of ground contacts per session (therefore when jumping each foot strike is counted as a ground contact). Remember, more is not better...better is better. Therefore insist on high quality reps for EVERY plyometric movement.

- New to plyometrics (less than 3-months plyo-training) = 40 contacts per session

- 3-months to 1-year experience with plyometrics = 30 to 80 contacts per session

- 1-year to 5-years' experience with plyometrics = 60 to 160 ground contacts per session

- Elite & Professional players = 90 to 200 ground contacts per session (depending on exercises and load)

When to Add Plyometrics into Training

Unlike strength training and various other kinds of lifting, plyometrics should only be done several times per year as a "finishing" protocol. If you look at the yearly periodization chart in the Putting it all Together chapter, you will notice that I include two distinct times of the year that speed development comes into play (at least for the older athletes of Bantam age and above). I often link the last four weeks of this speed training with plyometric work to develop that last little bit of explosive power for hockey players. If you perform plyometrics year round (which many programs do), you expose athletes to a much higher risk of overuse injuries. By limiting the plyometric training to two times per year (once before training camp in the late July into August, and the other before the playoff from January to mid-February), for only 4-weeks at a time it greatly reduces the chance of injuries and maximizes the effectiveness of the plyometrics. The graph below shows when I might use plyometrics with a midget level hockey player.

Example of a 15-17 Year Old (Midget in Canada & the USA)
General Periodization Macro-Cycle (12-Months) for Speed Training

General Preparation Phase			Special Preparation Phase			Pre-Competition Phase			Competition Phase		PO	Rest
April	May	June	July	August	Sept	Oct	Nov	Dec	Jan	Feb		March
No Speed	Volume Speed		Intensity Speed			Maintain Speed			Intensity Speed		Limited Speed	

Diagram 17 – Example of Speed Periodization within a Midget age Macro-cycle

Plyometric Guidelines

- Make sure to perform plyometrics first thing in the workout so the quality of the action is the best possible. With plyometrics more is not better, better is better. Meaning, volume is not important, rather the quality of the actions. I would rather have 5 jumps done right than 30 jumps done wrong.

- Depending on how you integrate plyometrics into your training you can work them up to 4-times per week.

- When performing plyometrics sets I usually keep the number of repetitions per set at 5-jumps. This allows the player to focus on quality of action rather than thinking they have to "gut out" a gruelling set of 25 or 30 jumps. Of course with elite athletes if I use plyometrics as a conditioning drill (such as a set of 25-jump squats combined with kettlebell snatch, burpees and jump lunges) as my goal is to condition the player and the quality of the jump becomes secondary. You can make up the rules as you go along with some of the more advanced athletes, just know WHY you are deviating from the "rules", and whether it is in the best interest of the athlete at that time.

- Performing plyometrics should not feel like hard work. In fact, it should feel like most true sprinting workouts in that you should work quality actions with lots of rest between sets to recover fully. If players are sweating or breathing hard from plyometrics then either they are doing them wrong (with too many jumps per set) or they have awful conditioning and that should immediately become the focus of training for that athlete.

- If possible work plyometrics with a coach so they can observe and detect problems with jumping and landing that might pose future problems. If this is not possible, then try to work out with a training partner who can watch how you land and jump to ensure quality actions.

- Coaches who implement plyometrics should have players perform them on a case by case basis and only when they are ready. Each player should be on an individual schedule/plan rather than having the entire team following one protocol.

Chapter 11 - Strength Training Exercises

"Mighty oaks from little acorns grow"

~ unknown

I believe that hockey players should use certain key exercises to build a base of general strength and power, and then supplement that with a wide range of auxiliary exercises for injury prevention, grip training and most importantly, conditioning. When all of these kinds of training are integrated together a player will have a very powerful method of improving their level of play on the ice. In this chapter I have outlined some (not all) of my favorite strength training exercises that get results.

Lower Body Exercises

Quad Dominate Exercises

Squats

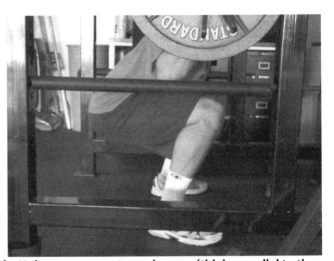

Cody demonstrates the proper squat technique (picture 1). Make sure you go to 90 degrees (thighs parallel to the ground) or lower in the bottom position of the squat (picture 2).

Squats are the **KING** of exercises for hockey players. Nothing else will build the kind of leg strength needed to play the game of hockey at a very high level like the squat...**NOTHING**. Start the squat by stepping under the bar, pulling the shoulder blades tightly together, arching the back, pushing outwards with the abdominal muscles, gripping the bar tightly and generally holding the body tight. Point the toes slightly outwards and make sure your <u>knees track over your toes</u>, ***but do not go past the toes*** (to prevent injury to the knees). Descend by breaking at the hips, and then the knees as you lower downwards. At the bottom position (at least 90-degrees parallel or <u>below if possible</u>), you will NOT bounce, but rather slowly move into and out of the "hole" or bottom of the squat. On the ascent make sure the hips and shoulders come up at the SAME TIME to prevent the back from losing its angle and putting more stress on the low back.

One of my favorite ways to use the squat is to put athletes through sets of 20-repetitions as suggested by strength and conditioning coach Randall Strossen in his book *Super Squats*. I use this method of training at the **end** of lower body workouts to really mentally and physically prepare players. Above all, just make sure the squat form is correct and performed safely!

As a further method of sport specification I will from time to time have my players perform squats (all kinds), deadlifts, lunges (all kinds), x-over deads, etc. **with skates on** (tied loosely). Try this (with a spotter) to develop tremendous ankle strength and higher levels of sport specific strength/balance. Just make sure your gym allows this and you do it safely!

Nick Kooiker (Eastern Washington University) squatting 225lbs for 12-reps well below parallel

Moose Jaw Warriors (WHL) goaltender Brandon Stone comes out of the bottom position in the squat while being spotted by Coach Clint Hazen (picture 1). In picture 2 CIS Nipissing University goaltender Dan Spence demonstrates a low squat position "he gets his ass to the grass" as he warms up for a 1RM attempt.

Barbell Chain Squats

The addition of chains to a traditional barbell squat does two very important things to the squatting action. Number one, it provides additional weight to the bar that matches a player's natural strength curve. What does this mean? Well, when you start off the chains are off the floor (if loaded as shown in the pictures on the next page). As you descend into a full squat the chains rest on the floor which unloads some of the weight from the barbell (when you are in the weakest part of the lift). When standing back up the chains start to come off the ground and add more and more weight until you lock out the exercise (where you are at your strongest). This means this exercise follows your strength curve for this exercise.

The number two reason that chains are used is that as you perform a squat (or bench press, etc), the chains swing around and provide an uneven pull on the barbell (which challenges balance and stability). Adding chains is an advanced strength training movement, but can be VERY valuable when performed correctly.

NOTE: *When using chains the goal is not to lift a maximal weight, but rather to perform dynamic lifts (quick, explosive actions). Use 50% of your 1RM for chain squats. Lower the barbell slowly, and from the bottom position explode up to the top. Also, make sure not to use too much weight in the form of chains. Usually 50 to 70lbs of chains is PLENTY to provide a good stimulus.*

Chains provide not only a different kind of resistance, but test the
balance and body position as they swing when moved

Barbell Band Squats

Todd using Superbands along with 185lbs to provide the right tension for his power curve in the squat

Much like the addition of chains, the use of bands provides resistance that develops the player's natural strength curve. As you lower the barbell the bands relax and provide little resistance (if any), and as you stand up they provide a good deal of resistance to the barbell.

NOTE: Much like chains this is an advanced exercise and should be performed only when you are ready. Use 50% of your 1RM on the barbell in terms of weight and start off with light bands. Lower the barbell slowly and then explode upwards to lockout. At the most I would recommend no more than one 2 ¾ inch band on each side of the barbell which provides about 70lbs of force to the barbell. Make sure you have a spotter when doing band squats.

Close Stance Squats
With close stance squats the set-up is the same as with regular squats except that the feet are placed only 8-inches apart. In the pictures Cody is warming up with 135lbs onto a box to get the form down properly before getting into the workout. Notice how the knees never go forward over the toes (picture 1), and the back stays more upright than a regular squat. This places more focus on the quads and low back to stabilize that weight and perform the action correctly.

Cody performs close stance squats

Cyclist Squats

Cyclist squats are very similar to close stance squats, only the heels are elevated on a small board, weight plate or 2x4 piece of wood. The legs are still kept 6 to 10 inches apart for the exercise, but it is not important for the knees to remain behind the toes in the lowest position. With cyclist squats the focus is really on the quads and due to the knee position this should be used as a supplemental exercise, rather than a primary exercise…and therefore, lower weights should be used.

Kevin performs cyclist squats (notice the knees staying in line with the toes)

Eagle Squats

Eagle squats are great exercise to help with hip mobilization and flexibility, but are also a good strengthening exercise for the groin muscles. To perform an Eagle Squat you start with the feet 14-inches or more apart and with the toes pointed outwards (to the sides). From this position keep the upper body relatively upright and squat down while keeping the knees direction over the toes (pictures 1 & 2). The knees are NOT to cave inwards (as is seen with people who are not flexible or lack strength in the glutes). You want to focus on lowering and rising with the inner thighs and butt on this exercise (not the quads). This exercise can also be used with a barbell behind the neck (picture 1) or with a KB or similar object (picture 2). Start with a lighter weight until you get used to these and then add weight as you see fit.

NOTE: I like to use half-filled kegs with this exercise as now the body has to stabilize an unstable object while performing this key injury prevention exercise.

Kevin Flather does eagle squats with a barbell,
while Justin sinks low into the eagle squat with a kettlebell held in front of the body

Box Squats

The box squat should be a staple exercise for <u>every</u> player as it works very well to develop great leg and core area strength, and is an awesome way to learn how to squat properly. By squatting down onto a box the body gets used to the proper depth necessary in the normal squat, but it also breaks up the "rebound effect" that happens at the bottom of the squat when the muscles store kinetic energy and help to rebound the body upwards. Sitting on the box cancels this spring affect and makes the player work to overcome the weight of the barbell plus the body's own weight as it breaks from the box. Powerlifters use this great exercise to build immense leg strength, and so should every player.

Barbell Squat Press

Clint using a 135lb barbell for repeated squat press training in Richmond, BC

Start with a lighter barbell on the back in the same position as a traditional squat. From this position squat down ½ the distance of a normal squat, pause briefly and then explode upwards with the legs. As the legs start to straighten the shoulders and arms now must continue the push upwards to an extended position overhead. Lower the barbell to the shoulders, pause and repeat the action. For a more advanced version of the barbell squat press players should squat lower (to below parallel with the thighs). *Note: this exercise is much like the Push Press, only the barbell starts behind the neck.*

Wave Squat

The wave squat is an explosive exercise that looks to develop the posterior chain muscles in the lower body. Think of the exercise as a jump squat without the jump portion. To begin, squat down to a 1/3 squat position and then explosively spring upwards and onto the balls of the feet (without leaving the feet). Lower down to a flat foot position and repeat. I like to use the wave squat with higher than normal repetitions as a finishing exercise or as part of high volume programs.

Kevin performing high rep wave squats with 225lbs

Overhead Squat

The overhead squat is a very difficult lift that takes a great deal of strength throughout the body to do right. To perform this lift the barbell is lifted over the head into a stabilized position, and then the player lowers down into a full squat much the same as the traditional front squat or barbell squat. Once well past parallel (with the thighs), stand back up to the starting position.

Players should start with just a hockey stick to get the form correct, and then progress to a barbell before adding weight to the bar. Performing the over-head squat is a very tough but valuable assistance exercise (not a main developer like squats or deadlifts) or as a great warm-up to future training.

The picture shows the correct form for the low position of the overhead squat. Notice how the barbell is right above Jen's base of support in the middle of her feet.

Pistols (One-Leg Squats)

The one leg squat is a great exercise to improve balance, coordination and basic strength in the lower body and is one of my favourites for players. As skating is largely done on 1-leg, it is important to develop that kind of independent leg strength and balance not trained by traditional squats.

In order to perform this exercise correctly, and with the most benefit, you must try to go as low as possible in the squat depth (you may need to hold on to a fixed object at first). Use a high enough plyobox to get a full range of motion and start next to a squat rack so you can hold on if need be for balance. As the balance improves, move the squat box to an open area and perform 1-leg squats there. Holding the hands out in front of the body and leaning forward at the hip really helps to complete this tough exercise. If your flexibility will not allow a full range of motion then you have to stretch out the lower leg (calf, in a seated position) and the hips to accommodate this exercise.

Cody Kreger demonstrates his favourite exercise, one-leg squats

Front Squats

The front squat is a very important exercise for developing a high level of quadriceps, core and back strength. Due to the nature of the lift a player cannot lift the same weight as a back squat and the low back has to have a more upright posture so the chance of low back injury is reduced. Another advantage of this lift is if the athlete gets into trouble they can simply drop the weight in front of them (always into a squat rack or power rack) without the same potential risks associated with back squats. One of my favorite uses of the front squat is as a finisher to be used with Tabata type interval training as this is a lung and leg killer.

To perform the front squat, approach the bar in a squat rack and place it on the front part of the shoulders, with the hands either folded in front, or in the power clean type "rack" position (see picture 1). From this position, take the barbell out of the supports to the workout area and then squat down to a below parallel position (see picture 2). It is important to keep the back as upright as possible and really push from the legs to perform the exercise correctly. Start with a lower weight to develop good technique and move up as you get stronger and more able to handle heavier weights.

Kevin Flather warms up with 135lbs for 8 reps in the front squat

Zercher Squats

The Zercher squat is a tough but great exercise to develop the low back, legs and upper body with a lower than normal weight. To start I advise players to put the barbell in on the hooks on the outside of the squat rack. Un-rack the weight and hold the barbell in the crook of the arms (picture 1). Squat down into a below parallel position (with the thighs) and try to keep the upper body in an upright posture, (picture 2). Start out with light weights as this exercise is tough on the low back at first. Consistent use of the Zercher squat will definitely help the strength of your low back and with all of the other lifts. Just be careful as this is the kind of exercise you need to perform correctly and with a light to moderate weight in order to prevent a potential injury.

UCLA Assistant Strength Coach Todd Bostrom doing Zercher squats at Revolution Athletics

Hack Squat

Start the action on the toes with a block of wood under the heels. Lower to the ground by keeping the back flat and in a fully upright position (while staying on the toes). Rise up out of the bottom position slowly and return to the starting position. When holding a barbell or kettlebell behind your back try to keep perfect form during this exercise (back flat and upright). When done properly, this should be completely a quad dominate exercise.

When choosing a block of wood to use start off with a normal 2"x4" piece of wood (we use a 2-inch wedge at our facility) and build up the load on the bar. Some athletes like to use a higher piece of wood or wedge, but note that this does change the exercise and will decrease the loads one can lift. Regardless of the height you use under the heels it is still very important to maintain a flat and upright back.

Kevin using a barbell with his feet up on weight plates (pictures 1 & 2)

Bulgarian Split Squats (BSS)

Last time I looked, hockey was mostly played on one leg (about 85% of the time anyway). The Bulgarian split squat has a history of developing great single leg power and muscle balance in the legs as the Bulgarians used this exercise to eventually equal and defeat the Russians in Olympic weightlifting. To start the Bulgarian split squat make sure you step out far enough from the bench so you get a good range of motion. From the starting position lower down (by sitting back into the Bulgarian split squat) until your back knee is slightly off the ground (1-inch or so). Keep the upper body in an upright position so as to keep the focus on the front leg.

NCAA goaltender Chelsea Knapp does the Bulgarian Split Squat (BSS)

Elevated Front Leg Bulgarian Split Squats (EBSS)

The elevated Bulgarian split squat is an awesome single leg exercise for hockey players as it works the front leg through a huge range of motion while putting an incredible stretch on the hip flexor of the back leg and developing single leg balance. I like to train one leg at a time to correct any imbalances (from leg to leg), and this exercise lets me load a player up with a heavy weight and develop the legs without putting much strain on the low back (due to the more upright posture).

Start by putting a 6 to 10-inch step in front of a weight bench, and then from the start position (picture 1) lower down until the back knee almost touches the ground (picture 2). Maintain an upright posture of the trunk throughout the entire lift and when standing up from the bottom position push through the heel of the front foot rather than the balls of the foot.

With a pair of 40lb dumbbells Kevin soldiers through a set of elevated BSS

Lunge Variations

There are many kinds of lunges, and in this section I am presenting just 6-variations (the forward walking lunge with dumbbells, the forward walking lunge with a barbell, walking keg lunges, cross-over lunges, hockey lunges, and the front Bosu lunge).

Traditional lunges (picture 1), weighted walking lunges (picture 2), keg walking lunges (picture 3)

With all lunges make sure to take a big step when lunging, keep the trunk upright and try to get the back knee close to the ground (to ensure a full range of motion). When returning to the starting position always push from the heel so it activates more of the hamstring and glute muscles.

Justin does cross-over lunges (picture 1), hockey lunges (picture 2),
Pro-hockey player Mykul Haun does front Bosu lunges with a stick held overhead (picture 3)

NOTE: If using a keg or barbell for lunges be sure you can complete the exercise with the load you have planned as falling with a heavy barbell or keg can cause serious injury. It is best to have a spotter always nearby in case you get into trouble and learn the safe methods to "get rid of" a barbell or keg that is too heavy or potentially dangerous.

Reverse Lunge

Kevin warms up with 135lbs on the reverse lunge

I include the reverse lunge separately because I feel that the reverse lunge is the best version of all the lunges due to the potential for heavy loading (if done in a squat rack). I like players to get a good deal of work on one-leg exercises and the reverse lunge is a safe option that pays high dividends provided the load is substantial.

To perform the reverse lunge load up a heavy barbell, get in the starting position like with a squat and take a big step backwards dropping down into the lunge position. Be careful not to lean too far forward with the upper body during the lift. Push from the heel of the front foot to stand upright.

Step-ups

With step-ups simply hold onto weights (dumbbells, a barbell, keg or kettelbell) and step-up onto a bench or box. Make sure the box is high enough so the leg at least makes a 90 degree angle (figure 1) when starting out. Stepping onto a bench is good as the uneven surface of the bench provides an additional challenge. Repeat on both side (right and left leg).

Clint performs step-ups at Magic Hockey in Langley, BC

Cross-Over (Hockey) Step-ups

The cross-over step-up is similar to the normal step-up only you stand parallel to the box/bench and then cross the leg over in front (like a hockey cross-over) as seen in figure 1. Muscle your way up and then bring the other leg onto the box/bench at the top of the movement (figure 2). To get back to the starting position reverse the movement by lowering inside leg to the ground (figure 1). Use dumbbells, barbells or kegs with this exercise as necessary to provide additional loading.

Cross-over step-ups are a key exercise for hockey players

Hip/Hamstring Dominate Exercises

Deadlifts

The deadlift is a basic full body movement that every hockey player should learn, as this is the basis for so many other important lifts and it builds incredible strength throughout the posterior chain muscles, core and upper back. For packing on mass, smaller players should use dumbbells to do sets of 20 reps in the deadlift. Generally though, repetitions in the deadlift with a barbell should be in the strength development range of 1 to 6 reps with a heavy load for multiple sets.

To perform the deadlift, start with the shoulders over the bar (critical), back flat, head up and with an alternating grip (one hand with palms facing forward and the other facing backwards). Rise up from the start (the head and shoulders must rise the SAME TIME as the hips). Continue to a full lockout (not shown in these pictures). Return to the start position (under control) and repeat. In this picture Justin uses 315 for repetitions of 6.

Wentworth Institute (NCAA Division III) hockey player Justin Anonas lifts 315lbs for reps in Banff, AB

Snatch Grip Deadlifts

Justin pulls 225lbs from the floor during warm-ups at Revolution Athletics

Very similar to the deadlift, the snatch grip deadlift uses a wider than shoulder width, overhand grip. To start grab the bar to the outside of the shoulders with an overhand grip and the shoulders overtop of the barbell (picture 1). From this position contract the glutes, legs and low back to pull the weight upwards to the top position (picture 2).

To execute this lift correctly you will need to lower the back down further than with a traditional deadlift as the hands are further apart. This puts a greater strain on the low back so be careful and make sure you are "tight" before lifting the barbell from the floor.

Sumo Deadlift
The technique for sumo deadlifts is the same as with other deadlifts, only the hands are held close together (6 to 8-inches apart), and the feet are wider than shoulder width. The toes can also be

pointed outwards a little bit to make it easier on the hips. Make sure to get the shoulders over the bar in the bottom position and then pull from the posterior chain muscles (hamstrings, glutes, low back).

Justin using Sumo Deadlift form

Trap Bar Deadlift

When most hockey players are first learning the deadlift exercise I usually start them on the trap bar as the design of the bar puts the load in the middle of the body when lifting. This feature helps people get used to pulling a heavy weight from the floor. As the form and weight increases athletes can move to a straight bar to continue learning and perfecting deadlift form and increasing maximal weight on the bar. As with any deadlift, start out with a "tight" position prior to the lift and pull the barbell up with good form and a flat back that does not round when pulling upwards.

Trap bar deadlifts are a great exercise for building strength in the posterior chain muscles

The Suitcase Deadlift

The suitcase deadlift is really just a one handed deadlift. My favorite way of performing the suitcase dead is with a barbell lodged into the corner of the room, weights loaded on the far end near the athlete and the athlete holding the 2" outside portion of the barbell (see pictures below). The athlete picks up the loaded barbell from the floor (picture 1), with a flat back and shoulders over the toes until they are standing upright with the barbell by the side of the legs (picture 2). The barbell deadlift is a tremendous exercise for grip training, deadlift form and unilateral muscle development. Repetitions should be low (3 to 8-reps) with a heavier load on the barbell. Take care not to drop the barbell on your toes as you might not play hockey for a while!

SFU Assistant Strength Coach Clint Hazen performs the suitcase deadlift to perfection

Band Deadlifts

Band deadlifts are a strength training exercise that works primarily the posterior chain muscles of the hamstrings, glutes and low back with some involvement of the quadriceps, upper back and grip muscles to perform the action. The reason why I include the band deadlift into this section is that it is a very good conditioning drill for the posterior chain muscles and should be incorporated into any hockey dryland program.

Players should start with a 1¾ inch Superband, and move up to a 3-inch Superband as their strength improves. I recommend performing at least 30-repetitions or as many repetitions in a set amount of time (such as 30 to 45 seconds). Including deadlifts will help many players with low back conditioning which is the heart and soul of a hockey players training program.

Bantam AAA hockey player John Grenier demonstrates band deadlifts with a 2-inch Superband

RDL (Romanian Dead Lifts)

The RDL is a tremendous exercise for developing the low back, glutes and hamstrings but you MUST keep your back as flat as possible and your core area really tight throughout this motion (or you risk low back strain). Keep the head up and tighten your glutes as if you have a $100 dollar bill between your butt cheeks and someone is trying to pull it out. You do not have to keep your legs perfectly straight for this exercise, in fact they need to be bent a little bit (but not too much) during the action. **This exercise should never be done for more than 6-repetitions (as the core and stabilizers muscles will tire out and it won't support the low back).**

Justin finishes up a set of RDL's with 315 for 5 reps

Also shown below is the sumo-style RDL performed by Justin Anonas, which is the same as normal RDL's only the feet are 2 to 4-inches wider than shoulder width, and the feet can be angled outwards slightly if necessary with the hands close to the middle of the barbell.

College player Justin Anonas demonstrates sumo style RDL's

X-Over Deads

Cody performs a proper x-over deadlift (pictures 1 & 2), Clint does a set of x-overs at Magic Hockey

The x-over dead is basically a one-leg version of the RDL with a twist towards the leg on the ground. Start balancing on one-leg and then while keeping that leg near straight lower the weight (held in the opposite hand) to the toes of the leg on the ground. The back leg should come up in a straight line with the upper body to counterbalance the load. Rise back up to complete this exercise (not letting the free leg ever touch the ground) by contracting the hamstrings, glutes and low back. Remember to train both sides and keep the body very tight throughout this exercise.

Barbell X-Over Deads

Dan Spence uses a 115lbs barbell to perform X-over Deads

Very similar to the normal x-over deads, this exercise uses a barbell to further stress the posterior chain muscles (hamstring, glutes and low back) one leg at a time. With the barbell players are able to hold more weight (both hands are used), and provides a slightly different feel in the hamstrings and balance than with a dumbbell.

Good Mornings

The good morning exercise starts by holding a barbell on the shoulders (like the starting position of the squat). From this position bend forward and keep the legs relatively straight like a RDL. Make sure to tighten the glutes and core muscles as you bend forward to protect your lower back. When the back gets to parallel or as the hamstrings reach the end range stand back up. Take care to maintain a flat back throughout the lift (not rounded) to prevent injury.

Good mornings are a great low back, hamstring and glute exercise as Todd shows above

Windmills

Windmills are a nice hamstring, glute, low back, core and shoulder stabilizer exercise that will test most players flexibility and coordination. Start by pointing the toes to one side and holding a dumbbell or kettlebell straight over head (picture 1). Bend forward at the waist without bending the knees and touch the toe on the side the weight is not held (picture 2). Rise back up slowly by contracting the hip, hamstrings and core. Gradually build up to a decent weight in this exercise (50+ pounds).

Windmills with a 44lbs kettlebell

Modified Glute-Ham Raise

Justin shows a modified glute-ham raise

Most gyms do not have a glute ham raise (although they should), so for this exercise we will adapt to the equipment that is most likely found in a typical gym (a 45 degree back extension machine). Start off on the 45 degree machine in a fully flexed position (picture 1). From this position raise up by contracting the hamstring muscles ONLY. Keep the low back neutral and do not pull the hips backwards to aid the motion, simply contract the hamstrings to pull yourself back (picture 2 & 3).

These are a tough exercise and at first will produce a high level of muscle soreness in the hamstrings. As players get better at this exercise add weight as the hamstrings best responds to heavier loading and fewer repetitions.

Nordic Hamstring Negatives

The glute ham raise is one of the best exercises around for the hamstrings but many athletes are simply not strong enough to perform the action correctly (or have no access to the machine at a typical gym). With the Nordic Hamstring assisted negative exercise a player can develop eccentric strength (the lowering part) first, where they are the strongest, and then after time apply those to normal glute ham raises or a full range Nordic hamstring exercise going down and then back up.

In the picture Coach Pollitt holds the feet of Cody Kreger as he performs assisted Nordic hamstring negatives on an Airex pad.

To do this exercise the player either has another person hold their ankles or hooks the ankles under a fixed object (like the side of a squat rack). Put a pad down for the knees and start off with the body upright and hands held out in the push-up ready position. From here, keep the body straight and lower down (picture above), as far as possible before the hamstring muscles give out and you fall to the ground. Using the arms get back to the starting position and repeat. As you grow stronger you should be able to lower yourself further and further towards the ground without falling. Ideally, you want to slowly lower yourself to the ground (without using your hands), and then rise back up to the starting position (again, without using your hands). This is a <u>tough</u> exercise that requires a very good strength to body weight ratio.

Slide Board Curls

  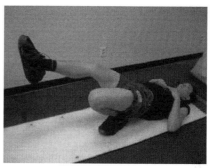

Justin demonstrating slide board curls (pictures 1&2), Bryan does 1-leg slideboard curls (picture 3)

The slide board curl is a very good stabilization and strengthening exercise for the hamstrings. One leg or both legs can be worked at a time depending on a player's strength and coordination. Players start lying on a slide board with the special nylon booties on (which slide easily on the board). Start with legs extended and the hips off the ground (3 inches or so). From this position keep the hips stable and in the same position while you curl the feet towards the butt (thus performing a hamstring curl). Personally I like to use this drill near the end of a workout for high repetitions to totally fatigue the hamstrings before I move to conditioning drills. If done right, players <u>hate</u> this exercise! Add a weight plate (held on the chest) if they don't hate this exercise…

Reverse Mountain Sliders
Another finishing exercise used at the end of a workout, (or for punishment for failing to win during conditioning workouts), the reverse mountain slider is a good hamstring conditioner. Much like the two-leg slide board curls, the player holds their hands across their chest (pictured above), raises the butt off the slide board by 3-inches, and slides the legs back and forth as fast as possible for a certain amount of time. Players must maintain the elevated hip throughout the motion and extend the legs through the fullest range of motion (both forward and back).

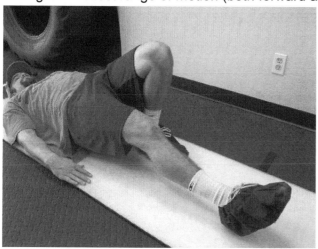 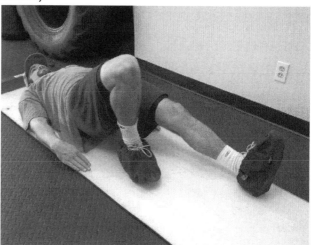

Cody starts his conditioning portion of the workout with a gruelling set of reverse mountain sliders

Stability Ball Hamstring Curls (1 & 2 Legs)

Julie curls in the hamstrings with both legs (pictures 1&2) and with one leg (picture 3)

Using the stability ball to perform hamstring curls presents a different challenge to the posterior chain muscles as they have to stabilize the hip and pull in the hamstrings at the same time. While this is more of a finishing exercise (to be performed at the end of a leg workout) due to the fact that the hamstrings cannot be loaded with weight (which the hamstrings best respond to), it is still valuable for hockey players.

Start on the floor with the heels on a stability ball and the hips held above the ground so a straight line forms between the shoulder blades and the heels (picture 1). Usually this is about 4-inches off the ground. Pull the hamstrings in towards the body while keeping the hips elevated above the ground (picture 2). To challenge the hamstrings even further try doing this exercise with only one-leg on the ball while the other one is held straight in the air (previous page picture 3).

Bench Band Hamstring Pull-Ins
The hamstring band pull-in is designed to trash the hamstrings which are responsible for a good deal of the power in the skating stride. Therefore I really like to work these muscles through the year and especially in the off-season when players are not on the ice as much, and therefore can recover and improve hamstring strength. Typically athletes should perform lower reps with higher loads with all hamstring training, but I like to use this exercise as a finisher (at the end of a workout).

Using a 1¾ inch Superband to perform bench hamstring band pull-ins

Hip Exercises

Machine Hip Flexion
The hip flexors are one of the most under-trained muscle groups in hockey players and **NEED** to be developed off the ice for correct muscle balance. So much time is spent improving the posterior chain muscles (the hamstrings, glutes and low back) that the small hip flexors (which bring the leg forward

with each skating stride) are terribly neglected. I work so much with players to make these muscles both strong and flexible it is not even funny. The multi-hip machine is a good way to continually increase the loading of the hip flexors, while not being locked into a set movement.

Using the multi-hip machine at Revolution Athletics

1-Leg Bench Band Pull-Ins
Much the same as the bench band pull-ins, this exercise is done with the player focusing on just one leg at a time. Use a lighter resistance band and try to pull as hard as possible with the hip flexor to complete this exercise correctly. In the photos below, Cody turns the toe outwards to perform the exercise as it might look during the skating action (the toes are pointed slightly outward during the skating recovery position).

It is important to start working this and other hip exercises early on in the off-season, and then throughout the year so that players build strong and stable hip flexors. This often neglected area is prone to injury in hockey, so do all you can to build strong and flexible hip flexors.

Fresh off a broken right ankle Cody works to rehab his legs prior to skating. Performing 1-Leg Band Pull-ins with turning the toe out on this exercise is a key point to simulate what happens in the skating stride

Cable Hip Flexion
Much the same as machine hip flexion, it is beneficial to use the cable and ankle attachment to work the hip flexor as there is more hip stabilization involved in this exercise. It helps if you have a chair or hockey stick for balance, but ideally you want to progress into not using any balance aids so you have to stand on one leg and then perform the exercise with balance.

Kevin using the cable hip flexion drill to prepare for pro tryouts

Assisted Band Hip Flexion

Hip flexor work is **VERY** important for hockey players and my **favorite** hip flexor exercise is the Assisted Band Hip Flexion drill. The reason I like this drill so much is that the partner/coach provides as much or as little resistance for the working player, and the player can focus on accelerating the hip (by bringing the knee forward quickly). It is essential to develop hip strength at the same rate of speed that occurs on the ice. If you use only slow movements on hip flexion drills then when you get on the ice and start to sprint the hips are not used to that amount of force and quickly become overworked and stretched too far. A lot of players hurt their hip flexors and groin muscles early in the year, and this is a big reason why. All through the off-season players should work the hip with this kind of drill to not only balance out the hip, but to work it with a high rate of speed that simulates skating.

Start this exercise in front of a squat rack so you can hold on to something solid. Wrap a Superband around the leg that is held back (picture 1), so the partner can hold the band. Accelerate from full extension to as high as possible (picture 2). Repetitions should be in the 4 to 10 range so the action is performed with quality repetitions.

Coach Pollitt works with Cody during sets of Assisted Band Hip Flexion

Lying Band Pull-ins

This exercise is a good way to improve hip flexor strength. In the picture below Justin lies down on his back, hooks a Superband on a fixed object and then around the top of the feet. Contract the hip flexors and pull the legs in as far as possible towards the chest. Both legs can be worked together (as pictured), or one leg can be worked to focus on muscle imbalances or specific strength.

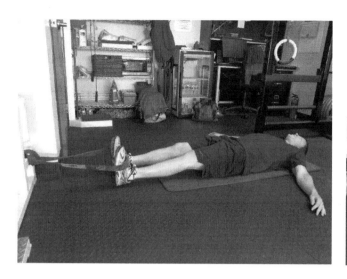 

Slideboard Lunges

The slideboard lunge works a variety of muscles but I have included it in the hip flexor section because of the tremendous stretch and use of the hips to perform this exercise correctly. Start standing up with one leg off the slideboard and the other leg on the slideboard with the "booties" on to allow that foot to slide. From this starting position (picture 1), slide the leg with the "booties" on backwards as far as possible (to the end range of motion of the hip, picture 2). Keep an upright body position and then contract the hips of the back leg and the hamstring and glutes of the stabilizing leg to return to the starting position, (picture 1). With this exercise I like to use higher than normal repetitions until the player gets used to the stretch and then sometimes I provide additional loading with a resistance band to the sliding leg, (not pictured).

Bryan performs slideboard lunges throughout off-season training to strengthen the hip flexors

Mountain Sliders

At the end of leg day workouts I like to add in conditioning drills for the hip flexors, hamstrings and groin. Mountain sliders are a great addition to any workout as they develop hip, abdominal, shoulder strength, as well as mental toughness. Many highly conditioned athletes fail to perform consistent sets of 2-minute mountain sliders as it is a tough exercise when performed correctly.

To do this drill a player will get down into the push-up position with the hands on the front of the slideboard. One leg is brought up as far as possible to the hands with the other leg extended as far behind as possible. At this point make sure to keep the hips down and slide the feet back and forth as quickly as possible through a full range of motion.

Bryan shows mountain sliders (picture 1 & 2), and single leg mountain sliders (pictures 3 & 4)

Another version of this exercise is the two leg mountain climber (not shown), that has the player keep both feet together while they bring them in and out as fast as possible. Start with 1 minute for this drill and increase this as necessary. I like to use this at the end of workouts and for punishment (for losing a race or event in the conditioning segment of a workout). It not only builds the hip flexor strength, but it helps develop the shoulders and abdominal muscle (as well as your mental grit).

To make this exercise more difficult I have my athletes perform this exercise with only one leg on the slideboard as the other is held in the air (pictures shown above).

Hip Adduction Exercises

Plate Drags
Plate drags are a staple exercise with **every** hockey player I work with as nothing else works the adduction muscles in the same motion as used on the ice. Most injuries in hockey are to the hip flexors or groin muscles so this is another area that MUST be worked hard to rebalance the body (throughout the year, not just in the off-season). Start off with a light plate (10lbs), get into a hockey type deep knee bend and extend the plate out to the side (like your hockey stride) as far as possible. From this position push down into the floor as hard as you can while you pull the weight in to the recovery position (next to the other leg, see figure 2). As you get stronger increase the weight plate to a 35lbs and then a 45lbs plate (while maintaining proper form and pushing hard into the floor).

Clint uses a 25lb plate for extended plate drags in Richmond, BC

Stability Ball Adduction
Very similar to plate drags, the stability ball adduction adds the element of stabilizing the body and the working limb into the mix. This exercise can be very challenging for most players but has a good carry-over affect because it not only simulates the skating specific muscles but with the balance thrown into the equation it is absolutely awesome for developing the adduction muscles of the skating stride. If players need resistance a rubber band or tubing can be added to the working leg (the one on the ball) and held by a training partner or coach. Note that doing this presents a potential risk of

116

injury if you are not careful so use your best judgement prior to including this exercise into your routine. I like to use higher than normal reps for this exercise (in the 20 to 30 range) at the end of a workout as a finisher. Try to get the maximum range of motion possible during this exercise to stimulate the skating adduction muscles fully.

Kevin performs stability ball adductions as a warm-up before the workout

Skating Cross-Overs

This drill involves attaching a low cable strap to the ankle and performing skating cross-overs as you might on the ice. Try to make the movement as real and authentic as possible so that there is a maximum carryover to the ice. To add variety add more and more weight to this drill or perform it very quickly using explosive type movements during the drill.

Kevin uses the cable to work the skating cross-over drill

Band Hockey Adductions

The groin and hip flexor muscles is the most injured area with hockey players. To help prevent injury these muscles must be strong and flexible so that players never hit an "end range" of motion, and have plenty of strength in those muscles to protect against injury. Using a 3-dollar mini-band attached around a post or squat rack allows a player to work the exact skating stride through an extended range of motion. Combined with other exercises for this area and lots of flexibility work players (and teams) should be able to greatly reduce injuries to this area.

Injury prevention starts with working the groin, hip flexor muscles used in the skating stride

Hip Abduction Exercises

Skating Abduction Drill

Attach the cable to the outside ankle and start on one leg with the other leg crossed over behind (picture 1). Forcefully extend the leg to the side in the same manor you would on the ice (picture 2). The trick is to stay low, move the hip quickly and through a full range of motion while you balance on the one leg. Done properly, this is an amazing drill for specific ice hockey development of the hip.

Skating abductions are a great drill to work the lateral portion of the hip and glutes, just like in hockey

Band Lateral Strides

While hockey players work a great deal on the external rotation component of the hip it is important to still work the glute muscles in a lateral motion with bent knees to improve stability and strength in the hips. Start by putting a mini-band around the ankles (picture 1) and then while keeping a deep knee bend step sideways as far as possible (picture 2).

This is a great exercise to use at the end of a workout when the legs are essentially done, but you still need to work the injury prevention exercises. After a hockey practice is also a good time to throw in this drill to fully exhaust the abduction muscles of the hip. Repetitions should be in the 20+ range and when that gets easy change the resistance level of the band.

Mini-bands put to good use in training the glute medius and maximus

Ankle/Calf Exercises

Seated Calf Raises

While I don't usually choose individual muscle groups to train I believe that the seated calf raise has a place in any hockey players training routine. As the knee in the hockey stride is mostly bent, you need to work that muscle in the bent position (like a seated calf raise). The muscles trained in the seated calf raise (the Soleus), traditionally has slow twitch muscle fibres that respond best to higher than average time under tension (15 to 20 repetitions), but players should also feel free to load up this exercise for low reps with heavy weight to develop top-end strength. Make sure you get a full range of motion (a big stretch at the bottom and a full toe raise to the top). If possible train one-leg at a time for maximal effort and focus.

Clint warming up with 2 plates on the seated calf raise

Standing Calf Raises

The standing calf raise is a simple exercise that should be used only at the end of a strength training session. Stand on one foot and sink down into a deep stretch of the calf muscle before extending upwards onto the tips of the toes. Add weight to this exercise by holding a heavy dumbbell or kettlebell. At the end of exercise try performing quick hops (1 to 2 inches in height), and keep hopping until you simply cannot hop any more. This will burn a lot, but over the course of a couple months the calf muscles will develop great strength to help the push phase in the skating stride.

For variety, use a standing calf raise machine (where both legs are trained together and a lot of weight is used to stimulate growth and strength).

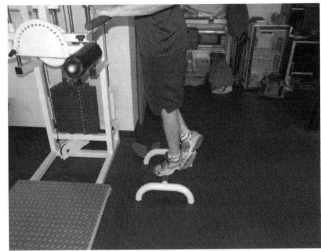

Using a round bar calf roller extends the range of motion of the calf muscles

Airex Balance Training

I like to use the Airex balance pad as a warm-up for the ankles, especially before doing agility and speed work. It really works all the little muscles in the ankle/calf, that control balance and stability. Start out standing on an Airex pad for a certain amount of time (for each leg). Once you do 2-sets of 15 to 30 seconds per leg, set the Airex pad on an incline (I use a balance board as a wedge), and repeat standing on the pad for a set amount of time. At this point I usually include a single leg ¼ squats or a drill where the athlete throws a small ball to a partner back and forth so that the player must not only balance, but work on other skills while balancing.

Balance pad work is also useful at the end of a calf training session as it knocks off the low threshold muscle fibers after hard work on strength development.

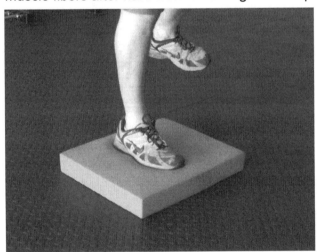

Balancing on the Airex pad (picture 1), and with the Airex pad on an angle (picture 2)

Balance Board Circles

At the end of training I like to really exhaust players ankles so I have them stand on a circular balance board and complete balance board circles. The idea is that they balance on one leg (on the board) and rotate the board clockwise, and then counter-clockwise. To complete a full circle the ankle must work through a wide range of motion in multiple planes of movement. For beginner athletes this drill can also be used with two legs until sufficient balance is developed.

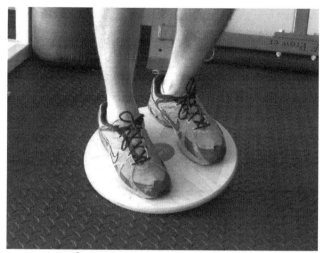

Perform circles around and around to train the 2-leg balance (picture 1) or 1-leg balance (picture 2)

Band Ankle Development

Hockey players need strong ankles...no doubt. Traditional exercises such as plyometrics, body weight exercises and such are very good for promoting general strength but the ankle is not often trained in a circular or side to side manor. Start by sitting on a bench wrapping a Superband around the ankle and then wrap the other end around the waist. Grab both ends of the band and concentrate the focus of the pull on either the outer side or inner side of the ankle. From this position perform ankle rotations, as well as inversion/eversion (side to side) so the ankle becomes strong in all planes of motion (just like it moves on the ice).

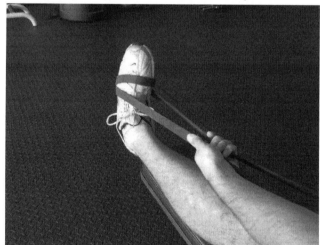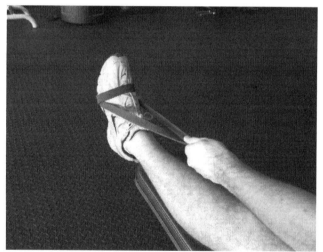

John Grenier uses a 1-inch Superband to develop ankle strength

Dard II

The Dard II is a device used to train the tibialis anterior by working the primary action of this muscle (to dorsiflexi the foot). This small muscle on the front side of the lower leg is the muscle that is worked when recovering the leg during the skating action (to pull the toe of the skate up for full recovery by the ankle). A lot of attention is spent developing the posterior muscles of the soleus and gastrocnemius (the calf muscles of the lower leg), but very little work is ever done on the front tibialis anterior muscles. Over time this will develop into an imbalance and potentially cause injury (shin splints).

To start, sit on a bench and slide the feet in to the device (as pictured). Contract the quadriceps muscles so the legs are suspended in the air and then extend the toes as far out as possible (picture 1). Contract the toes towards the knee to engage this muscle (picture 2). At first I recommend 12-20 repetitions with light weight and as strength improves reduce the reps and add weight.

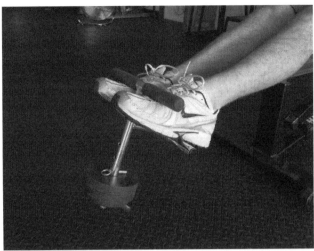

Training the tibialis anterior with the Dard II training device helps to prevent shin splints

Upper Body Exercises

Chest/Pressing Exercises

Bench Press

The bench press is one of the best ways to develop upper body strength. To start make sure to pull the shoulder blades together (and keep this position) throughout the lift. Really squeeze the bar tightly and have the feeling like you are trying to rip the bar in half (by pulling outwards with the hands). Lower the bar to the nipples (figure 2) and then press the weight back up over your mouth (this should be a diagonal line from the nipples to the mouth), (figure 1). Hold your feet out to the side and try to tighten the whole body during the lift. You can move your hand in (8 inches apart) for a close grip variety (figure 3), or with your pinky fingers on the bar knurling (for a traditional bench press) or with a very wide grip (index fingers on the bar knurling). Always use a spotter on heavy weights.

Clint shows good bench press form (pictures 1 & 2), and close grip bench press (picture 3)

Floor Press

The floor press is an awesome exercise to build strength in the middle and lockout portion of the bench press. At DP Hockey we use this exercise as one of the primary exercises (or as supplementary exercises) for the bench press and have players work up to 1-5 Repetition Maximum (RM). To complete this exercise set up the barbell in the power rack with the supports at arm's length, and the safety bars off. Un-rack the weight, lower it until your elbows contact the floor (picture 1 below) and then push upwards to lockout (picture 2 below).

Justin using the floor press during 2008 summer training for pro tryouts

2-Board Press

The 2-board press is an awesome powerlifting exercise that helps to train specific ranges of the horizontal pressing motion to help improve maximal bench press strength. The athlete (or training partner as shown above) will place a board over the chest, and then un-rack the barbell to begin the bench press action. Lower the barbell to the board, pause for a moment and then press the weight bar up to lock-out. In the exercise below Cody uses 2-2x4 wooden boards, but athletes can and should vary this up with 1 board, 2 boards, 3 boards, up to 4 boards. All of these boards provide a great deal of variation to the bench press action so that players never over train just one lift.

Bryan holds the board for Cody performing the 2-board press

Bench Press Lock-out

Bench press lock-outs are another variation of the traditional bench press. This action works to develop the lock-out strength of the triceps that many lifters lack. Make sure to use a squat rack with the safety pins so that heavy weights can be used. To start put a flat bench in the rack and set the pins so that when you extend the arms you only have 5 to 7 inches of travel (see pictures). Start with the bar on the safety pins, grip the bar and then lift it upwards to lock-out. Lower the bar to the pins, loosen your grip on the bar and then re-grip and press the weight again. With this exercise you can really work with heavy weights (repetitions in the 1-6 range) as the range of motion is small and at the final extension of the lift (where you should be strongest).

123

Using the Elite FTS classic 3x3 rack to perform bench press lock-outs

Incline Dumbbell Press

Incline dumbbell press is a good exercise to develop the upper part of the chest and shoulders. Players will not be able to use as much weight as either the standard bench press, or decline bench press so adjust this appropriately.

To perform this exercise, lie back on a bench that is set to about 45 degrees, grab a pair of dumbbells and raise them up to the starting position (picture 1). Push the dumbbells straight up (don't bang the dumbbells together), and then lower to the shoulders to repeat.

Justin grinds out 20 repetitions with 55lbs in the incline DB bench press

Decline Dumbbell Press

The decline dumbbell press is an exercise for the middle-lower portion of the chest, and one in which players can use a lot of weight to develop the pressing muscles of the chest, shoulders and triceps.

Find a bench that declines, or put blocks under a flat style bench and then lay back on the bench with dumbbells in the ready position (picture 1). Press the dumbbells up to lockout to complete the motion (picture 2). When you are done, drop the dumbbells safely to the side (watch your hands).

Dan Spence crankin' out a set of 70lb DB decline press's at the Gold's Gym in Langley, BC

Swiss Ball Dumbbell Press

Clint uses dumbbells for the chest press at Magic Hockey (pictures 1 & 2) and only one dumbbell (picture 3)

In the starting position make sure you are balanced and stable before you lower the weights. Start off with a lighter weight until you get used to the ball before you use heavy dumbbells. Be sure to use a quality stability ball that is burst proof so you won't get hurt. If you are able try to perform this exercise one handed (figure 3). To add more of a challenge for balance try bringing the feet together or raise one leg up slightly while performing this exercise to engage the core area.

Push-ups

Shown below are 6-kinds of push-ups that are much different from the regular version you are used to performing. You can increase the difficulty of push-ups by speeding them up, slowing them down, adding a jump into the motion (where you try to lift the hands off the ground when you push-up), making the hands less stable (ring push-ups), or by placing a resistance band around your back and hold with both hands. Push-ups should be included in every hockey players program so get to work!

Band resisted push-ups (picture 1), feet up push-ups (picture 2), roller push-ups (picture 3)

Justin doing ring push-ups (picture 1), Cody does push-ups with one hand up on a medicine ball (picture 2), 18-AAA Midget player Bryce Nielsen completes a set of Bosu push-ups (picture 3)

Plyometric Push-ups

This variation of plyometric push-ups is called "jumps"

Think of plyometric push-ups as the explosive and highly efficient version of the traditional push-up. Done correctly it builds incredible power throughout the upper body and used as a conditioning exercise it grinds even the most in shape athletes into the ground. There are many types of plyometric push-ups from clapping the hands in between the repetitions, to using small steps or boxes on either side of the hands and pushing up onto the boxes. The variation shown in the above pictures demonstrates a bent arm version where the athlete "jumps" from the ground to the boxes and back to the ground (without really extending the arms).

Hindu Push-ups

Start in a push-up type position with your butt in the air and your upper body/arm in a straight line (figure 1). From this position descend on an angle towards your hands (figure 2), and then push up towards the end of the exercise (figure 3). To get back to the start slowly follow the SAME PATH back to the start.

Hindu push-ups are a slow and deliberate exercise

126

Weighted Push-up Drags

Assume the push-up position with your feet on a 25 to 100lb Olympic weight plate. Walk yourself forward with your hands while your feet drag the weight plate. This is a great exercise for developing the upper body and core endurance.

Overall this is a pretty tough exercise that demands mental focus and endurance throughout the upper body. Try dragging the plate for distance and after you can do this for 50 yards up the weight to a larger plate. Some gyms have the 100lb plate which is a beast for this exercise. Dragging on rubber mats, carpet or concrete is advised over grass.

Back Exercises

Seated Rows

Seated rows are a good exercise for the middle and upper back, and will do a lot to help balance the muscles developed by forward pressing exercises. Players should do slightly more work on the pulling muscles of the back than the pressing actions of the chest and shoulders. Start this exercise by sitting down in front of a cable column and using a V-grip handle or some other attachment and while keeping the back flat and knees slightly bent pull the weight toward the chest. Do not sway back and forth while trying to pull a heavy weight as this works the low back muscles rather than the middle and upper back as it should.

Performing seated rows with a fat grip handle

Chest Supported Rows

The chest supported row is an easy exercise to learn as you simply load the machine up with weight plates, extend your arms fully while leaning on the support pad and then contract the muscles of the mid back as far as you are able. This exercise can be used with some pretty heavy weights (500+lbs). Just make sure you use a full range of motion.

For variety try performing chest supported rows with one-arm and really focus on the retraction of the scapula and following through with the elbow (like when throwing an elbow on the ice).

Athletes <u>should</u> develop an <u>equal</u> amount of strength between this exercise & bench press

T-Bar Rows

Clint performs T-bar rows at a facility in Richmond, BC

This simple to perform exercise is a good developer of the entire back as the low back and legs have to stabilize the body as the middle and upper back perform the action. Put an Olympic barbell into the corner of the wall or squat cage, and then load up the other end with weight plates. Grab a V-bar handle and put this around the barbell. Straddle the barbell, bend over and grab the V-bar handle to pull the weight towards the chest. Personally I prefer athletes use lower repetitions with this weight to minimize low back strain, and make sure to contract the core muscles and glutes to help anchor the spine during this lift.

Horizontal Hanging Rows

Horizontal rows use the players own body weight as the load that they have to pull upwards towards the hands. Start with the feet on a box and hanging from rings (as pictured) or from a bar and pull yourself up so the rings (or bar) touch the chest. When this becomes easy then add weight by putting on a weight vest or by having a training partner place a weigh plate on the chest. You can also strap bands around the chest and anchor them to the bottom of the squat rack for added resistance.

Hanging horizontal rows are a great pulling exercise for the back

Lying Dumbbell Rows

If you have access to a solid board (or top portion of a bench), place this across the safety pins in a squat rack. Grab two dumbbells (or a barbell) and while letting the arms hang in a fully extended position (picture 1), contract the muscles of the back and pull the weight up (picture 2). This is a tremendous exercise for building a solid mid-back area as you cannot cheat and it provides a full range of motion for the action if you really try to extend the hands prior to pulling the weight up to the end of the exercise.

Strength Coach Jean-Guy Gobeil performs lying dumbbell rows at the Community Centre, Banff, AB

One Arm Rows

Professional hockey player Mark Thomas of the Sheffield Steelers (EIHL) performing dumbbell rows

129

Really try to hang the weight as low as possible and then pull the weight up as high as you can. Notice how the back stays straight during this lift and the core area (abdominals and low back) are held tightly. Try using a "fat handle" dumbbell to help train the gripping muscles when performing 1-arm rows.

Face Pulls

Face pulls done with the elbows held high

This exercise is a good upper back action that most players should use to balance the push/pull muscles of the upper torso. With both hands grab a triceps rope that is attached to a cable weight stack above the head and pull towards the face, keeping the elbows held high throughout the motion. At first a light weight will be all you can handle but try to build up to a decent weight (100lbs+) over time.

Scarecrows

The scarecrow exercise, like face pulls work the scapula retractor muscles and the upper back in general. Start with either a cable and two single handles or a rubber band (pictured), and hold the arms straight while pulling them backwards to the side (picture 2). Depending on the kind of band you use this can be a very difficult exercise. I tend to use this more as a high-rep type of conditioning exercise for the upper back muscles.

Band scarecrows are a very difficult exercise to perform properly

Chin-ups

Justin performs 24 chin-up repetitions during summer testing

Chin-ups are one of the best upper body builders of strength that can be performed. Every athlete should use chin-ups as a staple exercise to strengthen the upper back musculature. Start by hanging from the bar with your arms straight. Really squeeze your grip and then pull yourself up so that your chin rises over the bar (and then lower back down and repeat). To change the exercise rotate your hands so the palms are facing away from you (pull-ups) or use a V-shaped bar to perform neutral grip chin-ups. Vary your hand positions and width of the grip frequently. Add weight between your legs (either holding a dumbbell or with a dip belt) for extra resistance.

Pull-ups

Cody performs pull-ups (pictures 1 & 2),

Pull-ups may be one of the hardest exercises to do in the gym, but also one of the best exercises to put meat on your upper back. Understand that at first you may not be able to do many of them, but with lots of repetitions it does get easier. Start with many sets of low reps (10+ sets of 3 to 5 reps) until you build a good foundation before you start crankin' out lots of repetitions with this exercise.

From the starting position where you are hanging with legs and arms straight, lift yourself up and bring your chin over the bar (see below) without moving your legs all over the place. Lower yourself back down to a straight arm hang and repeat this action.

Triathlete William Young does neutral grip pull-ups (picture 1),
while Long Beach State hockey player Cody Kreger does weighted pull-ups (picture 2),
Cody demonstrates using a superband hooked around the pull-up bar to provide extra lift for chin-ups (picture 3)

Pull-Downs

Performing pull-downs with a 4' lat-bar attachment

Sit down in front of a cable weight stack and grab the attachment (V-handle, lat-bar, triceps rope, etc.). Start from a fully stretched position (picture 1), and pull down towards the upper chest in front of the body, (picture 2). As this is a much easier version compared to chin-up (where you pull your own bodyweight) players should be able to load up the machine and pull a good deal of weight.

NOTE: Pull-downs or any variation is definitely <u>NOT</u> *a substitute for either chin-ups or pull-ups. This exercise should be used with people who are starting out with strength training and/or have poor upper body strength, or with athletes who are injured in the shoulder area and cannot complete a proper pull-up or chin-up without pain. Otherwise, ALL athletes should learn and get good at performing chin-ups and pull-ups for the majority of their upper back development.*

Shoulder Training

Shoulder Press
Start with the weights as low as possible (resting on the shoulder or below if possible) in the front part of the shoulders (under the chin). From this position raise the dumbbells (or barbell) to overhead and lock out the movement (picture 3). Make sure to have a good base of support and a strong core when pressing the weight overhead as the load is moving further away from the center of mass and therefore becomes more and more unstable.

Clint shoulder pressing dumbbells (pictures 1 & 2), Todd warm-ups up with barbell shoulder press (picture 3)

Kettlebell Shoulder Press

Balancing a kettlebell and then pressing it overhead

The shoulder press is a good overall upper body exercise to use with a dumbbell. Using a kettlebell turned upside down, this exercise becomes a very challenging grip and balance exercise for the upper body. Start with the kettlebell turned upside down and at shoulder height (picture 1) and then push it upwards to extend the arm overhead (picture 2). Start off with a lighter kettlebell and use a progressively heavier kettlebell as necessary.

Wide Military Press & Shrug

Justin uses a lighter barbell for 20-rep wide grip military press & shrug

Using wide grip military press & shrugs are a great developer for the shoulders and trapezius muscles. Hold an Olympic barbell with the hands wider than shoulder width and in front of the shoulders. Raise the barbell overhead and when the elbows lock out, shrug the shoulders. Lower the barbell and repeat. Generally I like to have athletes use lighter weight for more repetitions with this exercise to really put in the necessary volume to strengthen the shoulder girdle.

Bradford Press

Used and presented by the guys at Westside Barbell, the Bradford press is a simple movement that really destroys the shoulders. Sit on a bench inside of a squat rack and load up a heavy barbell. Start with the hands slightly wider than shoulder width and behind your head (picture 1). Contract the shoulders and raise the weight up to just over your head and then lower it in front of your face. Now raise it back over the head and onto the shoulders. Repeat this back and forth motion until you cannot push the weight any more. Enjoy this one...

Justin performing a Bradford press with 135lbs

Shoulder Press Lockouts

Start out sitting on a bench inside a squat rack with the safety pins set so that when you put your hands on the barbell (just outside of the shoulders) the upper arm/forearm make a 90 degree angle. Keep the back nice and straight, push out your abdominal muscles (to anchor the spine) and lift the barbell until your elbow locks out. Lower the barbell back to the safety pins and set it down before starting over again.

Clint working the shoulders with 135lbs

Upright Rows

Use a barbell or kettlebell to perform upright rows. Stand with the hands facing down holding onto the weight and start with the weight held in front at the waist (not shown). Pull upwards and extend the elbows out to the sides and upwards so the weight comes up just under the chin (see picture). Do not use your legs with this exercise as the focus is on the shoulders.

Clint using a barbell for upright rows (picture 1),
Lisa Newcomb uses the 35lb kettlebell for upright rows at Huntington Beach, CA

Cable Front/Side Raises

Kevin uses the low cable option for kneeling front raises (pictures 1 & 2), & side raises (pictures 3 & 4)

To develop the shoulders through a <u>full range of motion</u> individually I like to use the low cable row with a single handle attachment. Set the machine in the lowest position and with light weight to start.

For a front shoulder raise, grab the handle; kneel down in front of the cable stack (or step forward if using a different machine) so the working arm is behind you (picture 1). Raise with handle upwards as you keep the arm straight (while a slight bend in the elbow), to a 45 degree angle. Repeat for the required number of reps.

To work the side shoulder stand perpendicular to the weight stack with the arm held behind the back as far as possible (picture 3). Raise the cable up with the arm slightly bent to a 45 degree angle (picture 4). With all of the exercises make sure to really get the stretch in the starting position and then extend through the end of the arm motion.

External Rotations on Knee

Stacey using a light dumbbell for external rotations on the knee

The external rotation on knee exercise is probably my favorite shoulder exercise for the external rotators of the shoulder. Development of these muscles **greatly** helps to keep the shoulder stable and injury free. Start with a light weight on your knee and lower it as far as possible (getting the full stretch in the external rotators of the shoulder). Raise the weight back up to the starting position slowly. Use light weights with this exercise (5 to 40lbs) to start and build up as the shoulder girdle gets stronger. As with all external rotator exercises these muscles can become quite strong over time but an injury to this area takes longer than average to heal.

Bar External Rotations

Hang your arm over the bar to perform a bar external rotation

Bar external rotations are very similar to knee external rotations as the idea is to use a light weight for many repetitions on each arm through the largest possible range of motion. To perform this exercise stand next to a barbell in the squat rack with a dumbbell in hand. Rest the elbow of that arm on the barbell so the upper arm is perpendicular to the ground and while keeping a 90 degree angle in the arm, lower the weight through a full range of motion (see picture 1). Slowly raise the weight up to the starting position (picture 2) and repeat.

Use a light weight (8 to 40lbs) for at least 8 reps per arm to start. As with all external rotation exercises it is important to build up the strength in these muscles over time and not to rush their development with heavier weights than you can use without excessive strain. Ideally the goal is to use heavier weights for lower reps as the external rotators are made up of fast twitch muscle fibres. Just be careful as these muscles also take a long time to heal if injured.

Modified Cuban Press

Make sure to use a full range of motion with this exercise

Starting with a light bar (15 to 40lbs) start out with the hands spaced far enough apart that a 90 degree angle is made when lowering the bar (figure 1). Get a good stretch with this exercise and slowly rotate the bar up (in a half circle type motion) and finish over your head. This exercise should be used with light weights until you get used to the action. When this becomes easier you can progress to a heavier barbell for reduced reps (5 to 15) and/or more sets. Make sure the technique with this exercise is correct as athletes tend to cheat when the weight gets heavier.

Side External Rotations

 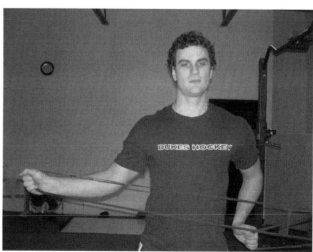

Hook light bands around a squat rack or solid post to perform side external rotations

Using a light rubber band or tubing start with the arm rotated inward towards the opposite shoulder (figure 1). Contract the rotators, keeping the elbow as close to the body as possible and extend the hand outwards (figure 2). Use a lighter band with this exercise and plenty of repetitions (12 to 20+) per set, much like during rehab at the physical therapist. As the shoulder gets stronger a heavier band is necessary to develop more strength in this action with reduced reps into the 5 to 12 range.

Arm Training

Dips
Dips are one of the best exercises to develop both size and strength in the upper body. Start out on the dip bar with the arms straight. Dip down as far as possible (at least to 90-degree flexion in the arms) and then push yourself back to the starting position without swinging or leaning forward. When you get used to this exercise add weight (by holding a dumbbell between your legs or with a dip belt and weight plates in the range of 50 to 100+lbs).

Clint uses dips as a main part of his upper body workouts (pictures 1 & 2),
Cody uses a 50lbs dumbbell held between the legs to crank out a set of dips (picture 3)

Skull Crushers
Skull crushers are a good assistance exercise for helping to develop the triceps muscles. Lie back on a bench and start with an EZ curl bar loaded up and the hands relatively close together. Keep the elbows pointed at the ceiling, bend at the elbows and lower the weight as far down as possible to get a good stretch in the triceps. Raise the weight up without moving the elbows and the arms angled slightly backwards (picture 2). This exercise can and should also be performed on a decline bench so the triceps are hit with a slightly different angle.

Flat bench skull crushers

Overhead Dumbbell Triceps Extension
This exercise works the triceps muscles in a semi-stretched position and is really a decent overall strengthening exercise for all three heads of the triceps. Hold a dumbbell with a neutral grip (palms facing each other), at the top of the dumbbell and then lower it as far as possible downward while keeping the elbows pointed straight up to the sky. Also make sure to keep the elbows in (towards the

138

head), not flaring out away from the head. Warm-up with lighter weights at first before you go heavy on this exercise as the elbow can sometimes not function well until it is warmed up.

Lisa holds a dumbbell to complete overhead triceps extensions

Band Triceps Press-down, and/or Triceps Press-Downs

Superband press-downs are a killer finishing exercise for the triceps (pictures 1 & 2)

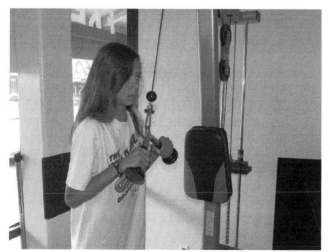 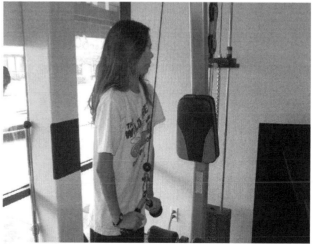

Kayla does a triceps press-down with a weight stack/cable system (pictures 3 & 4)

139

Another helpful triceps exercise is the Superband press-down. Start by looping a Superband around the top of a squat rack and grab the band with both hands (picture 1, previous page). Hold the core muscles firmly and extend the arms to lockout position.

I have also included the standard Triceps Press-down exercise (pictures 3 & 4, previous page) that is available at most gyms that have a weight stack/cable column. This exercise is more for triceps development rather than a finisher exercise because you can crank up the weight. Generally speaking however, the triceps muscles respond best to lower repetitions (1-8 reps) with heavier weights.

Barbell Biceps Curl

Cody performing strict barbell biceps curls with 135lbs

While many young hockey players do entirely too many bicep curls I have included them into this book as they do serve a purpose if you really load up the weight and focus on building strength in the biceps with low repetitions rather than just doing a lot of volume to build huge bicep muscles. All of the pulling actions such as chin-ups and rows require strong biceps, so spending one or two sets at the end of a workout to build the general strength in this area is not a horrible idea. Just don't approach bicep training like a bodybuilder by doing endless repetitions in order to build huge muscles…this is not important to hockey players, strength develop is important!

Perform biceps curls with a barbell, EZ curl bar, dumbbell or kettlebell. Start with the hands in a supinated (palms facing upward) grip, with the elbows tucked in to the side of the body and arms held straight. From this position curl the weight up to the chin without moving the elbows outward, forward or backwards. This attention to strict form is what makes a biceps curl a decent exercise. Barbell biceps curls work the mid-range of the force curve in the biceps and provide a good way to load the upper arms with heavy weight.

Incline DB Biceps Curls

Unlike barbell curls which hit the mid-range of the biceps force curve, incline curls focus on the upper range of the force curl. The key to performing this exercise correctly is to keep the upper portion of the arm hanging straight down throughout the entire movement so only the biceps muscles lift the dumbbells. Set the incline on the bench so that it ranges from 30 degrees to 70 degrees, and start off with lighter weights to really develop good form in this exercise. Begin by hanging the weights to the side of the body (picture 1), and curl up the weight as far as possible without moving the upper part of the arm (picture 2).

Kayla demonstrates incline curls as part of her upper body conditioning program

Scott Curls

1-handed Scott curls on an incline bench (picture 1), using a preacher bench with dumbbells (picture 2)

Scott curls are named after famous bodybuilder Larry Scott who used this exercise to help develop an awesome set of 20" arms in the mid 1960's. This exercise works the lower force curve of the biceps muscles and is a solid overall exercise for hockey players looking to add strength in the arm flexors. Start out on a Scott bench (also known as a Preacher bench) with the arms extended and curl the weight up so the lower portion of the arm is vertical. Start off with a light weight and progress up in weight slowly as this exercise tends to put strain on the elbow in the extended position. Over training with heavy weights can cause elbow related problems if you're not careful. Players can use a straight barbell, EZ curl bar or dumbbells to complete this exercise.

Reverse Curls

Working reverse curls is one of the best ways to work the Brachialis muscles of the arm which lay between the biceps in front of the arm, and the triceps at the back of the arm. They are typically an under-trained muscle group in most athletes and for hockey it can be very beneficial to develop this area (especially if you fight at all).

Start with the palm of the hands facing downward, with arms to the sides of the body and straight (picture 1). Curl the weight up as you keep your wrist in a neutral position (do not bend the wrist), and keep the elbows as close to the body as possible (picture 2). This is a tough exercise at first, and you can really injure the brachialis with overloading the muscles too soon (when injured it feels like you have tennis elbow). It is important to note that the Brachialis muscles are made up of more fast twitch

141

muscle fibres than other muscles groups so heavy loading with lower repetitions for more sets is the best course of program design for maximal benefit.

EZ bar reverse curls are a great exercise to develop the brachialis muscles

Hammer Curls

Bryan shows normal hammer curls (picture 1 & 2)

Hammer curls and incline hammer curls are two more variations of methods to develop the Brachialis muscles. With hammer curls you will feel this in the same area that is used when you hold a glass or scoop food into your mouth. As mentioned above these muscles are used extensively in hockey to shoot, or hold off an opponent so it is important to develop these areas. Exercises like pull-ups, neutral grip pull-ups and rows of any kind work these muscles, but some direct work with exercises like hammer curls or incline hammer curls can be very helpful to a player.

Start by holding the dumbbells at the sides of the body (picture 1), elbows in close and the palms in a neutral grip position (palms should face each other, and the thumb should be on top towards the sky). Curl the weight up as you keep the elbows close the body and without moving (picture 2). I often like to combine DB hammer curls with a shoulder press so I work multiple muscles groups at once.

Incline Hammer Curls

With incline hammer curls it is a similar action between a normal hammer curl and an incline biceps curl. Hold the dumbbells like you would the incline biceps curl, hang the arm straight down to the sides (picture 1), and from this position curl the weight up to the shoulder (picture 2). Keep the elbows pointed down and close to the body throughout the movement.

Long Beach State hockey player Cody Kreger demonstrates Incline Hammer curls (pictures 1 & 2)

Neck Work

Since hockey is a physical game (even for goalies) a strong neck to protect against concussions from body contact and checks is still advisable. Working the neck a little bit each day will not make you sore, but it can provide great strength and added security for you while on the ice. Start off using very little weight and progress the loading as you see fit (making sure the neck is never sore after training). With most of these exercises try to keep the repetitions in the 8 to 15 range, and perform at least two sets each day you workout. Make sure you equally train the neck in all four directions (front, back, and to each side), so no muscle imbalances are created.

Neck Harness

Put the neck harness on and load the chains with a very light weight to start (5lbs). Standing with a semi-bent-over stance you will move your head as forward as possible and then extend backwards as far as you can. I try to hold the weight so it doesn't move all around but you do what you like. On heavy days load the weight up on this harness and perform 8 repetitions or less, and on lighter days use a light load and perform 15+ repetitions.

To work the front part of the neck, lie down on a bench holding your head hanging over the end, with a neck harness strapped on backwards. From this position lower your head so you can "curl" the weight up and down with a full range of motion. Make sure you don't assist your neck muscles by helping with your hands.

Justin using a neck harness to develop the back (picture 1) and the front of the neck (picture 2)

Manual Resisted Neck Exercises (side to side, or front & back)
In order to train the neck in all ranges of motion the easiest method of development is to manually push on your neck from the front, sides, back with your hands. Push slowly and allow the muscle to move through a full range of motion in both the concentric and eccentric actions (in other words, with a contraction and then allowing the neck to go back to a starting position under load of the pushing from the hands). Performing 2 to 3 sets of 10 to 15 repetitions every two or three days will ensure a very strong neck which is very useful to have in hockey.

Another method of manual resistance is to put a bath towel around your head and hold it with one arm. From this position move your neck back and forth under a constant and gentle resistance from your hand. The idea is to work the side of the neck so try to extend the neck as far as you can both ways under resistance for maximum training affect.

Junior-A hockey player Chris Mason, now with the Kingston Voyageurs of the Ontario Junior Hockey League

Chapter 12 - Core Training

"A pint of sweat saves a gallon of blood"

~ United States 4-Star General George Patton, talking about physical preparation for battle

The core area which consists of all the abdominal muscles, hip flexors and low back are a **very important key** to hockey performance. Without a strong core you cannot stabilize movements and transfer energy effectively throughout the body (such as bracing for a body-check or shooting a slap shot). I learned the value of training the core area many years ago working with my former training partner & friend, Olympic Gold Medalist and World Champion (in Skeleton racing), Duff Gibson. Duff is one of the strongest and most conditioned people I know, and he preached the idea of a strong core every day in our training sessions. **EVERY SINGLE DAY** we worked the core area, and every week we made progress in just about every single lift. When I applied these principals to the other athletes I work with (especially hockey players) it is amazing to see the results.

As I won't be there to supervise your training I expect some personal initiative to accomplish the goal of training the core area every day. With each workout you will choose 2-exercises for 2-sets each (to start) and work these exercises with a variety of repetitions, loads, and rest periods. The one rule I have is that you never train the same exercise two days in a row. Make sure you understand that the purpose of this daily core training is not to kill your core area or exhaust it with a gruelling workout, but rather to hit it with a short (4 to 8-minute), challenging routine every day. An example of a 7-day period is provided at the end of this chapter.

Sit-ups

Julie Young (Arizona State Basketball, NCAA D1) does LOTS, and LOTS of sit-ups as part of her training

To perform a sit-up, hold your hands on your head, feet held under a fixed object and the shoulder blades on the ground (picture 1). Curl up without lifting the hips from the ground to bring your elbows over your knees (picture 2). Repeat...lots! Add a weight plate over your chest or a dumbbell behind your head for extra resistance. When this gets easy, move to incline sit-ups (next exercise).

Incline Sit-ups
Start out on an incline board, with your feet held firmly, knees bent to 90-degrees and hands over the ears. From this starting position (figure 1) rise up and bring your elbows over your knees without spreading your legs (figure 2). As this exercise becomes easy add a weight plate over your chest (or held over your head), adjust the angle of the incline bench so that it becomes more difficult, or have a partner resist you movements by holding your shoulders.

145

For a great alternative to normal incline sit-ups try doing 1-leg incline sit-ups. One leg will remain held by the board, while the other leg should be held out straight (not pictured). This variation will challenge most everyone. If this is still not enough and you're form is still decent, add weight over the chest or held overhead.

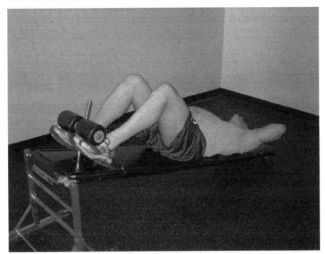 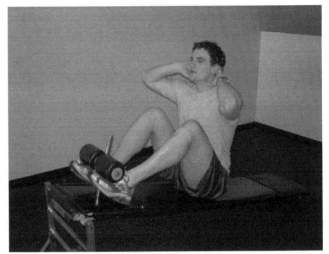

Avoid lifting your butt off the bench and focus on proper form with incline sit-ups

Straight Leg Sit-ups

By keeping the legs straight with this exercise it forces the hip flexors (used to a great extent in hockey) to really work hard. Start off with no weight and add a plate as this exercise becomes easier. You have to really hold the core area tight throughout this exercise to prevent low back strain.

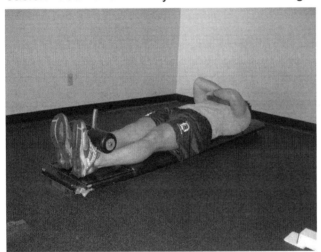 

Anchor the feet and hold a weight plate to add resistance to this exercise if possible

Stability Ball Crunches

The reason why stability ball crunches have gained such a following is that it allows the user to perform sit-ups over a full range of motion, rather than the ¾ range of motion seen with traditional sit-ups. Secondary to this, using a ball forces the user to engage and use all the hip stabilizer muscles to keep upright on the ball. This combination is a true winner for core training.

When starting out on the ball try to get the biggest range of motion possible by leaning way back, so your head faces behind you, (picture 1). Put your hands on your ears and rise up **WITHOUT MOVING THE BALL** to a full sitting position (picture 2). To make this exercise harder, bring your feet closer together (or balance on one foot).

Make sure to get a full range of motion on stability ball crunches as shown above by Clint

Weighted Stability Ball Crunches

Bryan Hodges holds a 25lb ball during a workout at Revolution Athletics in Orange County, CA

Weighted stability ball crunches are one of the best abdominal exercises around...period. The fact that you get a full range of motion of the rectus abdominus while under a load is tremendous for developing these muscles. Start with hooking your feet under a solid object (like a squat rack), and sit on the edge of the ball so you can bend around the ball and get a full stretch. Put a weight behind your head and bend backwards so the weight almost touches the floor (picture 1). From this stretched position, curl up **without moving the ball** until your trunk is vertical (picture 2).

Ball Hits

Ball hits are a very similar exercise to weighted ball crunches or ball crunches except for the element of acceleration in the action. Start fully extended on the ball with the small ball or dumbbell on the ground (picture 1), and then forcefully contract the abdominal muscles are hard as possible (like you are chopping wood right in front of you) and swing the small ball to the end point (picture 2). The reason this exercise is called hits is because a trainer or another player can hold a boxing mitt in front of the person exercising so they can "hit" the boxing mitt and therefore really develop more power in the abdominal muscles. I like to work players up to a 30lb ball and have them perform up to 50 repetitions with this exercise.

Julie starts with a full stretch on the ball (picture 1), and then maximally accelerates the ball to the end position (picture 2). What you don't see with these pictures is the action, which is like chopping wood as you come up.

Ab Pull-downs

Stand next to an overhead cable machine and set the weight load to a decent level (50 to 130lbs). Use a triceps rope type attachment and grasp the rope firmly with both hands. While keeping the hips stable in one place crunch your abdominals forward without bending your knees. Try to go as low as you physically are able. Rise up to the start position (again without moving the hips) and repeat. This is one of the best core exercises as you work the core while standing (much like what happens in hockey).

With Ab pull-downs don't be afraid to load up the cable stack and crank this exercise hard

Hanging Abdominal Raise

The hanging abdominal raise is a great exercise that will just trash the core area of almost any goaltender. Start out hanging from an overhead chin-up bar or squat rack and simply raise your feet/ankles/shin up to touch the bar (without bending your legs if possible). Make sure not to swing back and forth during this exercise too much, just rise upward and downward under control. To make this a harder exercise you can swing the legs to the side of the top of the hands, or add weight with a dumbbell. A good number to shoot for before adding weight is 20-repetitions. Enjoy this one…

My favorite abdominal exercise shown by triathlete William Young is a killer when done right!

Turkish Get-up

Clint uses a lighter 40lb dumbbell to perform the Turkish Get-up

The Turkish Get-up is one of those exercises that looks easy until you do it. Start out on a mat on your side with the weight directly overhead (with arm straight) and your other arm out to the side next to your head (figure 1). From this point rise up any way you like (as long as you keep the weight pointed straight overhead with the arm fully locked out), to a standing position (figure 3). To get to the start reverse the entire exercise by carefully kneeling down and then lying out to the start position again (figure 1). Start off with a light weight until you feel comfortable but know that over time elite athletes should be able to use 100+ lbs for this exercise.

Ab Roller

Extending as far as possible with the ab roller is <u>key</u> for this exercise

149

With the ab roller you start off holding the ab roller close to the body (picture 1) and then roll out as far as you can go, making sure to extend the arms and flatten out the hips (picture 2). The feeling should be that you are curling the weight in towards the body with the abs, not the arms. If you feel low back pain during this exercise it's because you are not (or can't) holding your abs in tightly.

Sledgehammer Hits

Justin hits the tire for 50 repetitions with a 10 or 16lbs sledgehammer

Using a heavy object to hit another object is perhaps one of the greatest feelings on earth. When properly implemented into a hockey players training sledge hammer hits can be a very valuable contribution to core strength, shoulder and back development along with cardiovascular conditioning. It takes a big effort to slam the 16lb sledge onto a tire over and over again, and this will help make any player into a beast if performed regularly. I like to have players start with a 10lbs sledge and work up from there. A company called *Torque Athletics* sells oversized "war hammers", which are big sledge hammers up to 150lbs. If you are ready to use a larger sledge I would definitely give them a call at 812-673-4490.

When using sledge hammers make sure that safety is the number one priority as you can smash a toe or shin bone to bits if you're not careful. Another tip is to hit the sledge onto a tire as the impact of the hit will go through the sledge to the hands and hurt like hell if you don't hit a softer object like a tire which has some rebounding properties.

Abdominal Leg Throws

Coach Steve Phillips throws down the legs of midget hockey player Alec James to the side randomly with this core training drill performed at the Hockey Contractor training facility in Simi Valley, CA.

Abdominal side throws involve a player lying on their back holding on to a partner or coach's legs while keeping the legs up in the air (picture 1). From this position the partner or coach throws the legs downward to the ground to the left, right or center with great force (picture 2). The player on the ground must slow the legs down before they touch the ground and then contract the core area to bring the legs back up to the starting position.

Knee-Ins

Balance, strength and coordination are all developed with knee-ins

Start the Knee-in by balancing in the push-up position with your feet up on the ball (figure 1). Try to bring your feet in as far as possible while staying in control (figure 2). For an added challenge try performing this exercise with one leg (figure 3). For another challenge include a push-up into this exercise when the legs are extended (picture 1).

Weighted Straight Leg Curl-ups

This is a really good core and hip flexor exercise that can be done with almost any kind of weight (dumbbell, kettlebell, medicine ball, etc.). Start with the feet held down (in the picture Justin uses two kettlebells looped around the foot), and hold another weight in the hands. Squeeze the hamstrings and glutes tightly while keeping the toes aimed at the ceiling. Rise up slowly by contracting the abdominal and hip flexor muscles while holding the weight extended overhead throughout the exercise (see pictures). Lower back slowly to the mat and repeat.

Weighted straight leg curl-up performed by Justin

45-Degree Side Abs

On a 45-degree back extension machine face sideways making sure the hip has enough room so you can complete a full range of motion. From the starting position flex sideways <u>as far as possible</u> and then rise back up to the starting position. Ensure that you go straight sideways with no twisting in the action. If this exercise is done right it should trash your core area without too much trouble. When this exercise becomes easier then it's time to add a dumbbell or weight plate (either on your chest or held overhead). Make sure to train both side (left and right).

45-degree side abs are a great exercise to develop the muscles of the core

Overhead Abs

With the overhead abs exercise you grab a light dumbbell (5 to 20lbs), hold it overhead with arms straight and then bend as far as possible from side to side. The goal is the range of motion with this exercise, not the amount of weight you can use. Bend straight to the side without turning the body inward or twisting at all. As you develop you can use heavier loads as long as the form stays perfect. Work both sides (left and right).

Stretch as far as possible to perform overhead abs correctly

Side Abdominal Bends

Dumbbell side bends work the core area on the side of the body. Hockey players often have to bend to the side to stick-handle, shoot, or pass the puck, so this is a necessary exercise. Start by holding a dumbbell in one hand and bend to that side as far as possible. Stay in a relatively straight line as you lower the weight to the side, without leaning forward or backwards. With this exercise don't be afraid to crank up the weight (some athletes use up to 150lbs dumbbells or heavily loaded barbells held in one hand with this exercise). Remember to work both sides (left and right).

Working the side abdominals with a heavy dumbbell

Barbell Side Holds

With barbell side holds we are building the static (or isometric) ability of the core area and grip strength. Simply grab a loaded barbell (in a power rack for safety) and hold on for as long as possible. Set the safety pins so that when the barbell falls (because you can't hold it any more) it doesn't travel very far before hitting the pins. Make sure to stand as straight as you can as you want to ensure correct posture. Build up in both weight and time holding the barbell with each hand. A good barbell side hold is 135lbs (in one hand) for 60 seconds.

Strength coach & good friend Chris Herner demonstrates barbell side holds
with 135lbs at Pasadena Fitness in Penticton, BC.

Russian Twists

The standard Russian twist is a decent exercise to develop the slight rotational aspect of the lower spine (it doesn't move very much, only 10%), along with the stabilizing nature of the core area. Grab a weight plate and on an incline sit-up bench move to a 45-degree angle (see picture) and then twist the weight plate from side to side, holding the end position on each rep. This is NOT a fast exercise (do this one very slowly). Start off with 30-seconds and a light weight and gradually increase until you are using a heavier weight for 60 to 120 seconds.

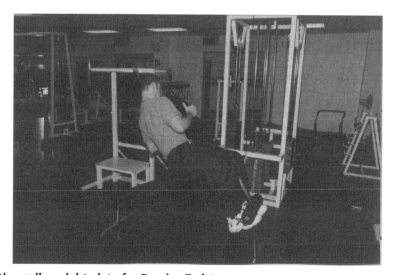

Chris training with a 45lb weight plate for Russian Twists

Back Extension

Clint shows good form on the start and finish of the back extension (pictures 1 & 2), while Julie uses a 20lbs medicine ball to complete a set of back extensions (picture 3)

Back extensions are a great exercise for all hockey players to develop and strengthen the low back. On a 45-degree back extension machine lower down with the fullest possible range of motion and then rise back up to a full hyper extension. Hold a weight plate on your chest to add resistance if necessary and don't be afraid to use a heavy plate with this exercise. On certain machines a Superband can be looped around the base and then put over the player's neck to create a good deal of resistance.

Band Twists

Using a heavy duty band requires a lot of core strength to turn and stabilize

The band twist is with a heavy resistance band and is only done over a short range of motion (see in the pictures). Typically I only want you to twist from the inside shoulder to the outside shoulder. Keep the lower body solid, the arms straight and move the band only by stabilizing and contracting the abdominals. With this exercise I usually have players do this as fast as they can for 20 to 50 reps on each side. In some drills I have players twist from the inside shoulder to a full turn to the side, depending on the goals for the session and the player.

Tornado Ball Hits

Tornado balls and similar balls like them with a rope attached to the ball act like a swinging implement that can only be moved by rotary action from the body. In other words, you have to rotate the body from side to side to get it moving and keep it moving, which trains the core musculature, hip flexors and shoulders very well. To perform this exercise players sit down on the floor with knees slightly bent and the upper body held at 45-degrees. From this position swing the ball with two hands from side to side making a half circle with the hands back and forth. To get the most from this exercise you have to really hit the hard rubber ball into the floor so it will rebound and you can start it moving to the other side without it hitting you in the head.

With the Tornado Ball you can also perform this same exercise standing with your back against a brick wall and hitting it from side to side (just as in the picture, only standing). Players can also use the Tornado Ball as a form of a sledge hammer and hit down against a curl or ground. The only thing to watch for is when the Tornado Ball rebounds just make sure it doesn't hit you in the head as it weighs 8lbs and when moving quickly that will definitely hurt.

Justin swings the Tornado Ball side to side in an arc type pattern as hard as possible

Diagonal Woodchop

This exercise simulates the side striking power of a woodchop with an axe

Start by holding a band or cable attachment head-height and to the side of the body (picture 1). In a diagonal pattern swing the arms straight and in front of the body by turning the hips to finish below the knees (picture 2). As you take a step to the side to complete this exercise make sure it is the core area that does most of the work. You can build up to a lot of weight in this exercise, or use a lighter weight for explosive movements to develop power and speed in these muscles.

Sledgehammer Side Hits

Swinging a sledgehammer is a tremendous conditioning workout, but hitting a large tire from the side works the core muscles, legs, upper back and shoulders to a large extent. Make sure a heavy duty tire is used (not a log or other solid object) as this will hurt the wrists from the forceful impact. Players must remember to train both sides of the body with this exercise and put as much force into each hit as possible. Multiple sets of 20-hits per side are a good start with a 10lbs sledgehammer. As strength and conditioning increases a larger sledgehammer can be used, the rest between sets can be reduced or the action can be sped up. Some players might want to use leather gloves to protect the hands from blisters with this exercise as it tends to beat up the hands.

Swinging a sledge hammer against a big tire is hard work for the shoulders and core musculature

Water Twists

Water twists with a 30lb water jug

The water twist is an exercise that works the rotational muscles of the core by accelerating and decelerating the water jug as quickly as possible. Stand holding a 5-gallon jug of water (not filled completely), or a semi-filled keg (40 to 90lbs) and twist the object side to side as quickly as possible. I like to have athletes twist for 30 to 60 seconds at a time and see how many repetitions can be done in that time. Make sure that the twist is not a full twist to the side, but rather a partial twist so the spine is not compromised or damaged during training.

Barbell Twists
The abdominal area is mostly a supporting structure built to stabilize the spine and transfer energy up or down the body. The barbell twist works this stabilizing nature of the core area as the player rotates a loaded barbell back and forth without letting the core really twist or move…just stabilize. To perform this exercise lodge an Olympic barbell into the corner of the gym or against a squat rack, and load one end with a weight plate. Grab the end with the weight plate and then in a large circular path rotate the barbell back and forth while trying to keep the abdominal area tight and resisting the movements side to side and rotationally.

The key to correctly performing barbell twists is to simply stabilize the core

Planks

Lisa does planks (picture 1), and planks with an arm and leg held up (picture 2)

The plank is a decent core exercise as you have to hold this area firm or you fall down. Make sure to tighten the abdominal muscles and hold the rest of your body as firm as possible for this exercise. Do this for a set amount of time starting off at 60 seconds and moving up from there. If this is really easy you can have someone put a weight plate on your back for extra resistance. Another way of making this more difficult is to hold an arm, leg, or both off the ground during the plank (see above).

If you want to make this exercise competitive then have two players facing each other in the plank position and when you start timing try to knock the other person down by hitting the elbows or arms, or push them over. This will build balance in addition to training the core area and can be a fun finishing exercise at the end of a workout.

Stability Ball Kneeling Twists
This exercise is like a reverse Russian twist in that one part of the body twists while another stays stable. This exercise also requires great balance throughout the core and stabilizer muscles throughout the hip and torso. Start by kneeling on a ball and put the hands down in the push-up position (see pictures). From this set-up twist the knees from side to side as the rest of the upper body is kept stable. Have a partner spot you for the first few times you perform this exercise as most people fall off the ball during the movement. Try to keep the angle between the body and the knees at 90 degrees so the core has to work that much harder during the action.

Wesley performs a stability ball kneeling twist

Sample Workouts

While many different activities such as playing hockey, weight training and most conditioning work will train the core area I think that **daily conditioning** of this area is a good idea for all hockey players. To start off I recommend picking 2 exercises from the list of abdominal exercises listed above and complete 2 sets of these 2 exercises. Always remember you can create great variety to abdominal training by adding more of a load, using a tougher band, changing the speed of muscle contraction, alter the pair of exercises or decreasing the amount of rest you take between sets to make your core training workouts harder. As you get comfortable with daily core training you can add a set or two to the workout just as long as the time it takes to complete doesn't take more than 10-minutes (you don't need to spend more than that on core training). The following are some sample workouts:

Monday
A1 Ab Roller   2 sets x 25 repetitions
A2 Russian Twists   2 sets x 15 repetitions/side

Tuesday
A1 Turkish Get-Up   2 sets x 5 repetitions/side
A2 Woodchops   2 sets x 20 repetitions

Wednesday
A1 Sledgehammer   2 sets x 15 hits/side
A2 Side Abs   2 sets x 12 reps/side

Thursday
A1 Hanging Curls   2 sets x 10 repetitions
A2 KB Windmills   2 sets x 5 repetitions/side

Friday
A1 Weighted Sit-ups   2 sets x 8 reps
A2 Side Abs   2 sets x 5 reps/side

Saturday
A1 Medicine Ball Throws   2 sets x 15 reps/side
A2 Straight Leg Curl-ups   2 sets x 30 repetitions

Sunday
A1 Stability Ball Crunches 2 sets x 15 repetitions
A2 Band Twists   2 sets x 20 reps/side

Chapter 13 - Grip Training

"Forget about style; worry about results."

~ Bobby Orr, Hall of fame NHL hockey player

In hockey you need a strong grip and wrist muscles for a variety of motions on the ice from shooting to battling opponents. The grip muscles will be worked when you perform regular strength training and conditioning routines but further work in this area will pay off. Much like core training you learned about in a previous chapter, I expect this to be done every day and with plenty of variety. As with injury prevention exercises and core training I do not schedule formal training time for grip training as this can be done in short training sessions of 5 to 10-minutes every day, or every other day for 15-minutes. Perform two exercises for repetitions of 5 to 50 (depending on your training age, load you choose and strength), making sure to change the exercises and the number of reps you do each day. The following exercises are simply some of the exercises you can do to strengthen the forearms.

Hand Roller

The hand roller works the finger muscles as they have to grip the outside of the weight plates (see picture) while the forearms work to turn the unit. I built my own hand roller using simple materials you can find in a hardware store (good rope, 2-2.5lbs plates, a round wood 1.5 inch circle and some Gorilla glue).

Start off with a lighter weight and make sure to turn the weight plates in sets forwards, and backwards. Adjust the weight used as you see fit, sometimes using a heavy weight for only a few turns, and other times using a lighter weight for many turns of the plates.

Wrist Roller

The traditional wrist roller (picture 1) and the wrist roller that is mounted to a squat rack (picture 2)

The wrist roller should be a staple piece of training equipment for every hockey player, at all levels. To use the roller you grip it on the outsides and turn the pipe either forwards or backwards until the weight that is attached is pulled from the ground to the handle. As with the hand roller (listed on the next page) I expect you to adjust the weight so sometimes you use a heavy weight for only a few turns and sometimes use a lighter weight for many turns of the handle.

Kettlebell wrist rotations

Kettlebell wrist rotations are a good wrist conditioning exercise

This basic exercise is meant to strengthen the wrist with plyometric type motions (fast change of direction type movements). Grab onto a kettlebell (or dumbbell) and hang it at your side. From this position rotate the weight to the left and then to the right as quickly as possible but only through a small range of motion. Do not twist as far as you can go as this will actually hurt your wrist muscles. Rather, I want you to twist the weight <u>quickly</u> over a 2 to 3-inch range of motion. Always be adjusting the range of motion so that it works all aspects of the wrist, but just make sure to keep it in the 2 to 3 inch range.

Kettlebell Grip Training

This is a ballistic grip training exercise, as hockey players need exceptional strength in the wrists and forearm to produce high velocity shots. Simply grab a heavy kettlebell and while holding it to one side of the body (outside on the grass or over a sandy beach) start to pull up the weight and then let go of the kettlebell, and as it begins to drop catch it. Repeat this lifting, releasing and catching over and over, without slowing down or stopping until you feel like dropping the kettlebell. For a change of pace try switching hands between "throws" from right to left and left to right. Do these drills on the grass and watch out if you miss...a broken toe is only one drop away!

Jerk the kettlebell upwards, let go, and then catch it! With the thick grip of the kettlebell, this is grip training.

160

Heavy Hammer

I believe that every hockey player should use this exercise to develop exceptional wrist strength for maximal shooting power. In the photo's below I am using the heavy hammer from the Ironmind Company but you can use a heavy wrench, fence post (that has been filled with cement), or a hockey stick held at the end to achieve the same objective. The idea is to rotate the object back and forth slowly which will train the rotational muscles of your forearm.

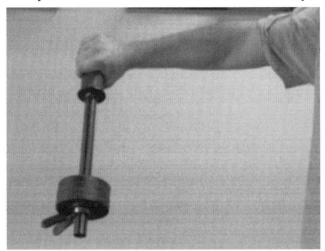 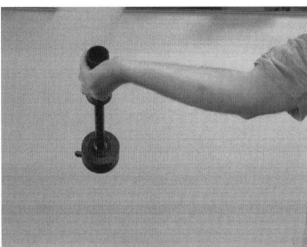

One of the best wrist training exercise for hockey players

Grippers

The **only** grippers I suggest are called the "Captains of Crush" and they are built by a company called Ironmind. These grippers will put any man's grip to the test as the easiest gripper they make provides 60-pounds of force to close, and the top gripper requires 365lbs of force to close (only about 10 men on earth have closed this gripper). Needless to say, they do make a gripper that is right for you! I suggest you start off with the entry gripper and perform many repetitions with that until you feel confident in moving up to the next level. These grippers are $19.95, plus shipping, but are well worth it for what they provide. In case you are wondering...a typical gripper you might find at Walmart requires only 25lbs of force to close.

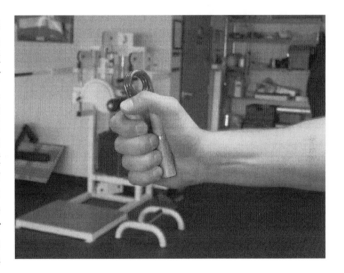

Barbell Pad Holds

Fat grip holds are a good exercise to work the gripping strength of the forearms. Wrap a bar pad around a barbell and then grip the bar pad for as long as possible. Start off with relatively light weight (45 to 75lbs) and build up to a good amount of weight. This exercise can also be done by using only one hand holding the barbell but this is very difficult and many players will not be able to use much more than 45 to 60lbs for holds.

Farmers Walk

With the farmers walk you grab a pair of heavy dumbbells or kettlebells and go for a walk. The goal should be to walk for about 60+ seconds without dropping the weights on the floor. Be careful as your grip starts to fail that you find a safe place to drop the weights (not on your toes or legs as that will be very painful). Ideally you would want to do this outside and on a dirt or grass area so dropping the weight isn't such a problem. Keep increasing the weight as you get stronger and stronger. I like to use this exercise as a finishing exercise at the end of workouts so athletes can compete to win.

Coach Pollitt walking with 2-inch thick-grip 75lb dumbbells

Barbell Holds

The barbell hold is a relatively simple exercise in which you load up a barbell with a pre-determined weight and simply hold it for as long as possible, until it drops out of your hands. I would strongly recommend you use a power rack or some kind of support so the barbell does not go crashing to the ground (gym owners don't like that). Instead, set the support pins so that the barbell is only an inch or two above the pins and has only a short distance to fall. Start off with a lighter weight with both hands such as 135lbs, and try to hold that for 60-seconds. If this is easy, then increase the weight as you see fit.

If you use one hand I suggest starting with just the 45lbs barbell as the balance of the barbell may be a problem. Hold just the barbell for 60+ seconds, then add weight to the bar (on both ends to balance the weight). In the picture above, Justin holds a 225lb barbell for maximal time.

Fat Gripz

In 2010 I bought a pair of Fat Gripz on the recommendation of another Strength & Conditioning Coach in Canada and was very impressed with the quality and functionality of this training device. Basically it turns any barbell or dumbbell into a fat handled training implement. As it is very challenging to hold a fat grip (in this case it's 2¼ inches in diameter) it provides a great training effect on all barbell and dumbbell exercises. I strongly recommend you get a pair...for more information check out their website at **www.fatgripz.com**.

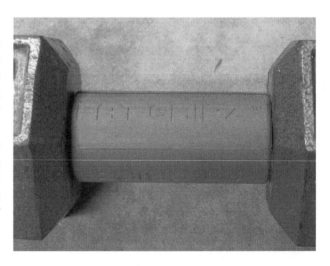

162

Mini-Sledge Hammer Hits

Take a mini 2lbs sledge hammer which you can buy at your local hardware store for less than 15 dollars and an old tire (or find one) for this training. Hold the hammer as far to the end of the handle as possible and with short, quick hits you want to strike the tire as fast as possible until you give up. Holding at the end of the 2lbs weight adds up and creates incredible tension in the forearm and gripping muscles. Repeat for a total of 2-sets (to failure, just watch the hammer doesn't fly out of your hand), with each hand.

Gripping Exercises

While the sport of hockey demands that the forearms possess good turning strength (to shoot the puck) it is also important to work the muscles involved in gripping the stick to provide balanced strength. At Revolution Athletics we have a wide variety of tools to work the gripping muscles such as the rolling thunder, pinch grip block, finger loops, etc. The idea is to grip a thick bar or block and hold that weight for as long as possible before it falls out of your hand. Below are just some of these implements.

The rolling thunder 3-inch grip tool (left) or the 3-inch metal pinch block (right)

Grip Training Suggestions

Just about everything you hold or move involves grip training but to get the most out of your efforts here are some other ideas on how to develop the forearm area for hockey:

- *To build the holding type of grip you can use softball sized rocks in the backyard, bags of grass seed, or yard tools. Be creative in your grip training approach.*

- *If possible buy a thick rope to mount on some overhead object so you can perform pull-ups or horizontal rows while your hands must tightly squeeze the rope.*

- *Try filling a large 5-gallon bucket with either water and sand, or preferable sand alone to use as a method of resistance. Stick your hand in the bucket and move it around. Open and close your hand.*

163

Twist your hand around. Put a couple of golf balls in the bucket and try to retrieve the balls as quickly as possible as your hand fishes around in the sand.

- *An old-school method of grip training from grip master John Brookfield requires using that same 5-gallon bucket and filling it with water or sand. Hold a pair of pliers and grip the pliers around the handle to lift the heavy bucket as long as possible.*

- *To make a thick handle grip for the hockey stick simply wrap stick tape around the handle and shaft of the stick so that it becomes a thick handle. With that thick handle stick now you can practice shooting, stick-handling and passing. When you return to using your normal stick you will be able to grip it more firmly and shoot the puck harder.*

- *Understand that with grip training we are working the small muscles and tendons of the hand and forearm. While I suggest you do a little bit of training each day it is important to note that sometimes these areas can be over-worked. Start off slowly and work into regular grip training.*

- *Following grip training if possible players should shoot pucks between sets to further exhaust the wrist muscles. Several sets of wrist specific weight training and shooting a couple times per week will be a great way to develop a powerful shot.*

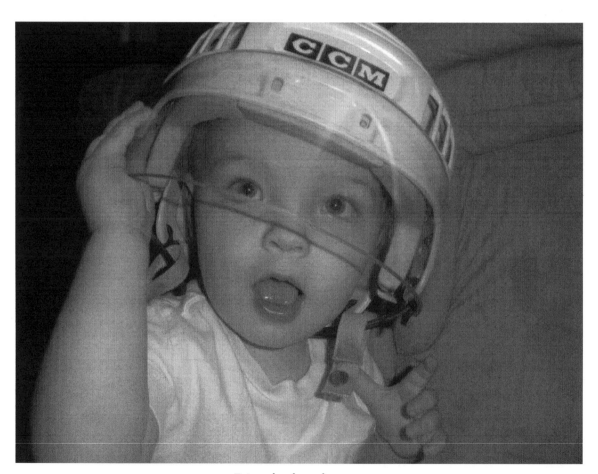

Future hockey player...

Chapter 14 - Speed & Agility Training

> "Nobody's a natural. You work hard to get good and then work to get better.
> It's hard to stay on top."
>
> **~ Paul Coffey, Hall of Fame NHL hockey player**

In the game of hockey both speed and agility are **game-changing skills**. They are qualities that allow players such as Sidney Crosby, Alexander Ovechkin and Teemu Selanne among many others to enjoy a great career in hockey. In order to play at the next level you simply **must get faster** in the first few steps (which I call quickness), faster at full speed and more agile at speed to be successful.

Now a certain amount of the ability to be quick, fast and agile comes from birth. Speedy athletes are born with certain genetic traits such as a higher percentage of fast twitch muscles, better muscle insertion points (to the bone), fast reflexes, or a higher percentage of strength to body weight ratio. Whatever the reason, these folks can become very fast as its part of their genetic make-up. For the rest of us this does not mean we will never be fast, it just means that either we will have to work very hard to become fast and when we are fast, it may not be as fast as others. Just remember that while you may never have the quickness or speed of a Paul Kariya, it doesn't mean you can't keep trying to improve on-ice speed as well as other physical attributes (size, strength, conditioning, flexibility, agility, etc.), that compliment hockey skills.

In the following sections I present only a few of the drills I use to develop speed and agility in players. While dryland training for speed/agility is useful; just make sure to work on sport specific speed and quickness skills on the ice as this is much more important. With dryland quickness I want you to get used to perfecting sprinting/movement techniques (with running and skating), as well as performing a quality workout each time you train (rather than working out just because it's written on the program).

Speed Training Key Points

I see so many training programs written by coaches or trainers that fail to address certain aspects of developing speed. You would think that every hockey player was a 100-meter track athlete by what I see during dryland workouts. The key that everyone needs to understand is that dryland training for speed is a supplement to improving speed, but ideally you have to work on skating skills and speed on the ice for it to really matter. In this section I present a list of speed training considerations that should be emphasised throughout the yearly training plan.

- The **KEY** to speed is **STRENGTH**. I have **NEVER** seen an athlete that was too strong for their sport. When a person's strength increases they positively change their strength to bodyweight ratio, (which means they are now able to produce more power). It's like putting a V-8 engine in a Honda Civic...that car would go like hell because you improved the power output of the engine relative to the size of the car. Work to develop great strength in the hips, quads and posterior chain muscles with heavy squats, deadlifts and RDL's. Also, remember to spend time to improve the strength in the hip flexors (the front part of the hip) as this area is usually overlooked in many training programs and is prone to injuries during the hockey season.

- Partial deadlifts with Olympic bumper plates are amazing for strength development (for speed work). Simply start in the bottom position and pull the weight to just below the knees and drop the weight. This works the concentric action of the deadlift only and allows you to train the deadlift many times per week without the negative effects of eccentric actions.

- In addition to performing exercises to improve strength you also must work explosiveness in the weight room, as developing speed is ALL about producing a high amount of force in a short period of time. Exercises such as power cleans, power pulls, hang cleans, hang snatches, kettlebell snatches, squat & press, jerks, Russian Box jumps, box jumps, squat jumps into box jump etc. are essential exercises to improve your ability to generate maximal power.

- Decreasing extra body fat will also affect the strength to bodyweight ratio as you have reduced the weight that has to be moved when skating/running. Ideally a hockey player should be between 8 to 12 percent body fat. If you are not, then get to work!

- Work on both skating technique and sprinting technique. Why do you think that most NHL teams employ a skating coach and every decent sprinter has a coach? Technique is critical to performance in sprinting. I could fill an entire chapter on this subject alone...so look to improving this aspect of your game by searching for a qualified skating coach. My recommendation on great skating coaches are Steffany Hanlen or Vanessa Hettinger at (**www.quantumspeed.ca**), or Laura Stamm (**www.laurastamm.com**)

- Hockey is a sport that 90% of the time demands short sprints (10 to 60-feet). Many times a sprint is required while skating along at a slow speed (like circling for a pass and then sprinting to catch the pass, or sprinting to intercept an opponent in the corner and battle for the puck). Therefore, to train correctly for hockey **FIRST STEP QUICKNESS** short bursts of **ACCELERATION** are critical. Make sure to perform sprints from many positions such as in a stopped position, slowly moving position and facing another direction turn/sprint position. Many coaches have players sprint like track athletes (performing repeated 60 to 100-meter sprints). This is the wrong approach. I rarely do sprints longer than 40 meters for this reason.

- Workouts **MUST** focus on quality of sprints rather than volume. Athletes should only sprint at 95+% of full speed. Working sprinting drills until speed decreases past this point becomes conditioning (which is fine too if that is the goal for the workout), but if developing raw speed is the goal then workout volume must be reduced and so quality can be the focus.

- You must have a great deal of flexibility to allow full contraction and extension of the hips. If the hips are tight you will not be a fast person and may ultimately injure yourself trying to run or skate faster.

- I have players use a variety of starting positions, such as facing forwards, backwards, sideways, or on the ground. This unpredictable starting position mimics hockey as players are not always square to the play when they are asked to move quickly to intercept a player or skate for a pass.

- The core area must be strong to hold the upper body in a correct position during the initial steps of any sprint or agility movement. Therefore players MUST work the core area.

- On days that sprint workouts are scheduled along with a strength workout, conditioning or a hockey practice it is important that sprinting ALWAYS is trained first that day. You must perform the speed, quickness and agility training when fresh or else the quality of the workout may suffer.

- Ideally players would schedule sprint training in the beginning part of the week when they are most fresh. This will change with every team or athlete.

- Short hill sprints are a great way to develop explosive sprint speed, leg strength and conditioning all in one workout. Just make sure that the sprints are done over short periods and performed as quickly as possible. Using a steep sand hill is also amazing to develop leg strength and turn-over rate in the legs (as the sand makes it hard to run).

Agility Training Key Points

The development of agility is very similar to improving speed in that many of the same qualities that are important to moving quickly apply to agility. As such, I generally combine both speed and agility training into one workout, and follow that up with a conditioning workout and flexibility session to get the most from each training workout. The following are some key points that should be looked at when training agility.

- Perhaps more than anything agility in hockey means changing directions (at any speed). During agility training the player should add drills that involve accelerating/decelerating as well as changing directions often.

- Players need to work on moving the feet quickly (in all directions) so that they can turn and move as quickly as possible. When moving players should try to be "light on their feet", which means setting the foot down and then moving it quickly. Agility ladder training, shadow drills, and close quarter hockey drills are best to develop these skills.

- With **ALL** agility training it is ESSENTIAL to have players complete the drills in an "athletic" low position that mimics the amount of knee bend used while skating.

- Some forms of agility training should include read and react type drills that force the player to read what is going on, make a quick decision and then react by moving. Agility ball training both on and off the ice is a good way to improve this skill.

- As hockey is not a straight ahead only sport I usually like to have players sprint to a cone and then make a slight turn either left or right, stop and back-pedal, or complete a 180 degree turn   so players get used to transitioning from forwards to backwards and vice-versa during off-ice speed work.

- Most importantly coaches should work on developing agility based actions on the ice (while stick-handling if possible), before integrating these skills to practices or games.

Speed & Agility Drills

Sprinting
The idea with sprinting workouts is that quality is the most important factor. If you can only perform 5 sprints before the quality decreases, then you can build your work capacity which will allow you to perform more and more over time. Ideally sprints should be between 10-feet and 100-feet so that the sprints are as fast as possible. Rarely do hockey players need sprints of more than 100-feet and never do they need this during dryland training. In the hockey workouts section you will find various sprinting workouts that will help your development as a hockey player.

Sprinting Drills
The use of sprinting drills is a good warm-up and general conditioning movement for sprinting or other speed work. There are many variations of sprinting drills as any good track and field coach will attest. Without including another entire section on sprinting here are four of the most common drills;

Butt Kickers
Taking small steps forward, try to bring the back leg up and kick your butt on each stride. It is not important how far you move with each stride, only the turnover of the legs (it should be fast) and how high the leg comes up and kicks the butt.

High Knees
Sprinting with the arms held out in front of the body at belly-button height; try to take small sprints while making sure the knees hit the hands. This forces the hip flexors to work much more than usual.

Bounding
Rather than sprinting, with every stride try to push off and jump as high as possible into the air. When you land, absorb the force of the jump and then jump again. Make sure to drive the non-jumping knee and opposite arm into the air so that the sprinting action is simulated.

High Knee Stretch

Similar to bounding, the high knee stretch drill is performed by taking a forward step and driving one knee high into the air. As this leg is in the air, the leg extends forward as if you are trying to hurdle an object and then it falls to the ground and the drill is repeated with the other leg. This drill is not easy and takes some practice to get right.

Start/Stop Drill

This drill involves straight ahead running on a track or in a park. The idea is to run forward as fast as possible for 10 to 50-feet and then at random decelerate to a stop. As soon as you stop, start back-pedalling for 5 to 10-feet, then change direction and sprint forwards again for 10 to 50-feet. Stop when the quality of the sprints or the change of direction drops off noticeably. This is a very simple change of direction drill that can be performed for sets of 5 to 15, and with a warm-up and cool-down should take no more than 20-minutes. This drill can also be combined with other running or conditioning drills to make up a circuit or giant set.

Hill Sprints

Hill sprinting is one of the most valuable methods of developing sheer power in the legs. As with hill jumping the reduced "air time" of the legs due to the angle of the hill and the need to flex the hip to get a good stride length make this an awesome exercise for all athletes. Hockey players especially will benefit from hill sprinting as it works the hip flexors in a wide range of motion (which is very valuable). Sprinting can be done forwards, backwards or other steps such as cross-overs, side shuffles or carioca steps. The length of each sprint can go from 20 feet to 200-meters, depending on the athletes conditioning and purpose (goal) of the workout. The important aspect of hill sprinting is to go 100% with each and every sprint to build the legs and cardiovascular power for hockey.

12' Agility Drill/Test

Justin runs through the 12' agility drill/test at Revolution Athletics

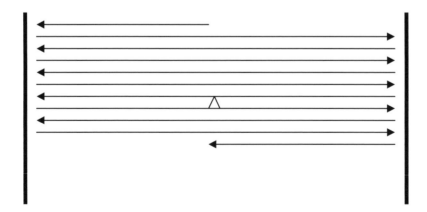

Diagram 18 – The 12' Lateral Agility Drill/Test

The 12-foot agility drill is one of my favourite tests of a player's ability to move side to side, accelerate and decelerate, and change directions quickly. To start, place two hockey sticks 12-feet apart with one cone in the middle. The player starts at the cone in the middle and runs to the right, touching one foot over the hockey stick, and then running left to the other hockey stick and crossing over that stick. This side to side running continues for 10 total repetitions (5-each way as shown in the diagram). Make sure that the player faces forward during the entire drill and holds a hockey stick in one hand to simulate an on-ice situation (see pictures below). The clock stops when the player returns to the middle cone after 10-repetitions. A good time in this test is around 12-seconds. Players who are heavier or do not possess adequate strength will have times in the 13 to 15-second range. I use this drill as both a test and a conditioning tool as it combines many different skills into one exercise.

12-Cone Agility Drill

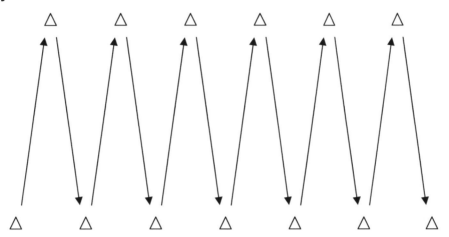

Diagram 19 – The standard 12-Cone Agility Drill

This is a forward and back agility drill that works the acceleration and deceleration components in hockey players. Place the twelve cones in a standard (as shown in diagram 19), and have players sprint from cone-1 to cone-2, around cone-2 and backwards to cone-3. Keep going from cone to cone, forwards and backwards until the player has gone around each cone. This is a drill the entire team can participate in or in smaller groups to keep athletes moving.

To add variation try a random pattern of cones (as pictured in diagram 20), so that distances between cones is always different. Run through this drill 5 to 15-times with short rest breaks in between for recovery. Players can also use a weighted vest with 10 to 80 extra pounds for additional conditioning.

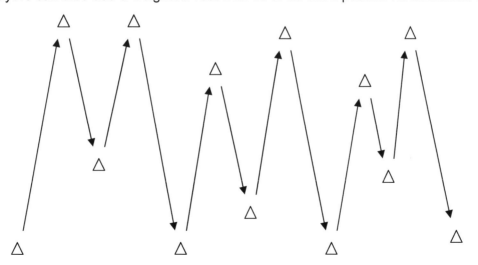

Diagram 20 – The random pattern of the 12-Cone Agility Drill

169

5-Line Drill

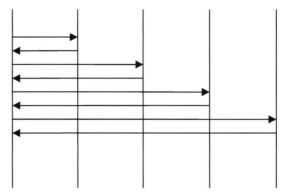

Diagram 21 – Line Drills

The line drill is a simple agility drill that works the acceleration and deceleration aspects of training. Players start on the first line and sprint to the first line and back, second line and back, third line and back, and then to the forth line and back. Players who are very fast will complete this drill in around 20-seconds. This drill should be used in conjunction with other drills to create a circuit of drills.

Forward/Backward Sprint Drill

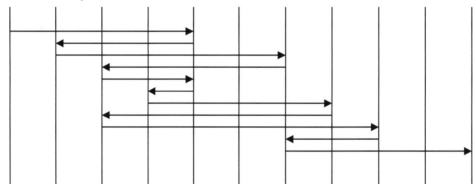

Diagram 22 – Forward/Backward Sprint Drill

The forward/backward sprint drill involves players sprinting forward to the designated line and then back-pedaling (run backwards) to the designated line. Follow the arrows on the above diagram or create your own drills with varying distances. The idea is to improve the acceleration and deceleration abilities both forwards and backwards, along with frequent changes of direction.

To set up this drill space the lines out 5-meters apart, which results in a 200 meter drill when all of the forward/backward sprints are calculated. To change this to a speed drill, simply reduce the spacing of the lines (to 5-feet) or change the distance of the lines to a lesser amount.

3-Cone Agility Drill

The 3-Cone agility drill is a simple sprinting and change of direction drill. Players start at a beginning cone and sprint 20 to 40-meters to the first cone, go around the cone and sprint 5 to 15-meters to cone number two, go around that cone and sprint to the finish line 20 to 40-meters away. This is a typical drill that might be found on the football field for receivers or tight ends, but works well with hockey as players need to be able to accelerate and decelerate quickly. Make sure that players do this drill going both ways so muscular balance is maintained. Record times for each distance of cones and in both directions to compare. Use this drill with bodyweight exercises, kettlebells or a sled to create a giant set of exercises.

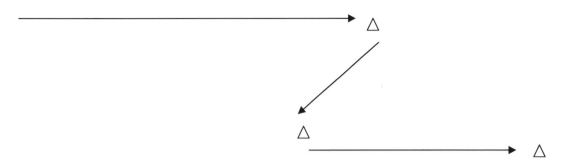

Diagram 23 – The 3-Cone Drill

5-Cone Agility Drill

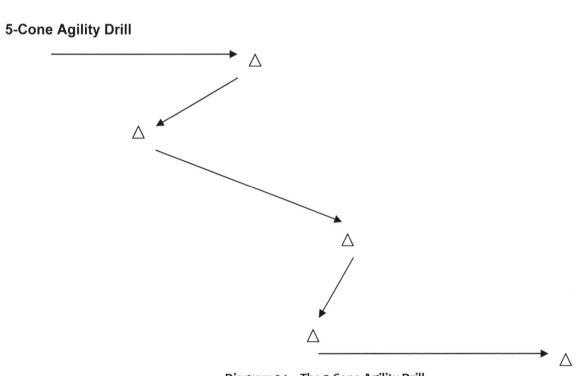

Diagram 24 – The 5-Cone Agility Drill

Much like the 3-Cone Agility Drill, the 5-Cone Agility Drill focuses on acceleration and deceleration as the player has to sprint to cones, and then change directions to sprint to the next cone. This drill can be set up however the coach or player wishes (changing distances between cones and the angle of the sprints) in order to vary the workout. Make sure that sprints are done both directions so that the muscles get the same workout on both sides. Record times for each distance of cones and in both directions to compare. Use this drill with sled dragging, combat workouts or band drills to create a giant set of exercises.

Dryland Figure-8 Drill
Set up the cones 4 to 8-feet apart and have players go through the cones to the right and to the left as if they were creating a figure-8 by running. This drill will help develop acceleration, deceleration plus pivoting and changing directions all with the same drill. As players get used to this drill have them stickhandle a street-hockey ball or Smart Hockey ball around the cones. Coaches can even have players make passes back and forth to other players who are standing or doing the same drill or set up a net to receive a pass and then shoot during the drills. Be creative and turn this simple drill into a very hockey specific method of dryland training.

John demonstrates the figure-8 drill

Partner Figure 8 Cone Drills

Kyle chases Alec during the partner figure-8 drill

The figure-8 cone drill involves players running around 2 cones in a figure-8 pattern. As this drill is performed the player faces one direction (towards another player or coach in the middle of the two cones, see picture). As the player runs through the cones in a figure-8 pattern the coach throws a ball to the player so that they can catch the ball and throw it back to the coach. This develops coordination of the feet while performing a drill but it also improves hand-eye coordination. The mind also has to learn to process many different variables at once which is similar to what happens on the ice when stick-handling with the puck.

Ring Avoiders

The ring avoiders is a drill I use to work the lateral agility in a hockey player as they must shuffle and move side to side around agility rings I put on the ground in various patterns. The goal of the drill is to move around each ring as fast as possible while keeping the body facing forward at all times. This drill can be done with either side shuffles or a cross-over type step to get around the rings. Used as a conditioning drill, the muscles of the hip develop great strength and quickness.

As with most of the other drills a coach/player can make this drill more hockey specific by adding stickhandling, passing or shooting. Be creative and have fun with this drill.

172

John and Kyle perform the ring avoider drill

Agility Ladder Drills

Just about every hockey program I know uses the agility ladder or a version of the agility ladder to work on quick feet and general coordination. Players need to get used to moving the legs quickly and through a wide variety of motions off the ice when a mistake will not matter. As players start skating more in the off-season this fundamental base of quickness can then be applied to the ice during drills and conditioning.

Various drills using the agility ladder such as alternating jumps (picture 1), 2-leg jumps (picture 2), lateral jumps (picture 3), cross-over jumps (picture 4)

Junior-A hockey player Ryan McInnis using the single agility ladder for quick feet drills

Many types of actions can be performed when using the agility ladder from hops with one or two legs, quick movements laterally, back and forth drills, etc. The cost of an agility ladder is about $80 for a good model, and the variety of exercises that can be performed is endless. Just like all other training, players should use the agility ladder for quick bursts of movements or for drills lasting no more than 40-seconds to ensure a quality movement on the ladder. Carolina Hurricane's Strength & Conditioning Coach Peter Friesen recommends that coaches "emphasis 2-step quickness and keeping the center of gravity low during all agility ladder drills". Be creative with this workout tool as it has some real benefits to hockey players.

Agility Ball Training

The agility ball is an **awesome** training tool for both players and goaltenders as it helps them work on first step quickness, lateral movement, and hand/eye coordination all at the same time. As I am a big fan of drills that incorporate 2 skills at once this exercise is a personal favourite. Have one or two players lined up facing a coach. The coach throws an agility ball towards the player and they have to change direction to try and catch the ball before it bounces twice or three times (whatever you choose). The shape of the agility ball creates an unpredictable bounce pattern so players cannot anticipate where the ball will go, they simply have to read and react to where it goes.

Notice from picture 1 to picture 2 how unpredictable the bounce is with the agility ball

To provide more of a challenge I like to have the players face a wall and I stand 10 feet behind them to throw the ball against the wall or ground. This limits the amount of time they have to read and react to the ball, which produces more of a training affect.

Acceleration Runs

Attaching a long band to a low post and then around a players weights with a hip belt can be used to provide great "first step" agility training for hockey players. Once the band is in place a wide range of agility drills such as side shuffles, cross-over steps, figure-8 cone drills, or even the 12' agility drill can be performed. Training agility this way forces the player to lower their center of gravity and use great power to overcome the band and to accelerate quickly during the drill. To add variety a coach can hold the long band at different angles to create off centered tension on the athlete.

Fix the band to a low post to help increase the challenge of this exercise

Juke Drill (Dryland)

The Juke drill is not a resistance exercise, but a very important agility drill for hockey players. Two athletes face each other several feet apart and are "tied" together with a strap that has a Velcro center which breaks apart if pulled. The drill ends when the Velcro breaks.

The Juke drill is exactly the same as the on-ice version (shown on the next page) only players are on a grass or rubber track surface wearing running shoes. The goal is the same, to break away from the other player who is shadowing you. This drill should be run with other drills to make up an agility circuit before performing conditioning work.

175

Juke Drill (On-Ice)

The on-ice version of the Juke drill is a challenging and highly beneficial agility drill that players can use anytime during practice to work on reaction time, read & react skills, proprioception, edge work, balance and explosive power. During the season I have my players do at least 5-rounds with the Juke three times per week during practice to keep improving all of the skills listed above. Get creative and see how this type of training will improve your game!

Austin Block (NCAA D1) works the Juke versus Junior-A player Mark Pustin

Shadow Drill (On-Ice)

A similar but low cost agility drill is to have two players stand a few feet apart and try to shadow each other. One player starts off trying to get away from the other player, while that player tries to mimic the same movements of the first player. After 20-seconds of the shadow drill take a quick break, and then switch places in the drill. This exercise can also be used with players in the open ice as one player follows another. Coaches can even make this a drill with a puck so now puck-handling skills are worked in addition to the read & react aspect of the drill.

Junior players Trent Takeuchi and Sean Keating practice agility drills on the mini-rink at the Banff Recreation Centre

Speed & Agility Workouts

With sprinting and agility workouts a great number of combinations can be performed. Use any of the drills listed above and be creative as long as the quality of the exercise is done at 100%. At the end of all speed & agility workouts you should add a conditioning workout such as sled dragging, kettlebell work, stick battling, partner drills or band resistance training. Here are some sample workouts.

Workout 1

A1 Forward sprints (from a standing position)   5 sets of 15 feet
B1 Backwards sprints (from a squat position, 90 degree knee bend)   5 sets of 15 feet
C1 Side shuffles   5 sets of 25 feet/side
NOTES: *Do not hurry through these drills to make sure the quality of the sprint stays high.*

Workout 2

A1 Forwards sprints (from a squat position, 90 degree knee bend)   5 sets of 15 feet
B1 Cross Over sprints (crossovers just like when skating)   3 sets of 15 feet/side
C1 12' Lateral Agility Drill   3 sets
NOTES: *Do not hurry through these drills to make sure the quality of the sprint stays high.*

Workout 3
A1 5-Line Drill	3 sets
B1 Ring Avoiders	5 sets of 12 rings
C1 Forward/Backwards Sprint Drill	5 sets

NOTES: Do not hurry through these drills to make sure the quality of the sprint stays high.

Workout 4
A1 12-Cone Agility Drill	5 sets
B1 Forward Sprints (50 feet from a lying starting position)	8 sets
C1 Agility Ladder Drill	5 sets

NOTES: Do not hurry through these drills to make sure the quality of the sprint stays high.

Workout 5
A1 3-Cone Agility Drill	6 sets (3 each way)
B1 5-Line Drill	5 sets
C1 Start/Stop Drill	5 minutes

NOTES: Do not hurry through these drills to make sure the quality of the sprint stays high.

Workout 6
A1 Juke (dryland)	5 total drills
B1 Acceleration Runs	3 drills each side
C1 Start/Stop Runs	5 runs of 200 meters
D1 Agility Ball Catches	50 total catches

NOTES: Do not hurry through these drills to make sure the quality of the sprint stays high.

Workout 7 (on-ice drills)
A1   Juke
B1   T-Test
C1   Band Forward Sprints
D1   Shadow Drill
NOTES: Do not hurry through these drills to make sure the quality of the sprint stays high.

Workout 8 (on-ice drills)
A1   Banff Agility Skating Drill
B1   Shadow Drill
C1   Forward Sprints (goal line to red line)
C1   Stick Battle
NOTES: Do not hurry through these drills to make sure the quality of the sprint stays high.

WHL prospect Bryan Hodges (Junior-A) leads out Bryce Nielsen (Junior-B) and Kayla Nielsen (16UAAA) during summer workouts in southern California (picture 1). Bryce battles Bryan in the 12' agility drill (picture 2)

Chapter 15 - Conditioning Basics for Hockey

"The difference between 'involvement' and 'commitment' is like an eggs-and-ham breakfast: the chicken was 'involved' - the pig was 'committed'."

~ unknown

The sport of hockey involves many different skills that must be seamlessly integrated on the ice in order to make a complete hockey player. One or two qualities cannot be developed at the expense of the others or problems are created. For example a fast player who is tight in the hips may tend to have hip flexor or groin injuries more often or a physically strong player might lack agility and quickness on the ice. The player who combines hockey skill and technique with strength, power, speed, agility, conditioning, flexibility, and desire to play the game at a high level are the athletes who move to the next level.

Having talked about the physical qualities that make up a solid hockey player it must be stated early and often that the goal of all training is to **make a better hockey player**. It does not matter what a player can bench press, how fast they can run a 40-meter sprint or run 1.5 miles on a track if this does not produce a better athlete on the ice. Too often coaches and trainers get hung up on the numbers of improvement (both on and off the ice) and fail to ask the important question: "Is this helping the product on the ice during the game?" If every drill, exercise or program has a clear purpose to create a better hockey player then make it happen…if not, rethink the strategy.

A Systematic Training Approach

Conditioning is the systematic training approach that takes into account many different factors such as strength, endurance, flexibility, power, agility, quickness, etc. The training model I prefer using is a Russian model of developing athletes that divide all physical training into General Physical Preparation (GPP) and Specific Physical Preparation (SPP). The purpose of these two methods of training provide an athlete with a solid base level of performance and then attempt to introduce sport specific actions that will ultimately help the player compete on the ice.

General Physical Preparation (GPP)

GPP is the overall, non-sport specific development of the athlete such as strength, joint mobility, aerobic & anaerobic endurance, body coordination, power, lateral quickness, read & reaction, and agility. The goal of GPP is to increase the athletes overall physical abilities in all areas to optimal levels before sport specific actions are introduced. This optimization of body resources provides a higher work capacity for the player and allows any type of physical work to be performed with greater success. Training methodologies such as sled dragging, tire dragging, kettlebell lifting, hill running, strongman exercises, and even combat training would be classified as general physical preparation as the goal of these workouts is to improve all areas of the hockey player. It should be noted that more GPP training is done to prepare the athlete than any other form of training, and this training is performed throughout the year to keep a players work capacity high.

Specific Physical Preparation

Legendary Russian sport scientist Verkhoshansky defined Special Physical Preparation (SPP) as: "the training that is specific to the sport's requirements in competition". This type of training takes the overall abilities that have been developed in prior GPP training and includes a sport specific component. This further prepares the player for competition. When players talk about "getting into game shape" they are referring to this type of training as it prepares them to play hockey at the highest level. Activities such as sled dragging, on-ice resistance work (bands, tires, parachutes, etc.), lateral training (such as slide boards or the Russian Box), and sport specific intervals that work acceleration, deceleration, and change of direction. SPP is used to a lesser degree than GPP, but it is still performed throughout the year to "grease the grove" by keeping players in game shape.

Conditioning is NOT only Aerobic Training

Over the years I have seen too many coaches, players and teams follow a significantly flawed off-season training program that focuses on long slow distance training to condition hockey players for in-season performance. To that end I will list 8 reasons why traditional training such as long distance running, cycling, inline skating or swimming is the wrong approach for hockey players:

- Aerobic training benefits plateau after 8-weeks. Unless more and more time is spent on building a larger aerobic base (as needed in sports like cross-country skiing, marathon racing, swimming, etc.) the aerobic system will not see significant improvements over time. In hockey the goal is to build aerobic fitness in order to recover from anaerobic shift intervals on the ice, not simply for aerobic fitness alone. Remember, hockey is an interval based sport, not a cyclical sport and should not be trained as such.

- Aerobic training makes you slower (both locally and system wide). The more you train to be slow (with long runs, inline skating or cycling), the more you **will** be slow. The muscles in the legs will not be accustom to hard work and moving quickly, thus predisposing them to injury. In a system wide situation the player who uses slow training never requires the central nervous system to fire quickly or improves signal output to the muscles and therefore trains the body and muscles to react slowly.

- With slow distance training (jogging, cycling, inline skating, etc) a full range of motion throughout the hip joint is never achieved, and this actually works to reduce the player's range of motion. The hip muscles in hockey MUST be flexible in all ranges of motion to help prevent injury. As hip and groin injuries account for a large percentage of all hockey injuries this must be taken into consideration when training hockey players.

- Hockey is a game of changing conditions (such as offense to defence, puck battling to skating, coasting to full out sprints). In all of these situations there exist elements of acceleration, deceleration and change of direction. During conditioning workouts these elements must be trained in order to prevent injury (especially during the beginning part of the season).

- Traditional aerobic training is hardly sport specific. A good hockey forward for example will play 15 to 18 minutes (20 to 24 45-second shifts) during a game at a very high intensity. During these hockey shifts lactic acid builds up in the working muscles (which feels like burning and gradually makes the legs feel heavy and non-responsive). Regular training of the anaerobic system helps to prolong the period of time before lactic acid build-up gets too high and the body cannot function properly. To work the anaerobic system for hockey intervals must be used that simulate game situations with very little aerobic recovery (accept the recovery on the bench, during a face-off, or when you are on the ice but not "working").

- We only have a limited amount of specific and general body recovery ability available to us (which is why you can't workout 12-hours a day and expect to get better). If we overload this ability to recover with long workouts or external stress (like prolonged aerobic training) the body will not be able to recover and improve. Why would you waste time on aerobic training that is not helping progress? Working the basics of on-ice skating skill, hockey skills, strength training, speed development and anaerobic conditioning will do far more for the player than long slow distance training.

- Aerobic training worsens testosterone/cortisol ratios. This limits the amount of lean muscle you will be able to add (which negatively impacts strength, power, agility) and reduces the ability to burn fat. None of these are good for the hockey player.

- With long sport specific workouts the skating technique falls apart very quickly. Have you ever noticed that at the start of a practice skating technique is the best? You have a deep knee bend, full extension, and great recovery in the stride. As you get tired, the knees start to straighten up,

179

the back goes horizontal and leg extension is terrible. The worst thing you can do is to keep training the body to skate with this "incorrect form", as you are training your central nervous system to use poor technique over and over again. With proper training you can increase the ability to hold proper form longer and longer, but I have never seen a hockey player display good technique for long periods of time.

Methodology Implementation
How a coach or player applies the two forms of GPP and SPP into the yearly training cycle is most important. Haphazardly including long distance running workouts or unsupervised SPP training sessions is not the correct method of athlete development. The following 4-step method of methodology implementation has worked with great results in my business as the players continue to develop throughout the year.

Evaluation
Without a thorough and scientifically valid evaluation it is very difficult to determine future progress and meet the needs of the hockey player. Using a wide variety of scientifically valid evaluation methods such as a functional movement screening, body composition measurements, and dryland physical testing, serves to create a "client blueprint" from which the right course of action can be determined for each individual person.

Periodized Training Progressions
Periodization is an organized approach to training that involves progressive cycling of various aspects of a training program during a specific period of time. Every major sports team (college and professional) uses a variation of periodization to achieve maximum results. Over the past 18-years I have come to rely on an advanced form of periodization called the Russian Conjugate Method to structure training cycles. This method essentially takes all of the GPP and SPP components of training (strength, agility, power, conditioning, endurance, etc.) and develops all of these attributes at the same time, rather than using a classical periodization style that works certain physical qualities during different times of the year.

Re-evaluation & Adjustment
Training is an important component of your success but if you do not re-evaluate, learn from your success and failures, and then move forward a training program will always fail to produce results. Every hockey player is different and that needs to be addressed during this stage as players may find or develop strong or weak areas from different training. Re-evaluation seeks to focus training and keep athletes on track for increased performance.

Motivation
A player or coach must understand that motivation to improve will be a large determining factor in the success or failure of a program. Simply wanting to make the next level without proper training is not enough. Motivation from training partners, trainers, coaches, teams, etc. must be included into every program so that maximum progress can be achieved.

During conditioning drills I will often employ the "it pays to be a winner" game. Players or teams face off against each other during a drill and the winners get to rest while the losers do another exercise or "punishment" type exercise. This is based on the US Navy SEALS philosophy and works very well.

General Conditioning Tips
I have several rules that I have every athlete follow with conditioning because it is very easy to get side-tracked and even hurt if you workout incorrectly. My main rule is that **I NEVER WANT PLAYERS TO GET HURT DURING TRAINING…EVER!!!** If you do get hurt, let it be on the ice during a game when it matters…during training you should never get hurt. Here are my basic rules of conditioning so that you get the most from your training.

- Make sure you warm-up prior to workouts and cool-down using light intensity exercises and other recovery methods outlined later in this book to speed recovery.

- Do conditioning work last in the day/workout (speed or on-ice skills always comes first, then strength training, followed by conditioning work).

- Vary the conditioning that is done, making sure to do at least 1-lateral workout (slide board or Russian Box) each week and 1-sled dragging/tire/band resistance workout per week.

- Make sure to use acceleration, deceleration and change of direction drills with just about every conditioning workout to simulate game conditions.

- Use recovery conditioning methods such as light sled dragging, swimming, water running, or band resistance to help repair the muscles and bring blood flow into the muscles.

- Conditioning work is not only aerobic in nature. Make each conditioning session as tough and challenging as possible so when you play in a game it will seem easy by comparison. With most of my conditioning workouts I have players competing against one other or multiple people in a race type of environment. I ALWAYS stress the motto of the Navy Seals "it pays to be a winner". Therefore the losers always do more work as punishment for not winning. I have fun dreaming up torturous punishment so the guys always work extra hard to finish first with every drill. Over time this builds a great athlete who becomes mentally and physically strong.

- During the season players will have their hands full with regular games, travel, practice's and perhaps school. Most players generally do not get enough sleep and tend to eat questionable meals on a regular basis. All of this stress adds up and at some point in the season a player or team may feel burned out or fatigued. At this point the only variable that can be reduced is general training (and that usually means strength and conditioning training), until the player or team has a chance to bounce back and recover. Remember that all training is to improve on-ice performance, not to improve the amount of weights lifted or increase your sit-up totals.

- Bantam & Midget players should focus on building general athleticism, coordination and general conditioning. Sport specificity should be used on a limited basis as the player should have a well-balanced physical training program. As players reach the later years in Midget hockey they can and should start working more on strength training, injury prevention (for hockey) and sport specificity.

- Off-ice training must mimic the conditions on the ice as much as possible. Calgary Flames strength and conditioning Coach Rich Hesketh states that: *"the human body reaches its anaerobic threshold following 30 to 45-seconds of intense physical activity, during which lactic acid builds up in the muscles and performance starts to decline. It makes sense then, based on these findings, that the average length of a pro shift is only 45-seconds. Focusing on training for speed, power, strength and conditioning off the ice, all of which enables athletes to own their 45-second shift."*

- Hockey conditioning coach Peter Twist suggests that "both on and off the ice teaching movement efficiency, being able to move from point A to point B with fewer steps, greater speed and more visual awareness, while expending less energy is key". GPP helps to improve the entire body's resources while raising work capacity, and SPP works to take that ability and channel it into a sport specific setting so movement efficiency that Coach Twist talks about can become an integrated approach to training.

- Younger hockey players with limited time might only want to work on conditioning drills from this book as it will help develop many different GPP and SPP attributes for hockey without having to commit to a full blown training program.

- Think of all training as a pyramid with GPP at the bottom, SPP above that, and on-ice hockey training (skills, tactics, drills, etc.) on the top. The bottom of the pyramid has to be solid and a large base of strength, endurance and general ability has to be developed before the next phase of training can be introduced. As the year progresses, the pyramid base must not be compromised (with reduced training) as this will reduce work capacity and overall conditioning.

- Practice like you play. If you play 15 shifts of 45-seconds the training should reflect this. Having said that I want players to build up to training for more time than you might need in case your coach suddenly puts you out on the ice for more shifts or the game goes in to overtime. You need a reserve of aerobic and anaerobic power and the ability to bounce back from prolonged work. Therefore I require players to complete at least 25% more training than they might need. In the case above a player who gets 15 shifts of 45-seconds will perform 11 minutes and 15 seconds of actual work in the game. In training if this player gave 25% more effort they would complete at least another 4-intervals (for a total of 19 shifts at 45-seconds). Ideally you will want to increase this amount as long as the quality of the intervals stays high (if you get slow and technique ever falls apart the workout is over).

- Train to reduce the rest intervals down to a 1 to 1 rest interval. This means if you work for 45 seconds, you will rest for 45-seconds. However, this should not be the rest interval you use at the start of your training. At first you should use a 1 to 3 rest interval (45 seconds work and 2 minutes & 15 seconds rest), which is a typical break in hockey without stoppages in play for penalties or whistles. After you get good at doing these (which means the speed is good and you feel good), then move to a 1 to 2 rest interval. When this is good, move down to a 1 to 1 rest interval. If during training sessions you consistently use a 1 to 1 work/rest interval just think about how much better you will be able to play hockey when the rest break is 2 to 3 minutes for every 45-second shift on the ice.

- All dryland workouts have to be done at 100% (just like when you play in a game). If you can't do that then don't workout, or adjust the time of the workout so you can go 100%. ***NOTE: The exception is when players perform recovery conditioning (such as easy sled dragging, swimming or cycling to recover from hard training).***

- Proper GPP & SPP drills that use hard bouts of training with short rest periods stimulates the EPOC response, fat burning and the body's resistance to lactic acid production.

- Using the dragging sled (as discussed in Chapter 16) during post season play might be the smartest thing you will ever do as a hockey player. Dragging or pushing the sled does not use an eccentric action, only concentric actions. These concentric actions bring blood flow and nutrients to the leg muscles (which aids recovery from games or practices) without tearing down or inflaming injuries caused during the playoffs. Athletes are able to keep up with conditioning and basic strength training in a sport specific manner, without worrying about these workouts affecting on-ice performance. It is highly recommended that players and teams use the sled during all post-season play with light weights and short workout sessions as this will have a very positive effect on performance.

- Realize that all the conditioning work, strength training, or summer hockey schools in the world are not going to make you a better hockey player without 100% commitment to physical, mental and hockey training. Commitment means running another sprint drill, adding weight to the bar when possible, performing one more repetition, shooting 10 more pucks at practice, asking the coaches for performance feedback, etc. You must take total and complete control of your development as a hockey player. It might mean contacting higher leagues and talking with coaches to get scouted. It is not a once in a while thing, it's an every day thing!

- Training with a teammate or friend is **always** a good idea. Working out alone can be challenging for even the most disciplined athletes. There are days in which you don't feel up to the challenge of hard training and a partner will help you make it to the rink/gym/field and hopefully inspire you to work hard during all workouts. If possible try to find a partner who is a slightly better athlete or hockey player than you are, as this will force you to keep up with them in all the conditioning drills, off-ice training and when you play hockey.

- When using kettlebells, sleds, sledgehammers, rocks or other heavy objects you may need to lightly chalk your hands prior to the exercise. Wet your hand slightly and then rub a light coating of chalk over the palm and heal of the hands. Re-chalk as necessary, especially if it is hot or if your hands sweat a lot.

- With my elite players I like to do 10 to 20-minutes of conditioning work at the end of most strength training sessions. My reasoning for this is that after they are tired and beat up from strength training I want to push them physically and mentally just like at the end of a game or in overtime. Players have to be able to dig deep and compete no matter what happens on the ice... this is made easier if they practice this all the time during dryland. If possible I pair up players to compete during conditioning drills. My method of racing is just like the US Navy Seals, "It pays to be a winner". Winners cool-down early, or get to rest. Losers always do more work. I find this fosters both a strong bond between the players and a healthy respect for going "balls out" on every drill.

On-Ice Training Suggestions

Coach Steve Phillips working hockey conditioning drills with the puck at the Easy Street Rink.

On the ice players, coaches and teams should use a variety of techniques to produce well-trained hockey players. As skating (and hockey) is such a technical skill it is critical to use drills that maximize hockey performance based on training physiology.

- Make sure a good warm-up is performed before every on-ice session. Far too often I see teams simply put on the gear and then head out onto the ice. Once on the ice players shoot around and may stretch for a couple of minutes before the coaches come out on the ice and practice starts. This IS a recipe for disaster. Players must warm-up the body gradually for a period of 10 to 15 minutes before getting on the ice.

- Skating technique breaks down after about 20-seconds of effort, and this effort cannot be repeated over and over without a system wide breakdown of skating form. This is the reason I am so against "bag skating" players if the goal is conditioning (I recommend it if you want to give a team a wake up call after several bad games, but this is different than everyday conditioning). When coaches use repeated skating drills for conditioning the form goes out the window and the

183

players train the central nervous system to perform slowly. Players skate with straight legs, the push phase becomes non-existent, and the upper body bends forward to help transfer weight from leg to leg.

- Hockey physiologist Jack Blatherwick (author of one of the best hockey training books ever, _Over-Speed_), recommends shorter on-ice drills and practices at a higher overall tempo so the quality of work being performed stays at a high level and the players never learn bad habits while skating in a fatigued state. I agree with this philosophy 100% and so should all hockey coaches.

- During the off-season skip the summer hockey league where you might play 15-games and touch the puck 90-seconds a game, and sign up for a 3-on-3 league where you get more "puck time", and practice all of your skills in a closed in area. Recently I watched the Anaheim Ducks pre-training camp workouts and most of the 1.5 hours spent on the ice was in a 3-on-3 format (on 1/3 of the ice rather than a full sheet). The result is more puck touches, higher level play and more development.

- In the summer players need to get on the ice 6 to 8-weeks before training camp begins and start running through all kinds of drills. Many players get used to shinny hockey in the off-season and that pace of play catches up with them when training camp starts as the pace of camp is so much higher than shinny hockey. Players need to perform drills at speed with a coach, other players or with an organized camp 3 to 5-times a week during this 6 to 8-week period so that they get use to the high pace of play before going to camp. Ideally at the end of each on-ice session during the summer 10-minutes should be spent at the end working on a players conditioning with some of the drills presented in this book.

Professional hockey player Tyler Doherty of the Mississippi Riverkings (CHL)

Chapter 16 - Sled Dragging Methodology & Exercises

"You see things; and you say 'Why?'
But I dream things that never were; and I say 'Why not?'"

~ George Bernard Shaw

Training for hockey is unique in that very few other sports require a similar amount of quickness, speed, power, strength, agility, flexibility and conditioning all within one athlete. One of the most important qualities that every player can improve is lower body strength in the quadriceps, hamstrings, glutes, adductors, abductors and lower back. The problem with all methods of gym or dryland training is that nothing specifically works the skating musculature as it is used on the ice…until now.

Dragging the sled, tire dragging or band resistance are closed-chain, ground-based concentric actions that help to develop the posterior chain muscles (hamstring, glutes and low back) as well as the skating muscles of the hip and quadriceps. Much like skating where 85% of the action is done on one-leg, using the sled works one leg at a time. Lateral strength and speed, along with basic strength and quickness can all be worked during a sled workout. UCLA assistant strength coach Todd Bostrom states:

> *"As a strength coaches goal is to improve an athletes performance while preventing injury, the sled is the perfect implement to employ. The sled can be used for multi-directional dragging which will improve strength in all muscles, tendons and ligaments utilized by an athlete for lower body mobilization. The resistance can also vary to cater to the specific exercise the athlete will be performing whether for speed, power, strength, conditioning or rehabilitation."*

Some of the benefits of dragging the sled include:

Recovery
Perhaps the greatest benefit of dragging a sled or tire is more efficient recovery. Following a game, hard practice, strength training session or speed workout the body can be tight, sore and generally beaten up. The most important thing is to increase the blood flow to the areas that have been worked. Light activity is considered one of the best methods of helping the body repair and recover from stressful training. Dynamically stretching the hips is also a critical area that must be considered during recovery. Using the sled or tire is a concentric oriented action, which means that the body will not be exposed to eccentric actions that further damage the muscles tissues. Rather, the concentric ground based action stimulates the muscle and helps to bring in blood flow to the injured area.

In fact I would highly recommend the sled as a recovery tool for teams in the playoffs instead of strength training, plyometrics, speed work and especially cycling (due to the tightening of the hips) as the body needs to recover by action…and the sled provides a concentric action for this purpose.

GPP (General Physical Preparation)
Using the sled is perhaps the best form of GPP as it works so many different areas of the body and helps build general body strength that no other form of training can match. The goal of GPP is to increase work capacity without negatively affecting the performance and recovery of the individual. The sled with a ground based, closed chain, concentric muscle action movement helps build work capacity in a low impact environment.

SPP (Specific Physical Preparation)

Few pieces of equipment can duplicate the sport specific nature of skating like the sled (or weighted tire, bands, etc.). Players can focus in on one area of the skating stride such as the adductors or abductors with lateral movements on the sled. The adjustable load provides a great variety in the sport specific actions that can be worked and the sled can use many different attachments to accomplish almost any hockey specific action. Machines like the Power Skater, Skating Treadmill, and Speed Traxx fail to train all the hockey specific actions like sled work can.

Speed Development

Many athletes need to work on their sprinting technique to get the most power applied to the ground (or ice). Using a sled, tire or band to provide a slight resistance to the action will help the athlete get into the optimal position for sprinting (almost automatically). Hockey strength and conditioning coach Michael Boyle is a big fan of the dragging sled as it helps improve a sprinters technique and correct forward lean during speed drills. With better technique comes better application of force to the ground and faster times while running or skating.

In conversations with skating experts Steffany Hanlen (www.quantumspeed.ca) and Steve Phillips they always stress how important a good forward lean, high knee position and complete recovery of the leg is to the skating stride when taking off in a quick start. Many of the drills they use are geared at developing these very techniques that can be hard to teach and have players learn effectively. Using the sled or tire can provide enough resistance so that proper technique is developed early on in skaters. Nothing else provides this type of benefit like the sled, tire or bands.

Strength Development

The sled, tire or bands can be used to develop great strength in players by forcing them to move heavier and heavier weights in a safe and productive manner. As with all types of training hockey players have to be able to take the strength and power developed in the weight room and apply that force to the ice. Dragging or pushing a heavy tire or sled (especially on the ice) will work to improve this specific ability to put force into the ground in a correct and efficient manner.

Injury Rehabilitation

When coming back from an injury many types of weight training are simply too much for players, and can make rehab a more difficult task. Most athletes can walk without trouble (depending on their injury), so using a very light sled and walking slowly can provide basic ground-based resistance to their rehab much sooner than if they went to the gym. Sled dragging helps to increase blood flow to the injured area and rebuild general strength in a low impact setting. I have had athletes who couldn't squat due to a recent knee surgery, but could pull and push a light sled just fine. Another client used the sled for rehab from a concussion (as traditional weight lifting caused too much pressure and his body was physically weak from 6 months of inactivity) with great success in just 2 months. With a week or two of sled work enough strength can be achieved to make a noticeable difference in the rehabilitation process and get athletes back on the ice sooner than without the sled.

Injury Prevention

Hockey is a fast moving game where injuries can occur by contact with other players (or the boards), as well as during skating actions (such as quick starts or fast turns). Typical injury sites for a hockey player include the groin (adductor muscles), hip flexor, hamstrings, quadriceps, shoulders and neck. Many of these areas can be trained with the sled, tire or band to provide a balance of muscle strength and flexibility in the body, which in turn helps to reduce the likelihood of a potential injury.

Sled Dragging Exercises

The following is a complete collection of the best dryland sled dragging and pushing exercises to improve your hockey abilities. Some exercises are for performance enhancement while others are more rehab (to build you back up from an injury) or pre-hab (to improve injury prone areas before they become injuries) based. Coaches should try each of these exercises and see why they work effectively to develop strong and well conditioned hockey players.

Forward Sled Dragging

Forward sled dragging is as simple as it gets. Simply use a shoulder harness or hip belt, load weights onto the sled and walk forward. The weight on the sled will determine how low you get to the ground (bending your knees) and how much force you have to put into pulling the sled forward. Try to drag the sled evenly, without jerky motions.

Depending on the goals you have established for the workout you can either use light weight (25-50lbs) on the sled for rehabilitative work, or load the sled up with heavy weights (118lbs to 208lbs +) for a great conditioning workout. Try to vary the weights you use, the distances traveled, and the speed of your movement on a regular basis to keep the sled workouts challenging. Every now and then add 5 to 25lbs on the sled to test your ability to perform more and more work. In the picture provided Justin Todd spends the entire summer dragging the sled in preparation for pro tryouts.

Forward Bent-Over Dragging

Similar to the traditional forward dragging, with the bent-over dragging a straight bar is held behind the back while the player bends over at the waist and in a low crouch position starts to pull the sled forward. This position really puts the body into a mechanical disadvantage and engages the posterior chain muscles (the hamstrings, glutes, and low back) to a larger extent. As the hands are behind the body the muscles in the torso have to stabilize the bar as the sled is pulled which further taxes the body.

Junior-A defencemen Matt Korotva crouches low to drag the sled in North Vancouver, British Columbia.

Loading for this exercise can be similar to regular forward sled dragging but due to the difficulty of the action most athletes will use 10 to 25% less weight on the sled. Make sure that the movement is done properly in a low crouch position to get the best results.

Forwards Sprinting

For most athletes using the sled to sprint will be an invaluable tool in their development as a hockey player. The resistance on the sled helps athletes learn to apply force to the ground (or ice in later development), and how to apply that force against resistance in order to develop sport specific strength. As a technique tool the light load on the sled allows the athlete to learn and apply the correct sprinting form (such as holding a 45 degree body lean and a high knee/toe recovery). Another benefit of the sled is that the quadriceps are forced into working harder in the beginning phases of the take-off, which is exactly what is desired from hockey players doing quick sprints on the ice (bending the knees and using the quads to push you forward).

It is critical however not to overload the sled during sprinting as this can and will create bad habits. Light loads that allow for proper run mechanics is optimal. A general rule of thumb I like to use is that the sled should slow the athlete down between 10 to 20% compared with non-resisted sprinting. Therefore the athlete will still use the same joint mechanics and actions that are involved with sprinting, without the shortened stride or variety of additional wasted movements that teach bad habits over time (from using a sled that is too heavy).

Sled Sprinting Drills

With the sled sprinting drill you can incorporate many different drills designed to improve certain attributes of the sprinting motion such as "high knees", "ass-kickers", or "high marching". The benefit of using a weighted sled to perform these drills is that the lower body must now learn how to apply force to the ground more effectively as it is being resisted by the light load on the sled. As with sprinting the goal is technique development and special strength enhancement, rather than pure strength and power development seen with other forms of sled dragging (such as forward sled dragging). There is a very positive carryover of strength built using the sled with these exercises as the actions are simply weighted versions of the same drills performed at the track, gym or ice.

Sled Crawls

The idea behind sled crawls is to lower the body's center of gravity and push with the quadriceps and posterior chain muscles of the hamstrings, glutes and low back. Start with a hip belt and a light to moderate weight on the sled. From a hands and knees position, begin to crawl forward, pulling the sled while keeping the hips low.

In the picture, NCAA Division-1 Hockey player Austin Block performs sled crawls at a field in Simi Valley, California.

Backwards Dragging

Backwards dragging is a very challenging exercise for the quadriceps muscles and core musculature. Players must bend the knees and sink low into a crouch while driving the feet and pulling the sled backwards (see picture). With the heavy weight that can (and should) be used with this exercise and the deep knee bend of the action many players find this to be one of the most challenging actions in sled dragging. Player can use a hip belt, harness or handle attachment to pull for backwards dragging sessions.

Justin pulling 118lbs backwards and uphill during a workout in Riverside, CA (picture 1), while Junior hockey player John Accardo uses a deep knee bend to pull a 100lbs sled in Banff, Alberta

Cross-Over Dragging

Using the cross-over dragging method is a great way to develop the inside and outside aspect of the hip musculature. Performing the cross-over technique properly on the ice uses a push from the outside leg around the corner but also from the inside leg as it crosses under the top leg and performs a secondary push. Good players will always display 2 distinct pushing phases during a cross-over which maximizes speed. Using the sled this skill can be developed as the player has no choice but to use both legs equally to pull the sled forward. To start a player can use a hip belt, shoulder attachment or single handle to move the sled forward. Light weights can be used at first but gradually the weights can be increased to very heavy amounts so the players learn to really drive with both legs equally. Below are two examples of cross over dragging.

Cross-over dragging performed by Justin (picture 1) and Coach Pollitt in Naramata, BC (picture 2)

Side Shuffle Dragging

Side shuffle dragging should be a staple exercise in any athlete's training as it works the adductors and abductors of the hip throughout a wide range of motion. To perform the action the athlete faces sideways to the sled and takes step sideways away from the sled. The back leg has to drive backwards to propel the body forward. Once the push is over the back leg reloads next to the front leg and pushes again.

Austin performs side shuffles with the dragging sled

Side Shuffle Hop-Drag

Much the same as the side shuffle drag, the side shuffle hop-drag incorporates a hopping action when the back leg pushes off (much the same as when do quick starts in skating). At the end of the push phase of the back leg you end the push with an explosive thrust and drive (which looks like a hop) as the back leg reloads next to the front foot). Lighter weights should be used with this exercise as the goal is the explosion of the back leg rather than the amount of weight loaded onto the sled. Also the hip belt should be the main attachment for this exercise as you want to have the arms free to swing and move (to help transfer force with the back leg as it explodes off the ground).

Hockey Lunge Dragging

The hockey dragging technique is used as an overall lower body drill for the hockey stride. With this exercise the player tries to simulate the skating action by lunging forward at a 45-degree angle and pushing off from the side/toe of the back foot (like in hockey). A stick can be used as a method of keeping the upper body quiet and stressing proper upright body positioning. Ideally players want to keep the knees bent and bring the feet together (ankle to ankle) in the recovery position so as to simulate the skating stride.

Adduction Dragging

Mark Pustin of the Fairbanks Ice Dogs (NAHL) practices ankle dragging.

Adduction dragging is a very hockey specific motion that will develop the inner thigh, groin and hip flexor muscles in the exact same manner as they are used on the ice. When creating training programs for hockey players I always include many different forms of training for the adductor

190

muscles (inner thigh, groin) as this area is prone to injuries in hockey players. It is **essential** to have strong and flexible adductors to be successful on the ice (especially for many years of playing).

To perform the adduction drag you simply attach an ankle strap and light weighted sled to one leg (picture 1), and then step forward with the free leg. Make sure to keep the hips open as you would a traditional skating stride and keep the back leg fully extended. From this position you pull the leg attached to the sled back towards the free leg as you would when recovering during a skating stride (picture 2). Try to keep the front leg bent and the upper body in a 45-degree bend as you would on the ice. When done properly this is the single greatest adduction exercise you can use to strengthen these under-trained muscles for hockey players.

Iron-Cross Dragging

Iron Cross sled dragging is one of the hardest forms of sled dragging because nearly all of the muscles of the upper body have to work to stabilize the shoulders as the arms are held out to the side (see picture). Start off with a light weight on the sled and using a double chain for the handle. Walk forward slowly making sure to contract and stabilize the entire upper body.

Reverse Iron Cross Dragging

If the Iron Cross is considered hard, then enjoy the reverse iron cross, as this sled dragging action is very difficult. The amount of scapula retraction strength needed to perform this drill in the shoulders, traps, core area and rotator cuff muscles is unreal. To start grip the double chain handles and hold the arms out to the sides while you walk slowly backwards.

In the picture, Todd Bostrom shows reverse iron cross dragging.

Sled Twists
Sled twists involve pulling the sled with a twisting lunge type action and then walking forward to pull the sled again. Players can build up to some pretty decent weight with this exercise and should remember to work both sides of the body to even out the musculature.

Sled twists at Revolution Athletics

Sled Rope Pulls

To add another dimension to sled dragging it is possible to attach a long rope (50 foot +) and pull (hand-over-hand) the sled in a tug-o-war type manner. This will greatly tax the muscles of the legs, core area and upper back as the sled is pulled toward the athlete. As the sled will hold up to 500lbs of weight this can be a very taxing exercise for any athlete.

Austin uses a long 100-foot rope to pull the sled during off-season training in 2008.

Lying Sled Pulls

Pulling the sled from a lying position works the muscles of the upper back in a similar manner to chin-ups or pull-downs. To start a player will lie on their back with the head facing the sled, holding a 50-foot length of rope (or more) outstretched and attached to a weighted sled. From this position the goal is to pull the sled towards you as quickly as possible. Using a thicker rope (1 ½ to 2 inches in diameter) is preferred as this will develop the gripping muscles in the forearm much faster than with smaller diameter ropes.

Todd pulling the sled with the long rope in Arcadia, CA

High Sled Pushing

The prowler is another tool in the sled dragging arsenal to help condition the lower body and skating muscular. While I am not a fan of the prowler for any pulling workouts, it works pretty well used as a pushing implement on concrete. For this exercise grab the handles near the top, lower the hips so the angle of push is straight forward and then push the prowler forward. This type of sled is difficult to use on grass which in my mind limits its effectiveness, but I wanted to include it in this manual as a possible training tool as it does work well for these specific exercises.

Low Sled Pushing

Low sled pushing requires athletes to lower their center of gravity much more and really push hard with the quadricep muscles to move the sled. This can be a gruelling exercise (especially on grass), but well worth the effort as this exercise builds the legs and cardiovascular conditioning very quickly. Players may want to use some type of cleat or even a golf shoe to maximize traction if pushing the sled on the grass. The Prowler does not push well on grass and should only be used on the concrete.

Justin using the low handles on the Prowler and Mark uses the DP Hockey Sled for low sled pushing

Tire Pulling (Dryland)

Pulling a tire is not as smooth or precise as dragging a sled, pulling a band or using a parachute, but it does get the job done. Due to the shape of the tire it will not provide the same type of constant resistance that a sled will offer, and in fact will jump around on the athlete, which is a great way to build variety into a sled dragging program. To execute this drill tie a rope or chain around a moderate to heavy tire, and then attach that rope to any kind of pulling harness, handle attachment, belt or rope to pull. If the tire is too light a piece of plywood can be cut to fit inside the tire, and weights, rocks or kettlebells can be placed inside the tire for additional weight. Note that for sprinting exercises the tire should be light enough to provide some resistance, but not impede the players sprinting mechanics.

Pavesled

The problem with traditional inline skating is that the glide phase of the inline skate is way too long compared to that of a hockey skate. Additionally most folks who inline skate push-off from the whole foot (for maximum traction), rather than pushing off with the toe at the end of the push phase (as seen in hockey). Both of these two "techniques" will kill a perfectly good skating stride in a very short period of time.

The Pavesled is a type of sled designed to be used on concrete while the athlete uses inline skates to pull the weighted sled. Usually I tell my athletes to never use inline skates as a method of training for hockey, but with the Pavesled I have a slightly different opinion provided it is done properly.

By using the Pavesled the first problem of the extended glide phase is fixed as the weight of the sled will control the length of time you spend gliding on the inline skate. The second problem tends to fix itself because the player is forced to use a proper form due to the weight on the sled and the shortened glide phase. Due to these reasons the Pavesled can be a valuable contribution to a hockey training regiment, provide correct technique is always maintained. In the above picture Pavesled founder Doug Kalvelage demonstrates ankle dragging drills.

Bryan Hodges (#21), with the Junior-A Kenai River Brown Bears, (NAHL)

Chapter 17 - On-Ice Tire Dragging Exercises

"Play for the logo on the front, not the name on the back."

~ unknown

With all forms of training I am always on the lookout for methods of training both general strength and athleticism as well as improving sport specific abilities. Building general strength in the gym or with the dryland sled is a key component to a successful hockey player. The athlete pictured on the next page (Justin Todd), has a 425lb squat for 3-repetitions and I am always trying to improve his performance in the weight room. Having said that, a player has to be able to take all of that strength, quickness and power, and learn to apply that energy to the ice. If this cannot be done then it doesn't really matter how much they can squat or lift as this will not help their hockey abilities.

For this reason I am a very strong advocate of using a skating coach or hockey expert to analyze the hockey stride (forwards, backwards, turning, pivoting, stopping, stick-handling, etc.), and then practicing the basics of edge work, balance, quick starts, etc. during **EVERY** hockey practice. By developing a solid technique all of that strength and power that is built up off the ice can then be applied to the on-ice skating stride correctly.

In addition to improving the correct skating mechanics and developing solid edge work in practice I also make sure that my athletes work the skating musculature on the ice (with full gear on). Players will drag a weighted sled, tire, use a parachute or pull resistance with bands or sticks in order to work the skating musculature. The following is a collection of on-ice exercises I use in conditioning the skating stride.

Forwards Tire Dragging

Using a tire is perhaps the best way to perform on-ice sled dragging as the tire will not beat up the ice and will not harm the boards if you cannot slow down the sled at the end of a pull. I like to use a variety of tire sizes to accomplish different tasks. If I am focusing on building general strength a heavy tire (100-150lbs) is appropriate for most junior aged players and above. If more weight is needed then a piece of plywood can be made to fit into the tire and then weight plates can be added to increase the resistance.

Dragging such a heavy object forces players to use their edges correctly and really bend the knees to dig into the ice and apply force correctly. You will not find a more hockey-specific strengthening exercise than pulling a heavy tire on the ice. In the above example Mark Pustin uses the handle attachment to drag the tire.

Pro hockey player Justin Todd pulling a heavy tire (100lbs) during summer training in Simi Valley, CA

Backwards Tire Dragging

Much like forward tire dragging a player can use either the heavy tire to develop power in the backwards stride, or a lighter tire to work on quick starts and skating mechanics. Many types of attachments can also be used such as the shoulder harness, hip belt, and a one or two handle attachment. Whatever weight you use, make sure to perform each repetition with correct form and really bend the legs to drive the skating edge into the ice. This will help reinforce good habits that can and should be applied to the skating stride. In the picture Austin Block pulls the tire while skating backwards.

Forward Tire Sprinting

With all sprinting drills using the sled, tire or on-ice sled it is important to mention that weight being pulled is heavy enough to provide some resistance, without being too heavy and wrecking the skating stride. For most athletes a small tire with 15 to 30lbs of weight will be plenty to provide the necessary resistance.

With sprinting drills the main focus will be on short sprints of no more than 50-feet (about the length from the goal line to the blue line), to build quickness and acceleration from a dead stop rather than top end speed. You want to work on sprinting mechanics which entails a good forward lean (roughly 45-degrees forward), high knee return, proper adduction of the legs to the heal of the weight bearing foot and a full extension of the back leg. In the above picture Justin Todd shows good form with a lighter 25lb tire at the Banff Recreation Centre.

Cross-Over Tire Dragging

Junior-A hockey player Peter Mercredi demonstrates cross-over tire dragging drills in Banff, Alberta. With cross over tire pulling the focus is on using the edges of the skates properly and stabilization of the core muscles rather than gliding (as with every other skating drill). This drill will help with a players overall ability to manoeuvres on the edges and improve balance as they pull the tire across the ice.

Variations of this drill are many and can include 2-quick steps followed by cross-overs, into skating or with a pivot and backwards skating.

Iron Cross Dragging

Players who are able to pull a heavy tire should also include iron cross dragging drills into their regiment. This drill works the stabilization muscles of the trunk and upper body while the lower body works hard to move the tire forward. Make sure to keep the arms held up to shoulder height throughout this drill for maximum effectiveness. Players should start off with a light weighted tire and progress to heavier loads over time as they learn to stabilize the shoulder girdle and trunk musculature.

Backwards Iron Cross Dragging

Reverse iron cross dragging is one of the hardest tire dragging exercises as many players have very weak upper back musculature to support and stabilize the arms during this type of drill.

To perform this drill players hold up their arms to the side of the body and skate backwards to pull the tire. The arms must stay up to shoulder height throughout this drill to execute it correctly. As with the forward iron cross drill players should start off with lighter weights and progress to heavier tires as necessary.

Tire Pushing

Much like pushing a car is a tremendous workout for the posterior chain muscles of the hamstrings, glutes and low back (as well as the quads), the heavy tire is an awesome exercise for all hockey players. The mechanics of pushing a heavy tire low to the ground forces a player to lower the hips and correctly use the skate edges to dig into the ice and produce force in a productive manner.

Pushing a 100lb tire forces the player to lower the hips and edge correctly to generate power (as shown by Austin Block)

Net Pushing

Similar to tire pushing, players can also push a hockey net to work the skating muscles. When using a net the angle of push is a little different so players must focus on bending the knees and driving with the legs to accelerate the net as much as possible over a 40 to 70-foot stretch. In order to train different muscles and actions players can push the net forward, pull it backwards or try to skate a face-off circle with the net.

Tire Pulling

Tire pulling is a great exercise to develop balance, stability and general body strength while on the ice. Players will drag a heavy weighted tire with a length of rope (50+ feet), while trying to maintain a stable position. This exercise will work the entire body and is an awesome conditioning workout for players or coaches to use at the end of practice for fun. I recommend using at least a 100lb tire or more to really develop strength throughout the body.

Mark pulls former team-mate Austin Block (a total of 275lbs) during training.

Tire Pushing Battle

To complete the tire pushing battle take the heavy tire and have two players on each side of the tire pushing (not shown). Set up 2 hockey sticks 10-feet apart (away from the battle area), as the purpose of the drill is to move the tire towards the opponents stick (much like in a tug-o-war match). To add resistance, a third player can sit in the heavy tire during the battle.

Chapter 18 - Band Resisted Exercises & Parachutes

"Success is not the result of spontaneous combustion.
You must set yourself on fire."

~ Reggie Leach, All-star NHL hockey player

The use of resistance bands in the training of athletes can be a very beneficial and productive type of strength, speed, balance and agility training. The combinations of how to use bands are limited only by the creativity of the coach or player using them. During hockey practices for instance a coach might use 10-bands and get in a highly sport specific strength training session with the entire team. At a hockey school or training camp coaches can find out about different players and their desire to persist through an exercise or bands can be used for fun team building type exercises.

For skating coaches, band training can provide a valuable method of teaching various skills in the skating stride such as the proper body lean, edge control, full extension and full recovery. Because the coach is being pulled along behind the player, they have a good view of what is going on with the hockey stride. The following are just some of the ways in which bands can be used as a form of resistance for hockey players both on and off the ice.

Forward Band Resistance (Dryland)

Very similar to dragging a sled or tire, using a band to provide resistance can be a very challenging workout. Unlike the sled or tire, the person holding the band can provide as much or as little resistance as necessary to work the athlete. In addition to this the person holding the band can move their hands side to side or up and down to provide an unstable line of pull for the working athlete, which ultimately challenges their ability to not only perform the task, but to stay balanced at the same time. During the off-season I like to use this type of training with large groups or teams because in a very short period of time a large group can get in an exceptional workout.

Forward Band Crawls (Dryland)

Resisted bear crawls start with the athlete placing the band around the waist and then dropping down onto the hands and feet position (see picture). A coach or player stands behind them and provides resistance to the bear crawl movement. As this is a more challenging exercise than forward running type drills the person in back providing the resistance has to make sure not to impede the action too much so the working player can at least do the drills.

The forward band crawl drill performed at the Hockey Contractor training facility.

Forward Band Sprints (Dryland)

Exactly the same as forward band resistance pulls; the sprinting variation requires the working athlete to violently explode from a start position and sprint as hard as possible while the back person provides tight resistance. The goal of these drills should not be technique enhancement (as with the sled or tire), but the development of raw power in the first 10-meters. When coaching this drill my expression is usually "unleash hell" as a description of how hard I want players to start off in this drill. As this will be a difficult exercise for the resisting coach or player, limit the sprints to 10-meters (which will develop quick starting power).

Backwards Band Resistance (Dryland)

Having the athlete turn around and walk backwards will target more of the quadriceps into the action and provide a good challenge for most athletes. Much the same as forward dragging, loop one end of the band around the athlete and then hold the other end. As the athlete moves backwards apply resistance by walking slowly. Try to vary the resistance and angle of pull to provide a different stimulus for the player.

Cross-Over Band Resistance (Dryland)

Cross-over strides with a coach resisting the players movement

Loop the one end of the band around the athlete and have them face perpendicular to the coach or athlete providing the resistance (see picture). From this position have the player cross the back leg over the front leg and pull the resistance person forward. Make sure the athlete uses a pronounced leg push with both legs (which maximizes speed on the ice). Keep crossing the back leg over the front leg until the necessary distance indicated in the training program is completed.

Side Shuffle Resistance (Dryland)

Side shuffles with a coach or team-mate providing resistance with a band is a good way to train the lateral muscles of the lower body. Start with the forward athlete facing perpendicular to the resisting person with the band looped around their waist. Have the athlete step forward with the front leg, and then bring the back leg up to the front leg (see picture).

Working the side shuffle to condition the skating stride

Hockey Lunge Band Resistance (Dryland)

Position the band around the forward athlete and have them face away from the backwards resistor at a 45-degree angle (forward). From this position the player will be in the ideal stance to work the skating musculature in a sport specific manner. Have the player step forward (keeping that 45-degree angle), and pushing off from the side/toe of the back foot (as in a hockey stride). The player will recover the back foot to the front foot and then repeat.

Long Band Resistance with Agility or Skating Drills (On-Ice)

Coach Steve Phillips works with Mark on backwards figure-8 drill around cones (picture 1), and around a circle performing cross-over's (picture 2), while being resisted by a long band

When training hockey players on the ice I like to use a longer resistance band attached to the athlete by way of a hip belt, and have them perform lightly resisted agility drills. The idea of this type of training is that the player will have to work hard to stabilize and maintain balance while skating around cones or performing a skating skill. This will develop a player's ability to be strong on their skates, and can be trained every day at practice if so desired. The two drills above are examples of skating drills that can be used with the long band by a coach/player or player/player.

Long Band Resisted Partner Skating (On-Ice)

Similar to the previous long band drill, two hockey players each put on a waist belt and are then connected to each other with a long resistance band. One player starts skating and the player in the second position skates behind the first skater and provides gentle resistance for the player in front. With this drill the two players can skate forward, around face-off circles, backwards or even through a set course on the ice (with cones) to provide more of a challenge. This exercise will test balance, agility, and strength.

Forward Resisted Skating (On-Ice)

Using a heavy gage Super-band (1¾ inches wide), loop one end of the band around a player's waist while a coach or another player holds the other end of the band. From this starting position have the player skate forward while the person in back provides resistance. The amount of resistance can vary depending on what goals the coach has for the session (example: speed training should have minimal resistance while strength training the back player should really dig in and provide a lot of resistance). The Super-band will hold up to just about any force applied by the pulling athlete so this should not be a concern.

Forward Resisted C-Cuts (On-Ice)

The C-cut is a great skating drill to develop the adductor muscles in the legs as well as learning how to edge correctly on the inside edge of the skate. Coaches can increase the effectiveness of this drill by looping a resistance band around the working player and providing a resisted pull during the exercise. As this drill is a slow drill the amount of resistance that is needed to further slow the player down is minimal, but worth the time as the adductors muscles get a really good workout with this drill.

Cross-Over Band Resistance Drill (On-Ice)

The cross-over band resistance drill involves a working player pulling another player around a face-off circle with a resistance band. The resisting player has to provide enough force on the band so that the working player learns to really load the leg edging into the ice, and drive off of both legs when crossing over. If only one leg crosses over and the other leg does little then the working player can be easily pulled over by the force of the band. This is a great drill when teaching and re-enforcing correct cross-over habits in the skating stride, both in the forward and backwards direction.

Skating circles both forwards and backwards with resistance bands

Backwards Resisted Skating (On-Ice)

Start with two athletes facing each other, band around the working athlete and held by the resisting athlete. The working athlete begins to skate backwards, pulling the resisting athlete as they provide braking power by using a forward snow-plough (see picture). The player who is working should use a variety of different methods to start off the backwards skating such as a cross-over technique (both directions) and the C-cut method (both directions). This helps build first step strength when starting off skating backwards and variations for training.

Resisted Juke Drill (On-Ice)

The resisted Juke drill is similar to the traditional Juke drill, but now a coach or player holds a resistance band around the player who is trying to follow or shadow the lead player. This makes this valuable drill even harder as the player shadowing the first player has to read and react to the first player while overcoming the resistance of the band held by the coach. This is tiring drill but players like how it works many different aspects of their skating.

The shadow player is resisted during this taxing drill that works balance, strength and skating

Band Abdominal Twists (On-Ice)

This exercise has been adapted from a dryland exercise where a light band is held by two players standing 4 feet apart (both facing the same direction). The purpose is to develop abdominal strength while on the ice by taking turns and trying to pull the other player off their feet (see picture). The drill is over when one player falls or the coach blows the whistle.

Players provide resistance for each other in this band abdominal twist drill

Forward & Reverse Parachute Sprints

The use of parachutes with hockey players can be a valuable addition to the training tool box. Parachutes offer a light form of constant resistance that does not involve dragging a tire or bands. Players can hook up a parachute on their own and run through a number of drills or skills with a parachute that can provide 20 to 50lbs of resistance.

The purpose of using a parachute is that when sprinting or performing drills the light resistance of the chute makes athletes lower their center of gravity, dig the edges of the skates in a little deeper and requires more muscular force from the skating muscles. With such a light resistance the parachute will not disrupt the quick starts that should be practiced with the chute, and will actually help players get into a forward leaning position which is favourable for quick starts.

Austin shown sprinting forward (picture 1) and backwards (picture 2) with a large parachute
which provides roughly 30lbs of resistance

Players can use the chute for backwards skating drills as it will not interfere with the skating mechanics or safety. These modern chutes fill up with air quickly so they will not drag on the ground much or get tangled in the skates. Start off in a backwards skating ready position while holding the chute. As you start skating backwards throw the chute in the air so it will fall and catch the air as you move backwards.

Parachute Circles or Cone Drills

The resistance parachute is best used when players are performing skating drills around cones, face-off circles or with line drills. The chute will fill up with air and as long as the player is moving forward (or backwards) the chute will stay open and off the ice. Players and coaches should use their imagination and creativity to see which drills the parachute may be used with.

Skating the figure-8 drill around the face-off circles is a great way to use the resistance parachute. Try adding a puck to stickhandle or pass to a partner for extra skill development.

Goaltender Andrew Volkening of the Air Force Academy (NCAA)

205

Chapter 19 - Stick Resistance Exercises

"I think the thing you always got to keep in mind, you know,
hockey is a game of one-on-one battles"

~ Mark Messier, Hall of fame NHL hockey player

Stick resistance drills are an excellent method of implementing on-ice strength, balance, change of direction and general conditioning in a very short period of time. Using hockey sticks players can work in pairs to provide unpredictable resistance for each other just like what might happen on the ice during games. Coaches can also combine these drills with skating drills, tire dragging or band exercises to make a very challenging on-ice training session for the entire team.

Stick Battle (On & Off-Ice)

On-ice stick battle (picture 1) and off-ice battle (picture 2)

Stick battling has to be one of my favourite on and off ice exercises for developing balance, strength and conditioning while on skates. Two players face each other over a face-off circle and hold one stick (perpendicular) between them. The goal of the drill is to take the stick away from the other person. The drill stops when the stick is taken away from one player. Battling for the stick players must overcome the other person and out work them to get the stick. Used as part of a team drill players can rotate from player to player on the entire team so they engage many different opponents during the course of a 10-minute drill.

Lunging Stick Battle

With the lunging stick battle drill one player settles into a standard lunge with a hockey stick held at arms length in front of the body. A second player stands in front of the lunging hockey player, holds onto the stick and tries to wrestle the stick away from the lunging player. As this drill can be very difficult for the lunging player it is recommended that players start off easy and work into this drill to get used to the balance and strength requirements of this exercise.

Castleton Spartans (NCAA Division III) goaltender Jay Seals battles against junior player Trent Takeuchi

Push/Pull Stick Drill

The push/pull stick battle involves two players holding opposite ends of a hockey stick, and trying to take it away from one another by pushing and pulling. The idea is to get players to lower their center of gravity and build strength in the legs, hips, core area and upper body as they try to control and out-perform an opponent.

Players need to lower their center of gravity and really work hard to win in a stick push/pull drill. Strong gripping muscles (the same kind of strength needed in shooting the puck), also helps to hold onto the stick.

2-Stick Battle Drill

Similar to the standard push/pull stick drill, the 2-handed push/pull drill uses 2 hockey sticks as the method of resistance between hockey players. The goal in this drill is to take one (or both) of the sticks from the opposing players, or knock them down to the ice. This drill takes a tremendous amount of balance, coordination, strength and perseverance for both players.

Forward Stick Pushing

The forward stick pushing drill helps work the skating stride as the player doing the work pushes against the stick of the other player who is facing backwards applying a reverse snow-plough to control the speed of the working player. As with band training the player providing the resistance can add or subtract the amount of resistance, or adjust the hand position so the working player has to constantly compensate the angle of push while skating.

Proper skating mechanics must be used during pushing drills or the player will not go far.

207

Resisted One-Leg Stick Pushing

In order to break down the skating stride and develop strength in one leg at a time it is nice to use the resisted one-leg stick pushing drill. Players face each other and the working player uses only one-leg to repeatedly push against the other players stick, as the non-working leg is pointed straight forward. This encourages a full push from the working leg and complete recovery to the non-working leg (as should be seen in a skating stride).

Backwards Stick Pulling

A great tool to work on the first step strength in the backwards skating motion, players face each other and hold a stick between them while one player skates backwards as the other resists this action. At first the resistance should be light, but as players get accustom to this type of training they can use more and more pressure to hold back the working skater.

Brothers Bryan & Mitchell Hodges

208

Chapter 20 - Lateral Conditioning

"It's a Great Day for Hockey."

~ "Badger Bob" Johnson, former Olympic, World Championship & NHL Head Coach

Many dryland programs that hockey players use simply do not include enough lateral movement to adequately train the skating specific muscles and rebalance the lower body. Running and biking are the primary focus for most players, along with frontal plane strength training movements such as squats, leg presses or deadlifts. While this does help, it fails to work the muscles used in skating, and can lead to injured players during training camp and into the season. Unfortunately very few pieces of training equipment work the lateral skating specific musculature. The following are two critical pieces of equipment that **EVERY** hockey player should use or have access to, in order to rebalance the skating muscles and train correctly for ice hockey.

Slide Boards

Originally invented by Scandinavian speed skaters more than 100-years ago to improve dryland conditioning (and popularized during the late 1970's by 5-time speed skating gold medalist, Eric Heiden), slide boards are perhaps the best piece of training equipment a hockey player can own. Unlike running, biking, stair machines or even my favourite - dragging sleds, a slide board is a highly effective piece of equipment. Using the slide board offers a ground based, low impact workout that is friendly on the joints and works the same muscles used in the skating stride. It trains the change of direction aspect that I think is critical to developing strong skating muscles, but with every slide an element of acceleration (or explosion) from one side to the other, followed by quick deceleration (as the player hits the end board and has to reverse direction) occur with the slide board.

Hockey strength & conditioning coach Michael Boyle has stated "the slide board may be the most important training device available for hockey". I certainly agree and would add that I notice many hockey teams and coaches never use the slide board with hockey training programs and this is a big mistake due to the many sport specific benefits the slide board can simulate in a dryland setting.

Slide boards can be purchased or made. Ultraslide makes a very good model of slide board with a solid wood base in two sizes that are adjustable in length from 6 to 8 feet and 8 to 10-feet. Another company (Power Slide), makes a decent model that rolls up between workouts and can easily be brought along during trips. The slide boards from the 80's that were popular with the aerobic fitness crowd are not that good as it is simply a piece of plastic that folds when you slide on it, and the surface is only 6 feet wide (which is too short for a hockey player to get in a proper stride).

Justin holds a hockey stick while on the slide board to work sport specific actions

While on the slide board players should use a mirror to evaluate proper 90-degree knee bend and the explosive sideways push that is produced during a slide board training session. Coaches can evaluate a player or even a team quickly and provide feedback immediately. Sets of 15 to 30 seconds should be used (any more than 30-seconds and most players cannot hold a proper knee flexion and/or use an explosive skating stride).

Many different variations can be used with the slide board to further the training affect. At our facility we like to use different lengths of slide boards to either create more stop/start speed in the action (with a shorter slide board of 6 to 8-feet) or build explosive power (with longer slide boards of 8 to 12-feet). Ideally, you would want to make a slideboard 12 to 14-feet long, and have a piece of sliding material in front of you to perform stickhandling, passing and shooting drills while on the board.

Using a weighted vest is also a tremendous addition to the slide board because it simulates the wearing of hockey gear unlike any other training tool, and it creates a little more body weight that the athlete has to move across the slide board. Weight vests of 10 to 80lbs can be used to accomplish a good workout on the slide board. Holding a plyotube, sandbag or kettlebell can also provide a good workout for slide board training. Sometimes for a real challenge I break out the medicine balls and have players bounce the ball on the ground or pass it to a partner or coach while sliding. Be creative with slide board training and make sure to add it to your hockey training immediately.

Other types of training that involve skill development such as stick-handling a golf ball, puck or Smart Hockey Ball can be useful to develop skills as a skating motion is performed (see picture of Steve Phillips below). Generally I have players set up two slide boards facing each other and have them pass a smart hockey ball between them as this builds hockey sense while working the legs in a hockey specific action. Make sure that players stay low during all training (in a deep skating stance) so there is a good carryover effect to the ice.

It should be noted that there are also many different types of strength training exercises such as mountain climbers, chest flys, lunges, twisting abdominal slides, and hamstring curls that can be done on a slide board. Teams or players in the market for a slide board should be aware of the vast amount of these exercises that can be done with this one piece of equipment in the decision process on whether or not to buy a slide board.

Coach Steve Phillips practicing the slide board while stick-handling a puck

Russian Box

As talked about in the Plyometrics Chapter, the Russian Box is a plyometric type of dryland equipment that forces hockey players to jump from platform to platform. In order to get a good jump (both laterally and upwards at a 45-degree angle) players must start off with a deep knee bend and really explode towards the other platform. Players using the Russian Box for multiple sets start to develop lactic acid and intense burning in the quads, calfs and posterior chain muscles. This helps expand a player's comfort with staying in a deep knee bend while skating and develops strength and endurance in the legs to repeatedly execute powerful explosive strides.

Noted hockey physiologist Jack Blatherwick PhD., who has worked with numerous NHL teams and the USA Olympic Hockey Team has stated:

> *"No matter how often you remind yourself to skate corners with greater knee bend, there are distractions such as pucks, opponents, fatigue, and competition… distractions that prevent you from maintaining optimum knee bend. That is why, I believe the Russian box is the best off-ice training tool for skating I've seen in four decades of searching… THE BEST! You are changing your comfort zone, developing strength and muscular endurance in a range of motion that is difficult to achieve on the ice."*

When starting to use the Russian Box the most important thing is to perform the jump from platform to platform properly. A small jump without height will not develop the skating stride very well. Players should get feedback from other players or coaches to ensure that a proper 90-degree knee bend, weight transfer and explosive jump are all performed during each repetition on the Russian Box. Anything less is wasted effort.

When training for conditioning I like to use sets of 15 to 30-seconds to guarantee each set will be a quality set. More than 30-seconds and most players cannot adequately jump with explosive power from side to side. For an additional training effect I like players to use a weight vest of 10 to 40lbs for sets of 15 to 20-seconds. Players can also hold a hockey stick if they choose or hold a sandbag or weight in their hands during the jumps as long as a quality jump is performed. Conditioning work ends on the Russian Box when a player's jumping quality starts to fall off.

NOTE: As stated in the plyometrics chapter, Russian Box training is a Level-9 method of plyometric training and therefore not recommended for everyone. Make sure athletes are ready for this exercise based on the 4-test method (readiness for plyometrics) as outlined. When players do use the Russian Box, make sure it is at a low setting (angled boards are placed close together), and teach correct form early on with ALL players.

Justin (pictures 1 & 2), and Mykul Haun (picture 3) practice off-season training at Revolution Athletics in Orange County, CA.

Chapter 21 - Strongman Conditioning

"You've got to love what you're doing. If you love it, you can overcome any handicap or the soreness or all the aches and pains, and continue to play for a long, long time"

~ Gordie Howe, Hall of fame NHL hockey player

The strongman based exercises use various implements and equipment that are odd shaped, unconventional, and fun to lift and move during a workout. Objects such as kegs, tires, rocks, logs, sledgehammers, and sandbags can be used by athletes as they work to develop strength in the gripping muscles, back, legs, and core area. These exercises can be very challenging but produce results as they improve mental toughness, competitiveness and team chemistry as players move through the workout. University of Florida strength and conditioning coach Mickey Marotti states "I value the chemistry and camaraderie that we build doing these strongman type events as a team, because it's rare to have that opportunity during traditional weight room training." At Michigan State University, strength and conditioning coach Ken Mannie has the hockey team complete the Spartan Challenge which is a 10-week strongman competition with activities held every Friday during the off-season.

Most of these workouts should be performed outside, and with a great deal of caution. Coaches should start off with lighter weights and really go over form on a regular basis. When performing a workout in a circuit each station should have a coach or injured athlete to monitor the form of the working players and when someone is struggling to complete a lift it should be stopped right away. Done correctly and with an emphasis on safety, strongman type training can be a fun and challenging method of developing hockey players.

Keg Lifting

Justin Todd picking up a 160lb keg in a deadlift position

Lifting a keg filled with water is a very challenging but fun exercise that all hockey players and athletes should use in their training on a regular basis. The uneven nature of lifting water (and a lot of it with a keg) makes this exercise difficult. I have my athletes lift the keg for repetitions (if it's not full), or for only several repetitions if full. A full 15.5 gallon keg should weight around 165lbs with water, 210lbs if filled with sand, and 270lbs with both sand and water mixed.

In using the keg I recommend the advice of strongman and author Brooks Kubik who says in his book *Dinosaur Training*:

> *"Start with a keg and fill it with water, sand, lead shot or anything else. Start out with 100-160lbs. Be conservative – this is going to be MUCH more challenging than you imagine. Then lift the thing. Clean it if you can. Press it if you are able. Deadlift it. Walk around with it. Curl it. Wrestle it. Bearhug the monster. Do singles or do reps. Anything you do with that big animal is going to work the devil out of your fingers, wrists, forearms, back, legs, and trunk. Handling a 100 pound keg is no easy task. A 150 pounder is murder."*

Keg Shouldering

The idea of shouldering a keg is to get that monster weight from the ground to the shoulder. Start with a parallel grip on the top of the keg and with a quick pull from the ground get the keg moving up towards one shoulder. You may need to bend the knees as the keg approaches the shoulder to "catch" the weight (much like in Olympic Weightlifting when performing a snatch or clean & jerk motion). Make sure to lift the keg to each shoulder equally, and start with a very light weight and work up to a full keg.

UCLA Assistant Strength & Conditioning Coach Todd Bostrom shoulders a keg

Keg Clean & Press

Much like a barbell clean & jerk the object is to get the keg lifted to full extension overhead. Start by holding the keg in an off-set position with the legs bent and back straight (picture 1). Explosively lift the keg by contracting the legs and anchoring the low back, spin the hands around and "catch" the weight at the shoulders, in front of your face. You will need to lean backwards slightly (picture 2), so you catch the weight at the shoulders. From this position bend the knees and forcefully drive upwards (as if you were jumping) and push the keg with the arms at the same time to extend it overhead.

A tip on lifting a water filled keg is to keep the keg tilted to one side to help prevent the water from sloshing around. A keg that is sloshing around will be MUCH more difficult to lift, especially overhead. As with every keg lift be very careful and drop the keg if you feel that lifting it will not happen or it is too heavy.

Keg clean & jerks are one of the most challenging strongman lifts for any athlete

Keg Lunges

As my goal is always to make training as difficult as possible for my athletes (so that games will be easy by comparison), I like to use what I call "moving weight" (water, sand, or another person) as resistance for training. This is much more difficult than lifting weights as you have to overcome the weight and unpredictable nature of the object to successfully lift or move it. When performing a standard lunge for instance I make the exercise more difficult by adding weight (in the form of dumbbells or a barbell), then gradually move into heavy sandbag and finally partially filled kegs (that slosh around and move while you lift them).

I buy my kegs from a local guy for $45 each, but you should be able to find them locally or online. My advice is to start slowly and add weight when you are ready. Be safe and have fun.

Justin performs over-head lunges with a 50lb keg, and Cody lunges with a 80lbs keg

Tire Flipping

Tire flipping is one of those great strongman exercises that work's the entire body along with the cardiovascular system like nothing else. A few flips of a heavy tire will leave even the most in shape athletes gasping for air. To begin, stand next to a heavy tire, bend over and deadlift the tire up so you can then push it over. Players should start with lighter tires (150-250lbs) and as they get stronger a heavier tire can be used. At the elite level players can use 700lb+ tires for great conditioning. Depending on the tire I have athletes flip it for only a few repetitions up to 20 if the tire is lighter.

Many companies that use heavy duty front end loaders or equipment have used heavy tires that they need to pay to have disposed. As long as you can pick it up in a truck many companies will simply give them away (which is great for your training options). In this picture, Todd flips a 700lb tractor tire.

Tire Wrestling

Tire wrestling drills involve two athletes on either side of a big tractor tire with the goal of trying to push the tire over. Players have to wrestle each other, and the tire to push it over. The player who lets the tire fall on their side loses. Battles should last for sets of 30-seconds or until one player wins.

Tire Rotation Throws

Much like throwing a discus, a tire throw works the rotational muscles of the trunk in addition to the lower body and upper body. To start, grab a normal car tire and in an open field throw the tire with spin throws the same as if you would throw a discus. Make sure to throw an equal amount on both sides of the body to maintain muscle balance.

Wheelbarrow Walking/Running

This simple exercise involves loading a wheelbarrow with 50 to 300lbs and then trying to walk or run with the wheelbarrow. Players must be able to lift the wheelbarrow off the ground, and then balance it while moving forward under control. Tipping it over is not an option because the wheelbarrow tends to dig into the pavement and stop suddenly (which hurts the shins). The neighbours may think you are nuts, but it's a great conditioning exercise.

To add weight you can add sandbags, bricks, stones, dirt, weight plates, kettlebells, tires, cement, or whatever heavy object you can find.

Sets of 20 to 60-seconds are a good starting point with a decent weight in the bucket. If kettlebells are loaded into the wheelbarrow you can stop every now and then to perform swings, snatches, clean & jerks, squat pulls, etc. For another kind of challenge players can find an uphill road (cement or gravel) and run the wheelbarrow up the hill (which is very challenging).

Shovelling Sand/Dirt/Snow

Anyone who has lived in a cold climate knows that shovelling snow is hard work, especially when the snow is that wet snow with a high moisture content. Growing up my driveway was 122-feet long…and let me tell you, it sucks when 6-inches of snow falls and you're the only person out shovelling.

So, your task is to find some snow, sand, or dirt and shovel for sets of 20 to 60-seconds as fast as possible. Make sure to switch sides to work both sides of the body equally.

Shovelling snow sucks… but it's a great conditioning exercise!

Sandbag Lifting

Lifting a sandbag is a very different experience from traditional dumbbells, barbells or kettlebells. If a sandbag is lifted the contents move and create an unpredictable object that is tough to move around. In the pictures below Wesley is moving around a 90lb sandbag, but even that is tough if many repetitions are performed.

Start sandbag training by picking up an army duffle bag from the local Army Surplus store or on Ebay. The US Army duffle bag I have cost $12.00 on Ebay, so it won't break the bank. Go to the hardware store and buy a couple bags of playground sand that has been washed and dried (so it won't rot and stink). Fill the Army bag with whatever amount of sand you want, use a rope and some duct tape to tie off the bag and get lifting. In addition to lifting the sandbag you can also throw the sandbag, run with the sandbag or have two players hold the sandbag between each other and wrestle for the bag. Be creative and have fun! As with all other forms of training start out with a relatively light weight and get used to the action of the sandbag.

Demonstrating how to pick up and shoulder a heavy sandbag (110lbs), and then squat

Rock Deadlifts
A rock deadlift is a very inexpensive way for strongman lifting that will build tremendous strength in the legs, core and gripping muscles. Grip a moderately sized rock (50 to 100lbs) and pick it up to waist height. To add variation to this exercise you can carry the rock around (held at waist height) for a certain distance, for a set amount of time or for as long as you can hold it without dropping it. Make sure not to drop the heavy rock on your foot...that might end your hockey season in a hurry if you aren't careful.

Rock Throws
Many different throws can be done with a heavy rock from a pick up and underhand toss type throw to a squat throw (like a medicine ball squat throw). Athlete's can perform spin throws with the rock or even slams to the ground (as the rock will not bounce). Use different sized rocks for throws and always try to better the throwing distance, or amount of repetitions performed during a workout. As with all rock training, make sure you are very careful when lifting or moving a heavy rock.

Farmers Walk

The farmers walk is a classic event in most strongman competitions for one reason...it's bloody hard. To start, load up an adjustable dumbbell (with a fat grip 2" grip if possible) with heavy weights and go for a walk. It's really that simple. Carry the dumbbells for as long as possible until your fingers finally let go of the weight (just don't drop it on your foot).

Other variations include using heavy kettlebells, loaded barbells, or heavy sandbags. I use this exercise as a "finisher" after a strength workout to train the gripping muscles, condition the legs and core muscles, and work an athlete's ability to push through the burning pain of muscles that want to let go of the weight. For a good conditioning workout include the farmers walk with other forms of training to create a circuit, and remember to use heavy weights to make athletes work hard! In the above picture I'm walking with 2-inch grip dumbbells that weigh 75lbs each for about 300-meters. Be creative with this "finisher" as it is fun and challenging for even the most advanced athletes.

Sledgehammer Hits

Justin hits the tire for 30 repetitions per side with a 10 or 16lbs sledgehammer
as part of his conditioning workouts

Using a heavy object to hit another object is perhaps one of the greatest feelings on earth. When properly implemented into a hockey players training sledge hammer hits can be a very valuable contribution to core strength, shoulder and back development along with cardiovascular conditioning. It takes a big effort to slam the 16lb sledge onto a tire over and over again, and this will help make any player into a beast if performed regularly. I like to have players start with a 10lbs sledge and work up from there. A company called *Torque Athletics* sells oversized "war hammers", which are big sledge hammers up to 150lbs. If you are ready to use a larger sledge call them at 812-673-4490.

When using sledge hammers make sure that safety is the number one priority as you can smash a toe or shin bone to bits if you're not careful. Another tip is to hit the sledge onto a tire as the impact of the hit will go through the sledge to the hands and hurt like hell if you don't hit a softer object like a tire which has some rebounding properties.

Sledgehammer Side Hits

Sledgehammer side hits are an awesome conditioning workout

See the explanation of sledgehammer side hits in the core training section, chapter 8.

Car Pushing

Todd pushing his car forwards and then backwards

Anyone who has ever driven in the snow knows the value of car pushing as a method of training athletes. The force it takes to start such a heavy object moving and keep it moving works the posterior chain muscles (the hamstring, glutes and low back) enormously. Athletes start by having a buddy, coach or girlfriend steer a car or truck without the engine on (to avoid choking to death), and the driver side door open if you are by yourself (in case the car goes the wrong way and you need to jump in and steer. As they steer the car or truck, you provide the engine and push as hard as possible.

My advice is to start with short distances and focus on getting the car moving as fast as possible for that distance. Start off slowly with this exercise and as you're conditioning gets better try pushing the car for longer and longer intervals (30-seconds pushing, 30-seconds rest or 1 minute pushing, 1 minute rest). For additional conditioning try combining car pushing with kettlebell lifting, plyometrics or a quick sprint.

Backwards car pushing is exactly the same as forward car pushing, only the player is turned around with the back facing the car/truck. In order to "get the car moving" the athlete has to really bend the legs and push with the quadriceps muscles. This is a painful exercise as it really burns the quads and makes even the strongest athletes gasp from the effort.

Cross-Over Car Pushing

Cross-over car pushing is the same as forward and backwards pushing. The key with this exercise though is to really exaggerate the pushing phase of BOTH legs, just as you would while performing cross-over's on the ice. A skating cross-over uses both feet to stride, not just the foot that crosses over, but the inside leg too!

Make sure to get a full extension with both legs on the cross-over car push so it simulates the skating motion as much as possible. For fun have a friend sit in the driver's seat and apply the brakes (gently) from time to time.

Heavy Bag Walks

Wesley using a 100lb heavy bag for training

This is a very simple exercise that can be used with a heavy punching bag, sand bag or military duffle bag loaded with rocks, sand or other weights. The idea is to hoist the bag up over your shoulder and carry it around the block. There are many different ways you can carry the bag, such as in a hugging type action (picture 1), over the shoulder, at arms length (picture 2) and pressed overhead. The distance the weighted bag is carried does not matter, as long as you put forth a tremendous effort to walk the bag as far as possible.

In some cases I have players pick up the bag and walk a short distance, then put the bag down, pick it up again and walk another short distance. Repeat this for a set amount of time or number of repetitions so that the athlete is exhausted by the end of the drill. Be careful with this drill as a heavy bag can injure athletes who are not ready for that type of load.

Heavy Bag Flip

This is a pretty tough exercise if you have a bag that weighs 80 to 100lbs, but it really works the core and shoulder musculature. Lift a heavy bag from the ground and flip the bag just as the bag gets to the shoulder. The idea is you have to catch the bag on the shoulder after a flip has been done. Ideally the bag should be a 50-100lbs heavy punching bag. A heavy sandbag or duffle bag filled with clothes or rocks can also work if you don't have a punching bag handy. Repeat the flipping and catching of the heavy bag for a set amount of time or a set number of repetitions.

Battling Ropes

I learned about this exercise from grip master John Brookfield. It's a pretty simple exercise but will trash the shoulders, back, hips and especially the core of just about anyone. The idea is that you take a heavy duty rope (a thick 1½ to 2 ½ inch rope used to anchor ships), and unroll it from 50 to 100 feet. Hook one end to a lamp post or heavy object (or wrap it around so you now hold both ends), go to the free end of the rope and with a full range of motion shake the rope up and down from your knees to over head as hard and as fast as possible.

Start off with sets of 20-seconds and build up as your body adapts to this stress. For additional training you can try shaking the rope with one end in each hand or twist the rope from side to side (like if you wanted to wrestle it away from someone). Find out more about this Battling Ropes exercise at www.battlingropes.com.

NFL players using the Battling Rope Tsunami exercise.
(Photo used by permission from John Brookfield)

Josh Everett, head strength & conditioning coach of *Naval Special Warfare Group 1* (SEAL Teams 1, 3, 5, 7) has this to say about his experience using the battling ropes:

> *"When it comes to the Battling Ropes system, doing is believing! When I tried out the exercises, it blasted my core and my heart rate shot up as well! There was so much more to the workout than my eyes had led me to believe. Talk about functional ab work. This training is perfect for athletes looking for a way to train their abs in a standing position to maintain midline stabilization and balance while absorbing tremendous outside forces."*

Chapter 22 - Partner Conditioning

"If you always put limit on everything you do, physical or anything else it will spread into your work and into your life. There are no limits. There are only plateaus, and you must not stay there, you must go beyond them"

~ Bruce Lee (legendary martial arts master)

With all forms of exercise I recommend training with a partner as they will often push you to higher levels of effort than by training alone. These drills are for working with a partner only. Give these a try or coaches might want to use some of these drills during training camp to build the team dynamics and condition players with fun workouts.

Fireman Carries

Fireman carries are a great way for athletes to work in small groups and work the basic musculature of the hip, core and upper body. To do this exercise one athlete bends down and hooks a leg and arm of their partner and from this position stands up so that the partner is draped across the working athlete's upper back (see picture 2). From this position the working athlete runs or walks a set distance, or if they are really strong they can perform squats or lunges with the partner on their back.

Fireman Squats

Much like the fireman carry drill one player hoists another player onto their shoulders and then performs a squat. This is an interesting exercise because lifting another person is more difficult than moving a barbell due to the fact that the weight shifts around during the action. Players should start off with light training partners and use a modified range of motion to get used to this exercise. Over time players can go lower and lower into the full squat action.

Partner Hill Running
Standing at the bottom of a long hill you sprint 50-feet up the hill and stop. Your partner runs the same 50-feet, and then 50-feet past you and stops. Now you run to your partner and past him 50-feet. Repeat until the hill is completed or both of you are exhausted. You can make this drill more challenging by carrying a heavy object up the hill or by using a parachute to slow the speed of the sprint slightly.

Piggyback Running

This simple exercise involves one player jumping on the back of another player, and then the player standing runs for a set distance or time. Combined with other partner drills or bodyweight exercises this is a good transition exercise during conditioning workouts.

Kyle runs with Alec on his back as part of conditioning drills after a hockey specific strength leg training workout. This is a great training option following a leg workout to "finish" the legs.

Rock Throws

Rock throws may be the simplest form of training, but very effective. Start by finding a large, heavy rock that weighs 30 to 100lbs. Two players stand facing each other and the rock is thrown from partner to partner by any means necessary (see picture from chapter 9). **DO NOT TRY TO CATCH THE ROCK!** It is heavy and will cause injury if it hits anyone. Let it fall to the ground and come to rest before picking it up and throwing it.

Tire Discus Throws

Players start by picking up a tire on the side like holding a discus (see picture from chapter 9). Anchor the feet and extend the tire behind in a rotational type movement before exploding out of this "coil" and throwing the tire in the exact same manner a discus is thrown in the Olympics. Try to throw the tire further and further each time. Throw with both sides to balance the musculature.

Make sure NOT to try and catch the tire as it will be a heavy object with significant force that will be very difficult to catch safely. Let it land on the ground before picking it up to throw.

Quad Band Conditioning

Partner quad band rowing (picture 1) and chest press (picture 2)

The Quad band is a rubber tube band that has 4-separate bands joined together in the middle (or two bands looped together) so that two people can workout at the same time. While this is a strength training exercise it becomes a conditioning drill when the exercises are done in a circuit, many repetitions are performed and little rest is allowed. Players can do pressing movements, curls, rows, abdominal twists, downward pulls or a large variety of exercises (as demonstrated above) to complete this workout.

Depending on the player and the strength of the band 20 to 50-repetitions can be performed per exercise or for a set amount of time (45-seconds work, then rest 45-seconds while the partner completes a set, then repeat with another exercise).

Start/Stop Runs
Go to the local track for this drill (or an open field or park). After a good warm-up one player runs while the other player calls out the instructions. Basically the non-working player yells either stop or start at random intervals for a period of 30 to 90-seconds. The working player has to listen to the commands of the non-working player and either run straight ahead or stop as instructed. This drill works both acceleration and deceleration (much like what can happen during a hockey shift).

Lateral Right/Left Runs
Similar to the straight ahead version of this drill the non-running partner calls out changes of direction at random and the working player follows those instructions by decelerating and changing directions as needed. Drills can last from 30 to 90-seconds. These drills work the lateral acceleration and deceleration of the body which is definitely a skill seen on the ice.

Hand Walks

One partner holds the working partners legs as the working athlete walks forward, backwards or to the side (picture 1). Generally with players I have them hand walk for a set distance and then switch partners. To add variety and a challenge coaches can create teams of athletes using the hand walking and have them compete in a race against each other. I have also made up timed circuits or races for athletes to perform such as hand walks for 100-feet, fireman carries for 100-feet, 100-hack squats, 100-feet of bear crawls, and 20-heavy tire flips.

Scramble Drill

Set up this drill by putting out 3 cones in a triangle type design or put down a large tractor tire on the ground. Have two partners face each other in a bear crawl type position on either side of the triangle or tire. To start one player yells a direction (left or right), and both players scramble in that direction (keeping a bear crawl type position), trying to catch each other. During the drill one player is in charge of yelling "reverse", where by both athletes reverse direction and go the other way. This works the hip and shoulder muscles in a lateral fashion as well as developing the stabilizing muscles of the core as the body is forced to change direction repeatedly.

Wheelbarrow Walks

One partner holds a wheelbarrow while the other partner gets into the hopper. The partner holding the wheelbarrow has to lift the handles to their sides and then run with the wheelbarrow a set amount of time. Upon completion, the partners switch places and continue with the workout. Try going around the block or around several blocks to begin with. Try to get further and further with each set.

Shield Shoulder Hits

One player holds a boxing/MMA type shield with an athletic stance while another player lines up and performs side body checks into the shield. Players should try to hit each other as hard as possible and try to knock each other over with the impact. As the striking shield is well padded nobody will get hurt, but both players will receive a good conditioning workout. After 10 to 20-hits, switch roles and have the person holding the shield now do the shoulder hits as the other player holds the shield.

Pro-hockey player Mykul Haun takes a face-off

224

Chapter 23 - Combat Conditioning

> "You do dat, you go to da box, you know, uh, two minutes by yourself,
> and you feel shame, you know, and then you get free."
>
> **~ Charlestown Chiefs goaltender Denis from the movie *Slap Shot***

Combat conditioning does not mean military training or preparing anyone for war. What is meant by combat conditioning is to improve conditioning by battling an opponent or fixed object to achieve a conditioning affect. Athletes in the sports of boxing, martial arts, MMA, and wrestling are some of the best conditioned athletes in the world and many of their same drills can be used for general physical preparation by hockey players.

Tug-O-War

The Tug-O-War drill is an old-fashioned test of strength that can be used for two or more athletes to work a variety of physical attributes. If coaches use repeated battles this test of strength can quickly become a conditioning exercise as players fight hard to try and win the contest. Gripping strength, balance, trunk stability, leg power, balance and mental toughness are all tested during this drill.

Two or more athletes can build tremendous strength, balance and coordination
in order to overcome and win the tug-o-war contest.

One Leg Boxing

Players looking for a great exercise to strengthen and balance the hip and core stabilization musculature, along with improving cardiovascular conditioning may want to try boxing a heavy bag while standing on one leg. The rotational forces produced by punching lead to an unstable situation for the balancing leg and if performed in sets with other forms of conditioning can be a valuable GPP drill.

Standing on one leg to hit a punching bag can be a challenging conditioning exercise.

Rapid Fire Boxing

Rapid fire boxing is conditioning form of traditional boxing in which the athlete tries to hit the heavy bag/target as many times as possible in a set amount of time. I generally like players to use a 30 to 60 second stopwatch and count how many punches are thrown in that period of time. Each set or workout the player tries to beat the previous number. With this exercise it is not important what the form is on the punches or the footwork that is used, simply the number of punches thrown in a set.

Knee Boxing

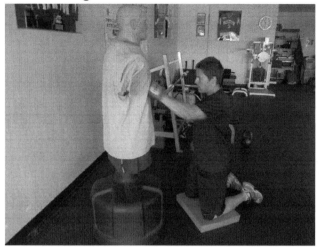

With knee boxing you take the legs out of the equation and box a heavy bag while on the knees. This method forces the abdominal and core muscles to work harder in order to generate punching power. Sets of 45 to 60-seconds work well for conditioning purposes.

Justin demonstrates knee boxing using an Airex pad cushion for the knees.

Mounted Punches (on heavy bag)

To perform the mounted punches exercise you take a heavy punching bag and put it on the ground. Mount the bag just like a MMA fighter mounts their opponent to deliver punches and from this position punch the bag with a variety of straight punches, round-house punches, elbow strikes, and hammer blows. The idea is to work the core area and maintain balance while striking a ground based target.

(As a side note I bought my 100lbs Everlast Punching bag on Craigslist for $35, so you can get a good bag for very little money these days).

Heavy Bag Kicks

Kicking is an awesome activity for hockey players as it involves working the hip flexors to raise the leg and the development of force to the target. The hip is one of the most undertrained and easily injured areas for hockey players so priority should be spent with strength and conditioning exercises that work this area. A roundhouse kick, Muay Thai kick, or high kick will all help work the hip flexors very well.

Boxing/Combat Training

While many people will criticize my use of boxing in training for hockey I understand the concern but also realize the potential for players to get in a great workout while learning how to defend themselves and battle an opponent through hand to hand combat. Many kids in midget and junior hockey fail to play hard because they fear getting in a fight or being hurt by a larger player. Lifting this "monkey off the back" allows some players to compete harder on the ice as they are not as afraid of being hurt. Former Junior hockey player and Canadian midget level hockey coach Mike Olson has this to say about teenagers learning basic combat/fighting skills:

> "I like it. It's very good for conditioning and confidence. For some guys just knowing that they can take care of themselves if need be can make a big difference. And now that I have tried a few new things like kickboxing and jiu-jitsu I'm amazed at how awesome these sports are for conditioning."

My thinking on boxing training is that I would rather a player learn how to defend themselves from an expert and practice in a safe environment as opposed to on the ice where someone could get seriously hurt (even if they are fooling around). The bottom line is that players do think about fighting (especially in the midget/junior age range) and it does impact the play of many young players who have not learned basic defensive combat type skills.

When setting up boxing type training I only recommend that a certified boxing coach be brought in to teach the player or team. Either that or have the player/team go to the boxing gym. All precautions must be taken (such as full head-gear, mouth guards, 16-ounce gloves, and a cup). Learn the basics first over time and then add light sparring matches and more hockey (fight) specific type tactics as time goes on.

Agility Ball Battle

The agility ball battle involves the use of the unpredictable bouncing agility ball from chapter 7. To perform the agility ball battle a coach has two players stand 10-feet in front of and facing him. The coach takes an agility ball (the kind of balls that are not perfectly round and bounce in weird directions), and throws that ball towards the players. The players have to react to the ball but also out manoeuvre each other and catch the ball. To add difficulty, two balls can be thrown by the coach so players have multiple targets to watch, react and move towards.

Swiss Ball/Medicine Ball Battles

Much like the stick battle, the ball battle involves two players holding a large Swiss ball or medicine ball between them, and on the whistle they fight for control of the ball. Make sure the ball is a durable ball so that it cannot easily be punctured by the force of the battle.

Rule the Circle (On-Ice)

One of the best drills ever to work a players balance, strength, conditioning, mental focus, grit and agility is the Rule the Circle drill. Two player's face each other over a face-off circle and on the whistle try to control or "rule" the circle by standing overtop of it. Players must use their entire body to push each other in order to win the drill. The exercise is over when one player rules the circle for 5-straight seconds or after a set amount of time (30 to 45-seconds is enough).

Coaches can pair up members of the entire team and have them face off against each other over and over again until each player has faced the rest of the team in battle. In 10-minutes a team can get in a great workout if no rest periods are allowed and coaches move the players along quickly from battle to battle. In the above drill Banff Hockey Academy junior players Sean Keating and Trent Takeuchi square off for "rule the circle" conditioning drills after practice.

Puck Battles (On-Ice)

More than a hockey drill, puck battles can be used as a form of conditioning in the latter stages of a hockey practice to work on balance, strength, coordination and mental toughness. To perform this drill two players line up 25-feet away from the boards and a puck is shot into the corner. The players skate towards the puck and battle in the corner for the puck with the goal of coming out of the corner with the puck. This drill can be combined with rule the circle drills, stick drills or band resistance drills to create a mini-circuit for a team or small group of players.

Junior players Trent Takeuchi and Sean Keating battle for the puck during this on-ice drill

Bear Crawl Battles

Bear crawl battles entail two players facing off against each other while performing a bear crawl exercise. The goal of each battle is to knock your opponent over by swiping a hand, foot or by leaning on them so they fall. Players can move around in any direction as they wish as long as they stay on their hands and feet in the bear crawl position. Rounds can be until a winner is declared or for a set amount of time (30 to 90-seconds).

Chapter 24 - Medicine Ball Training

"Strength does not come from winning. Your struggles develop your strengths. When you go through hardships and decide not to surrender, that is strength."

~ Arnold Schwarzenegger

Medicine ball training is an age old method of training eastern block athletes that is a great form of training for hockey players. To pass or throw a heavy ball requires explosive full body effort, or else the ball doesn't go anywhere. Catching a heavy ball thrown forcefully is also a unique skill that requires a certain amount of strength, coordination and balance. Players can use a wide variety of exercises to throw or slam the medicine balls against a wall or at a partner, and workouts can be a great team building or conditioning workout. Personally I have used medicine ball training with every single athlete I have coached (in all sports) with great success as a warm-up, explosive movements or with conditioning. Be creative but safe with medicine ball exercises!

Squat & Throw

This standard medicine ball exercise requires the player to hold the ball between the hands under the chin, squat down and then explode upwards throwing the ball as high as possible into the air. A deep squat and forceful explosion (that usually ends with the athlete jumping into the air) is required for a high throw. Make sure to throw the ball at a slight forward angle so it does not come down and hit you as it lands. Step forward, pick up the ball and repeat the throw for a set amount of time or a certain number of repetitions.

Generally I like to have players do 60-seconds of throwing or 25-squat throws as one set of a workout with a 8 to 20lb ball (depending on player level and ability).

In the picture professional hockey player Tyler Doherty of the Mississippi Riverkings (CHL) throws the 14lb medicine ball during early spring training in Banff, Alberta with Coach Pollitt.

Overhead Medicine Ball Squat Jump

Alec squats with the medicine ball and then with the arms extended overhead jumps as high as possible

Hold a medicine ball with both hands overhead, squat down and from this position rise up and throw the ball at the top of the motion. This is a more difficult version of the squat throw as the arms are extended overhead throughout the entire motion so only the legs really provide the force to throw the ball.

Slams

Clint Hazen slams a heavy D-Ball during off-season training in Richmond, British Columbia

Shown to me many years ago by United States Weightlifting Junior Team Head Coach Mike Burgener this exercise is a conditioning killer if you use a heavy D-Ball (a non-bouncing ball that can vary in weight between 20lbs to 150lbs). To perform a slam, simply pick up a D-Ball, raise it overhead with both hands and then slam it to the ground as hard as possible. Repeat this action for a set amount of time or for a certain number of repetitions. Athletes at my facility use a 50lb D-Ball as part of training circuits or during conditioning workouts, and sometimes I test athletes by having them slam the 50lb D-ball as many times as possible in 30-seconds.

Twisting Wall Pass

Alec repeatedly throws a 12lbs medicine ball against a block wall

This exercise is a very good exercise to develop the explosive aspect of the core area as it rotates to throw a heavy medicine ball and then is forced to absorb and throw the ball again. Rather than use this exercise as a slow movement I like to have athletes use a shorter range of motion and try to throw the ball as many times as possible over a set period of time (30 to 60-seconds) or time how long it takes to throw the ball 30-times against the wall. Make sure to train both sides of the body to help balance out the musculature.

230

Bounce Pass

Two players face each other standing 8 to 15-feet apart. One player takes a heavy medicine ball, brings it overhead and throws it like a soccer throw. The throw should bounce off the ground and into the hands of the partner. Try to really slam the ball into the ground so it gets a good bounce. This exercise can also be done against a brick wall or concrete building.

In the picture Kyle uses an overhead soccer throwing motion to bounce the 18lb medicine ball to Alec at the Hockey Contractor training facility.

Soccer Throw Pass

Partners stand facing each other and one player lifts a medicine ball overhead, steps forward and throws it towards the other player who catches the ball before it drops to the ground. Be careful when catching a heavy medicine ball as it tends to slip through the fingers rather easily. This drill can also be done against a brick wall or concrete building.

Chest Pass

Throwing the 18lbs medicine ball between training partners with a bounce pass

Partners stand 8-feet apart facing each other and use a chest pass (like passing a basketball) to throw the ball back and forth to each other. This really works the upper body pressing muscles of the chest, shoulders, triceps and core musculature.

Twisting Pass

Two players stand sideways with the same shoulder facing each other (see picture). With a twisting motion of the abdominal muscles and loading of the legs throw the ball to your partner as hard as possible. The partner must catch the ball, absorb the shock, coil up and throw the ball back to the first person as hard as possible. Make sure to perform throws on both sides of the body.

The medicine ball standing twist pass is a great core and stability exercise

Bosu Twisting Pass

John catches the ball and twists as far as possible (picture 1), then uncoils to throw the ball (picture 2)

Much the same as the regular twisting pass, a player now stands on a Bosu ball and performs the same twist pass action. The unstable surface of the Bosu ball helps to develop general balance and stability. Start off by standing on a Bosu ball and have a partner (or coach) throw you a medicine ball. From this position catch the ball to the side by twisting the core area and then throw the ball back forcefully by uncoiling the core area while staying balanced on the Bosu.

Skating Twist Pass

Junior hockey players Trent Takeuchi and Matt Korotva (Slavie) throw the 7kg medicine ball back and forth while skating. The drill can be a very challenging and effective way to improve on-ice coordination, balance, agility and general body strength. Players skate around the ice throwing the ball back and forth to each other in any pattern or setup (as long as it's safe). Used as part of the warm-up or during team building exercises players can be creative when throwing the ball as long as it's safe.

Skating Chest Pass

Two players face each other roughly 8 to 10-feet apart and from this position skate around the rink passing a medicine ball between them. The idea is to keep skating with good form while throwing and catching a heavy medicine ball as a means of strength and balance training. This can also be incorporated into the on-ice warm-up for a hockey practice so players can have some fun, warm-up and get in some functional training all at once.

Trent & Slavie throw the medicine ball back and forth while skating

Dan Spence formerly of the Calgary Hitmen (WHL). Photo by Dwayne Fletcher.

Chapter 25 - Running Drills

"Don't let what you cannot do interfere with what you can do."

~ **John Wooden (legendary UCLA Basketball Coach)**

Conditioning drills that involve ground based movements such as running or bodyweight movements are the preferred method for training hockey players. On the ice players must support and move their own weight, in addition to overcoming high lateral forces (such as in turns), so it only makes sense to use dryland training methods that replicate this weight bearing nature. The following is a collection of running drills that should form the backbone of any hockey training program and provide a superior conditioning affect compared to traditional aerobic training that most hockey players and teams currently use.

I strongly advise that coaches and players use these drills as races, or combined with other forms of GPP training to create an obstacle course so that players can compare their results with each other and the team can condition more than one player at a time. I usually will break down a team into an A and a B group and have individuals compete (for the benefit of the group) to determine a winner between groups. This provides a challenge of competitions to workouts and raises the intensity level.

Intervals
Intervals are perhaps the most important type of running drill as the sport of hockey involves intervals throughout the game. Players need to work this work/rest change of pace during dryland training so that line changes become easy in the hockey season.

All interval training is based on changing the amount of work that is performed, compared to the rest the athlete receives. This is shown as a ratio of 1 to 1 work/rest, but can be changed many different ways from a 1 to 2 ratio, 1 to 3 ratio, or even a 2 to 1 ratio. When starting with intervals players should start with easier intervals such as a 1 to 2 or 1 to 3 ratio as this gives more rest compared to the amount of work performed. This allows better recovery between sets so the quality of the work interval stays high. As the start of the season gets close players should work towards moving the interval to a 1 to 1 or a 2 to 1 work/rest ratio so that they are able to put in hard bouts of effort followed by little rest (as might occur in hockey when playing in game situations). In the hockey workouts chapter there are a number of running interval workouts that players can use to develop incredible conditioning.

Fartlek Drills
The word fartlek is a Swedish word that literally means "speed play", and involves slow to medium paced running intermixed with fast sprinting and hard interval work. The difference between this type of training and regular running is that the intensity of the running speed varies so that it works both the aerobic and anaerobic system. This is a good cardiovascular team warm-up drill for 5 to 10 minutes prior to a game or practice. Remember, after this the dynamic warm-up begins (see the Warm-ups Chapter for more information).

Start/Stop Drill
This drill involves straight ahead running on a track or in a park. The idea is to run forward as fast as possible for 10 to 50-feet and then at random decelerate to a stop. As soon as you stop, start backpedalling for 5 to 10-feet, then change direction and sprint forwards again for 10 to 50-feet. Stop when the quality of the sprints or the change of direction drops off noticeably. This is a very simple change of direction drill that can be performed for sets of 5 to 15, and with a warm-up and cool-down should take no more than 20-minutes. This drill can also be combined with other running or conditioning drills to make up a circuit or giant set.

Change of Direction Drills

I like to include runs that involve players changing from forwards to backwards, side to side, or diagonal to diagonal. As hockey has many different stops, starts and change of direction situations during a game this MUST be trained in the off-season with these types of drills. To simply run in a straight line is missing this critical ingredient of hockey training.

Much like the start/stop drill players will start out running at any speed and then when you come to a tree, lamp post, cone, etc., you will change directions and run backwards, turn around and run forwards, run diagonally, side shuffles, etc. The point is that each time you change direction it involves a stop and then a move into another movement in another direction. This drill should be done in park so that you can move in all directions without running into things. Players can include bodyweight drills such as burpees, push-ups, squat jumps, 1-leg hops, sit-ups, etc. when stopping to add variety and another challenge. This form of training allows you to be as creative as you want...enjoy!

Hill Sprints

Hill sprinting is one of the most valuable methods of developing sheer power in the legs. As with hill jumping the reduced "air time" of the legs due to the angle of the hill and the need to flex the hip to get a good stride length make this an awesome exercise for all athletes. Hockey players especially will benefit from hill sprinting as it works the hip flexors in a wide range of motion (which is very valuable). Sprinting can be done forwards, backwards or other steps such as cross-over's, side shuffles or carioca steps. The length of each sprint can go from 20 feet to 200-meters, depending on the conditioning of the athlete and the purpose of the workout. The important aspect of hill sprinting is to go 100% with each and every sprint to build the legs and cardiovascular power for hockey.

Hill Jumps

The reduced "air time" due to the incline of the hill, and the stress this puts on the calf and posterior chain muscles is good for working the legs. Players can use one leg jumps, two leg jumps, side jumps, bouncing, skate hops, side shuffles, cross-over jumps, or carioca steps to provide a wide variety of conditioning drills.

Stair Running

Since most hockey rinks have stairs this seems to be a no-brainer in terms of "in-house" conditioning. Many times I have had players perform stair sprints, jumps, quick feet drills or partner drills (such as incline partner wheelbarrow walks, fireman carries, lateral start/stop drills, etc.) as part of training. Coaches should be creative rather than just sending players to run the stairs. Drills should start with players required to step on every stair to improve quick feet and leg power. Move into drill where player run two stairs at a time, and then 3-stairs at a time. Each progression requires more and more power from the athlete in order to complete the drill.

To add variety player can turn sideways and run up the stairs laterally. One step at a time, two sets or even three steps can be very challenging and more sport specific to hockey. I also recommend quick feet drills while facing sideways. To perform these players step up 2-steps, then down 1, then up 2-steps and down one. Repeat to the top of the stairs and then switch sides. For another variation intervals can be used on the stairs with 20 to 40-seconds of hard work followed by a short interval of rest or active rest (such as core work or stick-handling with a ball).

Strongman Hill Running

Carrying a heavy object (a sandbag, rock, log, kettlebell or tire) while running up a hill is a tremendous conditioning workout. Add in some hill sprints, some hill jumps, line drills (on the hill) and a final 2-minute all out run up the hill and in a short time a great workout can be had by any hockey player. Be creative and find a hill that is long enough and with a steep enough incline to provide a real challenge.

Chapter 26 - Cross Training for Hockey

"A man can be as great as he wants to be.
If you believe in yourself and have the courage, the determination, the dedication,
the competitive drive and if you are willing to sacrifice the little things in life and pay
the price for the things that are worthwhile, it can be done."

~ Vince Lombardi (legendary NFL football coach)

All hockey players should engage in some form of cross training during the year to get away from ice hockey training and enjoy playing another sport or game with non-hockey friends or family. Many sports such as handball, racquetball, squash, tennis, judo, mixed martial arts, or jujitsu provide a great non-sport specific conditioning workout that does work quickness, agility, balance, hand-eye coordination and power. Used in the offseason or at the end of a season these activities can be a great way to stay in shape without specifically training for hockey.

Other than the sports suggested above, I have included several running based, team sports that can provide hockey players a good break from the ice and a reasonable alternative to summer hockey. Players looking to move up in hockey or maintain elite level conditioning should include these sports along with a solid strength and conditioning program in order to balance out the hockey musculature and get ready for the on-ice season.

Ball Hockey

Played on city streets and in parks for many years, organized ball hockey has only been around for about 30-years. Ball hockey is a sport in which the game of hockey is played on a rink that has no ice, so players must run instead of skate and a low bounce orange ball is used rather than a puck. Players must wear a helmet, gloves, jock and use a standard hockey stick. The rules are very similar to hockey with minor exceptions.

Ball hockey has become a very popular off-season alternative to hockey, and in Canada they have more than 50,000 players in the system annually. At least 200 NHL players (and numerous WHL, OHL, and QMJHL players), have played organized ball hockey as a method of summer conditioning, including Pavol Demitra, Michael Ryder, Derian Hatcher, Curtis Joseph, Craig McTavish, Steve Thomas, Tie Domi, George Laraque, Patrick Roy and Dino Ciccarelli.

As a means of hockey conditioning ball hockey can be very good for training. Players can learn positioning, how to battle for pucks, lateral agility, quickness and general hockey type conditioning. Team Canada head coach George Gortsos states that "hockey players often have trouble adapting to the speed and agility required to play high level ball hockey and bigger players (as hockey players are) have trouble with changing directions and being agile". With all of the similarities of hockey, the low cost involved and the tremendous carryover effect to ice hockey, ball hockey is a great method of summer conditioning along with a solid off-season strength and conditioning program.

Over the past few years I have really started to use more and more ball hockey type drills in my off-ice dryland training as I feel strongly that many hockey related skills can be learned effectively off the ice by ball hockey as the skating component of the skill has been taken out of the equation. Therefore, kids can learn how to stick-handle and move with the puck, without skating getting in the way. When you combine the two with some on-ice skill development the rate at which players acquire new skills and develop as hockey players is vastly increased. Ball hockey can also be a great option when teaching positioning and tactics to a team as this can be done over time off the ice (therefore at huge cost savings), which leads to better on-ice practice sessions.

More information can be found at: Canadian Ball Hockey Association, (www.cbha.com/), Street Hockey USA, (www.streethockeyusa.com/home.htm), or the International Street & Ball Hockey Association, (www.isbhf.com).

Inline Hockey (aka: Roller Hockey)

It took me a while to warm-up to inline hockey as a viable option for training hockey players as I always hated the way wheels seemed to screw up the skating stride of a hockey player. Having said that there has been a big development of roller hockey skates since my opinion was first formed and I have now become an inline hockey convert. It sure can't hurt that a number of NHL players (like Bobby Ryan, Luc Robitaille, Alec Hemsky, and Devin Setoguchi (to name just a few), have learned and refined their ice hockey skills by playing a lot of inline hockey.

In fact, with the various rule differences in inline hockey, games tend to be faster-paced and higher scoring. The focus on higher skill levels (stick-handling, puck control) and more speed of play (skating and passing) is evident. This all works well for players when they return to the ice in the fall. Learn more about Canadian Inline at **www.canadainline.com**, or at USA Hockey **www.usahockey.com**.

Lacrosse

Much like hockey, lacrosse requires that players carry a good deal of muscle mass in order to cope with the aggressive nature of the sport. Low body fat levels, quickness, agility, speed and smart team based strategy is key for successful participation of lacrosse. As a means of conditioning throughout the off-season lacrosse is a very appropriate sport for all hockey players. Young players looking to take a break from ice hockey and experience an outdoor sport for summer, while learning new skills and improving conditioning should look to lacrosse. The best quote in support of lacrosse as an off-season sport for hockey comes from hall of fame hockey player Wayne Gretzky when he once stated:

"One of the worst things to happen to the game, in my opinion, has been year-round hockey and, in particular, summer hockey. All it does for kids, as far as I can tell, is keep them out of sports they should be doing in warmer weather. I could hardly wait to get my lacrosse stick out and start throwing the ball around. It didn't matter how cold or rainy it would be, we'd be out firing the ball against walls and working on our moves as we played the lacrosse equivalent to road hockey. All the good hockey players seemed to play lacrosse in those days and every one of them learned something from the game to carry over to the other - things athletes can only learn by mixing up games they play when they are young."

More information on lacrosse can be found at: The Canadian Lacrosse Association (www.lacrosse.ca), and USA Lacrosse (www.uslacrosse.org).

Rugby

This popular mid-18th century sport developed in England is a fast moving game with few stoppages in the action and continuous possession changes from team to team. Every player on the field has to be able to run, pass, catch, kick, tackle and defend at all times during the match consisting of two 40-minute halves.

As a means of training for hockey Rugby is a summer sport that demands players develop good quickness, agility, and endurance, all while being a physically gruelling event.   For midget and junior players adding Rugby into a yearly strength and conditioning program would be a good method of staying in shape and having fun by playing a different sport in the summer. Learn more at: www.rugbyfootballhistory.com/national_unions.htm.

Field Hockey

One of the oldest team sports, modern day field hockey was developed in England during the 19th century and has been included in the Summer Olympic Games since 1908 (for men) and 1980 (for women). Today field hockey is one of the most popular sports in the world and a staple sport in most European countries.

As a method of training hockey players Field Hockey is similar to hockey in that a stick is used to move the ball and players must flex the knees to stickhandle correctly. The team sport environment requires that players work together and improve quickness, lateral agility, and conditioning as it relates to the strategy of the sport. As a summer sport including Field Hockey into a yearly program would be a suitable complement to the training for winter ice hockey.

More information can be found at the following national association websites: Field Hockey Canada (www.fieldhockey.ca) and USA Field Hockey (www.usfieldhockey.com).

Racquet Sports

Every hockey player needs to have a high degree of agility and possess exceptional hand-eye coordination. Racquet sports such as racquet ball, squash, tennis and non-racquet sport hand-ball are all useful methods of developing great conditioning, agility, and hand-eye coordination. As a form of additional training in a fun and competitive environment I highly recommend players learn and player racquet sports as part of their off-season conditioning. The lateral nature of the sport helps develop the legs in a very unique and effective way for skating sports. It is much more valuable than traditional training methods that old school coaches used to develop players, such as long distance running, cycling, swimming, and even general skating.

Tennis (left), squash (center) or handball (right) are great summer sports for players looking to develop superior agility & explosiveness

Gymnastics

Hockey players need a wide range of physical tools such as flexibility, agility, power, proprioception (the ability to know where your body is in space), and core strength. These are essential to be successful on the ice. The sport of gymnastics teaches many of these qualities in a gradual, fun method so children learn to move the body properly and build incredible athleticism. For young players (less than 12-years of age) I **highly** recommend gymnastics training as a compliment to their existing hockey training.

Martial Arts

While these sports are not for everyone they do build a great deal of the physical qualities that will benefit the hockey player. General conditioning, flexibility, speed and agility are perhaps the most noticeable. Martial arts' training is a wonderful addition to any training program as a player learns to develop individual skills in a group setting and for younger players it helps improve their self-confidence as they execute complex movements.

Dryland Hockey Skills Training

Skating Ramp

While I am not a fan of hockey training methods that I consider gimmicks, I must say I really like the skating ramp. The skating ramp is basically a slightly inclined ramp that has synthetic ice over it so that players can skate with minimal resistance indoors. The reason I like the ramp over the treadmill is that with the ramp you are skating up the surface, rather than the surface moving under your feet which pushes the skate backwards.

Players should look to get on the ice during the off-season, but for training purposes the skating ramp is a very good alternative conditioning and technique developing tool.

Steve demonstrates the skating ramp at his facility in Simi Valley, CA.

Mini-Rink (Synthetic Ice) or Ice

The Mini-rink is a synthetic ice surface with boards and nets. The glide on synthetic ice is about 85% of what natural ice has so players must skate harder and glide less in order to move properly on this surface. These smaller rinks are also perfect for 3-on-3 leagues as they develop players and teach people how to compete against each other in close, tight spaces. In my opinion, this type of small space training is a **critical** aspect of training that many players and coaches overlook.

Dryland Shooting

Practicing your shot is a key area that many players simply do not take advantage of in the off-season. With shooting the puck more, you get better at accuracy, shot velocity and most importantly the quick release from the stick that often will fool a goaltender. Players looking to make the jump to the next level should try to shoot pucks (not balls) every day. Taking just 100-shots a day would amount to over 15,000 shots in the off-season alone.

When practicing your dryland shot make sure you stand on a slightly elevated surface just like how Coach Steve Phillips does in the picture above (as a side note, Steve has a 106mph slap shot). The reason for this is that you are slightly higher on skates than bare feet and it is important you practice how you play as much as possible (either that or use a slightly shorter stick for dryland training). Use a real stick, real puck and really try to get good velocity on every shot (forehand, backhand, snap and slap shot).

Many of us do not have access to a rink or shooting surface every day so the answer is a tarp or specialized shooting background. I like the Insta-Net from Garage Hockey as they make a very high quality 10'x8' product that will stand up to even the hardest shots. You will also need an elevated surface to stand on and a small sheet of synthetic plastic ice that can be found at many local companies that make plastics.

Off-Ice Stick-Handling

There are <u>many</u> ways to improve your stick-handling ability, and players should look to be creative when practicing this vital component of hockey. When I grew up playing hockey we only used tennis or golf balls, but now they have all kinds of weighted pucks or Smart Hockey stick-handling balls that can be used to develop stick-handling. The goal of this type of practice is to improve your ability to move the puck around while keeping your head up. As your stick-handling ability improves you can work on moving the puck/ball faster and around objects but with all of these drills you must be able to **hold your head up** throughout the drill to get the maximum benefit.

Junior-A player Austin Block

241

Chapter 27 - Hockey Conditioning Workouts

"That which does not kill us makes us stronger"

~ Friedrich Nietzsche

In this section I have provided a collection of 76-hockey conditioning workouts that I use with my athletes. These are only conditioning workouts (not programs), and while they may contain strength training type movements and exercises this is not strength training (as that is a separate form of training all together). This is general conditioning. These workouts are meant to be physically and mentally gruelling, and will require a great deal of effort to complete as they are described. Please note that you can combine just about any of the exercises presented in this book with each other to create fun and challenging workouts. Read over my "conditioning rules" section in chapter-2 and craft your own workouts that will challenge your GPP and SPP.

I use a A1, A2, B1, C1 type system in describing my workouts. What this means is I would like people to complete all "A" numbers in a row, without a break until all are done, and then take a short break. Once all the "A" sets are complete, move to the "B" sets, finish those and then move on to the "D", "E", etc., sets. Therefore if I list the exercises as A1 = Squats, A2 = Sit-ups, A3 = Bench press, you would perform a set of squats, then move to sit-ups, then to bench press, without stopping (this is called a "giant set"), and then have a break. Repeat for the required number of sets, and then move to the "B" exercises.

For ease of use I have grouped the workouts under the topic they fall under. With each grouping of exercises I number each workout so that it is simple to integrate into your overall plan with just a number that corresponds to a workout.

Sled Dragging Workouts

Sled dragging workouts are the premier form of GPP training as it conditions many parts of the body simultaneously. Many of the athletes I work with have used the sled to further their strength training effectiveness and on-ice performance. Give these workouts a try and rest as much as needed to perform each set with 100% focus (just don't rest too long).

SD #1

A1 Forward Sprints (hip belt attachment)	4x40 meters (73lbs)
B1 Cross-Over Sprints (handle attachment)	4x30 meters (73lbs)
C1 Heavy Forward Dragging (shoulder harness)	6x50 meters (163-208lbs)
D1 Heavy Backward Drags (handle attachment)	4x30 meters (163-208lbs)
E1 Forward Sled Pushing	2x30 meters (72lbs)
E2 Kettlebell Snatches	2x15 reps/side
E3 Burpees	2x20 reps

SD #2

A1 Side Shuffle Sprints (single handle attachment)	4x20 meters/side (73lbs)
B1 Bent-Over Forward Drags (handle attachment)	4x50 meters (118-163lbs)
C1 Hockey Drags (single handle attachment)	4x30 meters/side (73-118lbs)
D1 Backward Drags (with shoulder harness)	4x50 meters (73-118lbs)
D2 Forward Sled Pushing	4x50 meters (73-118lbs)

SD #3

A1 Heavy Forward Dragging (shoulder harness)	10x50 meters (163-208lbs)
B1 Heavy Backwards Dragging (double-hand attachment)	6x50 meters (118-163lbs)
C1 Kettlebell Snatch Repeats (with 53lb kettlebell)*	10 sets of 10 reps/side

Notes: To complete the kettlebell snatch repeat a player starts a stop-watch, takes a kettlebell and performs a set of 10 snatches with one hand, then a set of 10 snatches with the other hand, and then puts down the kettlebell. At the start of every minute a new set of 10 repetitions per hand is started, until a total of 10 minutes is reached. The rest period is calculated by subtracting the time it takes to perform the 10 reps per side from 60 seconds. For example a player might take 25 seconds to perform the first set of 10/side, so they would get 35 seconds rest. When the clock hits the one minute mark, another set is performed and say it takes 28 seconds to perform, so the rest interval would be 32 seconds. Keep repeating this until you have done a total of 10 minutes (100 repetitions per side).

SD #4

- A1 Forward Sled Dragging   100 feet
- A2 2 Handed Kettlebell Swings   20 repetitions
- A3 Backwards Sled Dragging   100 feet
- A4 Snatches   10 repetitions/side

NOTES: Load the drag sled up with a heavy amount of weight (163lbs plus) and then attach your kettlebell to the top of the post. After dragging the sled 100 feet you take off the kettlebell and perform your swings before setting the kettlebell back on the sled and dragging it backwards for 100 feet. Then take off the kettlebell again and do the 20 snatches. At this point you can rest for 2 minutes and then repeat 2-4 more times (3-5 total).

SD #5

A1 Forward Sled Pushing	200 feet
A2 Cross Over Dragging (left side)	100 feet
A3 Cross Over Dragging (right side)	100 feet
A4 Sled Pushing	200 feet
A5 Backwards Dragging	200 feet
A6 Bent Forward Dragging	200 feet

NOTES: Use a standard weight for every set (start off with a 35lb weight plate, and add weight as you are able). Repeat this 1 to 3 more times, resting 5 minutes between giant sets.

SD #6

A1 Sled Pushing (heavy load on sled)	100 feet
A2 1-Arm Kettlebell Swings	10/side
A3 Sled Pushing (heavy load on sled)	100 feet
A4 1-Arm Kettlebell Squat Pulls	10/side

NOTES: Load the sled up with as much weight as you can push for 100 feet, and add the kettlebell to the sled by looping the handle over the weight holder. When you get done pushing the sled simply take the kettlebell off the weight holder and start your swings or squat pulls. Do not stop for a break until you have finished the entire A1-A4 circuit. Repeat 2-4 times, and vary the kettlebell exercises to snatches, jerks, windmills, 2-handed swings, etc. to add variety.

On-Ice Tire Workouts

With tire workouts I have players use full equipment (to simulate game actions as much as possible) and require them to do a full skating warm-up of inside edges, outside edges, balance drills, recovery leg drills, etc.

TW #1

A1 Forward tire sprints	6 x blue to blue
B1 Backwards heavy tire dragging	4 x blue to blue
C1 Heavy tire pushing	6 x goal line to red line
D1 Backwards tire iron cross	4 x blue to blue

TW #2

A1 Backward tire sprints	4 x blue to blue
B1 Heavy tire dragging	8 x goal line to red line
C1 Forwards tire iron cross	4 x blue to blue
D1 Backwards net pulling	4 x blue to blue

TW #3

A1 Tire pulling (with partner in the heavy tire)	4 x 50 feet (or whatever distance rope)
B1 2-Stick battles	2 sets of 30 seconds
B2 Tire pushing battle	2 sets of 30 seconds
C1 Rule the circle drill	2 sets of 45 seconds
D1 Forward heavy tire dragging	8 sets of goal line to goal line

TW #4

This workout involves using a small group of 3 partners. To start players stand on the goal lines (one on one side, and two on the other) and a heavy tire is dragged forward, backwards, using cross-over steps, repeated 1-leg pushes, and pushing the tire. Each player must push or pull the tire from goal line to goal line, where the next person does the same thing. With three or more people in a group this drill flows well and allows players to get a 1 to 3 work/rest ratio. Use whatever pulling/pushing exercise from chapter 4, just make sure that everyone does the same exercise each set.

Partner Workouts

Since many of these drills such as band resistance, stick battles, medicine ball throwing, combat drills, and various body weight exercises involve a partner I have put all of these workouts together in this format. You may want to single out one specific drill such as band work or stick battle and spend more time on that...it's up to you. These are some of my favourite partner workouts.

PW #1

A1 Stick battles	30 seconds
A2 Juke drill (agility drill off-ice)	30 seconds
A3 Frog squat jumps	30 seconds
A4 Band twists (dryland)	30 seconds
A5 Scramble drill	30 seconds

NOTES: Both players perform this drill at the same time and take a 2½ minute break at the end of the giant set. Finish a total of 3 to 5 giant sets and/or pair this up with sprinting, sled dragging, running intervals, etc.

PW #2

A1 Partner wheelbarrow running	30 seconds
A2 Band resisted forward sprinting	30 seconds
A3 Partner push-up walks	30 seconds
A4 2-Stick battle drill	30 seconds
A5 Fireman carries	30 seconds

NOTES: One person completes the entire set without rest, then the other partner does their set. Once both partners have finished take a 60 second break and then repeat for a total of 3 to 5 repetitions. To perform the partner wheelbarrow running have one partner get into the wheelbarrow while the other partner (who is working through the set) lifts the wheelbarrow and starts to run with it for 30 seconds.

PW #3

A1 Bear crawl battle	45 seconds
A2 Rule the circle drill	45 seconds
A3 Medicine ball twist passing	45 seconds
A4 Medicine ball soccer throw passing	45 seconds

NOTES: Both players perform this drill at the same time and take a 3 minute break at the end of the giant set. Finish a total of 3 to 5 giant sets and/or pair this up with sprinting, sled dragging, running intervals, etc.

PW #4

A1 Stick battle	30 seconds
A2 Frog squat jumps	30 seconds
A3 Stick battle	30 seconds
A4 Push-ups	30 seconds
A5 Stick battle	30 seconds

NOTES: Both players perform this drill at the same time and take a 3 minute break at the end of the giant set. Finish a total of 3 to 5 giant sets and/or pair this up with sprinting, sled dragging, running intervals, etc

PW #5

-Jump lunges	20 repetitions/side
-Band resisted bear crawls	100 feet
-Fireman carries	100 feet
-Partner wheelbarrow runs	100 feet
-Frog squat jumps	20 repetitions
-Stick battles	30 seconds
-Shadowing (one person mimics the movements of another player)	30 seconds
-Plyometric push-ups	20 repetitions
-Repeated standing long jump	10 repetitions

NOTES: This should be done with both partners running through the drill at the same time (on exercises such as fireman carry, and partner wheelbarrow runs each partner will take a turn while the other partner helps them complete the exercise). Move from exercise to exercise without rest. Repeat 2 times and rest 4 minutes between giant sets.

PW #6

A1	Band resisted forward sprint	40 meters
A2	Band resisted bear crawls	40 meters
A3	Band resisted side shuffle	40 meters
A4	Partner push-up walks	40 meters
A5	Fireman carries	40 meters
A6	Side shoulder hits	40 meters

NOTES: One person completes the entire set without rest, then the other partner does their set. Once both partners have finished take a 60 second break and then repeat for a total of 3 to 5 repetitions.

PW #7

A1	Partner sprints	40 meters
A2	Scramble drill	30 seconds
A3	Tug-o-war	until a winner is declared
A4	Stick battle	until a winner is declared

NOTES: Both players perform this drill at the same time and take a 3 minute break at the end of the giant set. Finish a total of 3 to 5 giant sets. The partner sprint drill at the end basically means that the partners will line up and try to beat each other in a 40 meter sprint. Pair this up with sprinting, sled dragging, running intervals, etc. for further conditioning.

PW #8

A1	Medicine ball underhand throws	30 total throws
A2	Band resisted twists	30 total repetitions
A3	Medicine ball squat throws	30 total throws
A4	Frog squat jumps	15 repetitions each partner
A5	Medicine ball chest pass throws	30 total throws
A6	Medicine ball twist passing	30 total throws
A7	Burpees	20 repetitions
A8	Medicine ball bounce pass	30 total throws

NOTES: Both players perform this drill at the same time and take a 3 minute break at the end of the giant set. Finish a total of 3 to 5 giant sets.

Lateral Workouts

Lateral workouts on the slide board or Russian box can be very challenging workouts for most hockey players. As your level of conditioning improves add a weight vest to provide another level of challenge. Ideally players should look to build up into a 1 to 1 work/rest interval (which means for every second you work, you rest one second). By building up to a 1 to 1 work/rest interval your conditioning will be at a very high level and playing a game of hockey that typically has a 1 to 3 work/rest interval (forwards), or a 1 to 2/3 work/rest interval (defence) will be much easier to handle.

LT #1

A1	Slide board	10 seconds work, 10 seconds rest
A2	Slide board	15 seconds work, 15 seconds rest
A3	Slide board	20 seconds work, 20 seconds rest
A4	Slide board	25 seconds work, 25 seconds rest
A5	Slide board	30 seconds work, 30 seconds rest
A6	Slide board	25 seconds work, 25 seconds rest
A7	Slide board	20 seconds work, 20 seconds rest
A8	Slide board	15 seconds work, 15 seconds rest
A9	Slide board	10 seconds work

NOTES: Complete this set as shown, take a 5 minute rest and repeat one or two more times. Make sure to use proper deep knee bend with all slide board training.

LT #2

A1	Slide board	30 seconds work, 30 seconds rest
A2	Slide board	10 seconds work, 10 seconds rest
A3	Slide board	30 seconds work, 30 seconds rest
A4	Slide board	10 seconds work, 10 seconds rest
A5	Slide board	30 seconds work, 30 seconds rest
A6	Slide board	10 seconds work, 10 seconds rest
A7	Slide board	30 seconds work, 30 seconds rest
A8	Slide board	10 seconds work, 10 seconds rest
A9	Slide board	30 seconds work

NOTES: Complete this set as shown, take a 3 minute rest and repeat one or two more times. Make sure to use proper deep knee bend with all slide board training.

LT #3

A1	Slide board	30 seconds work, 45 seconds rest
A2	Kettlebell Swings	30 seconds work, 45 seconds rest
A3	Slide board	30 seconds work, 45 seconds rest
A4	Kettlebell Squat Pulls	30 seconds work, 45 seconds rest
A5	Slide board	30 seconds work, 45 seconds rest
A6	Kettlebell Swings	30 seconds work, 45 seconds rest
A7	Slide board	30 seconds work, 45 seconds rest
A8	Kettlebell Squat Pulls	30 seconds work

NOTES: Complete this set as shown, take a 3 minute rest and repeat one or two more times. During A2 and A4 use the right hand, and during A6 and A8 use the left hand.

LT #4

A1	Slide board	20 seconds work, 20 seconds rest
A2	Plyo-Push-ups	20 seconds work, 20 seconds rest
A3	Slide board	20 seconds work, 20 seconds rest
A4	Weighted Push-up Drags	20 seconds work, 20 seconds rest
A5	Slide board	20 seconds work, 20 seconds rest
A6	Hindu Squats	20 seconds work

NOTES: Complete this set as shown, take a 3 minute rest and repeat one or two more times. Make sure to use proper deep knee bend with all slide board training.

LT #5

A1	Slide board	45 seconds, 45 seconds rest
A2	Tornado Ball Hits	45 seconds, 45 seconds rest
A3	Burpees	45 seconds

NOTES: Rest 2 minutes between giant sets and continue for 4 to 9 more giant sets. Think of this workout like a hockey shift with a 1 to 1 work/rest ratio.

LT #6

A1 Russian Box jumps	10 seconds work, 20 seconds rest
A2 Russian Box jumps	15 seconds work, 30 seconds rest
A3 Russian Box jumps	20 seconds work, 40 seconds rest
A4 Russian Box jumps	25 seconds work, 50 seconds rest
A5 Russian Box jumps	30 seconds work

NOTES: Complete all A1-A5 sets and then take a 2 minute rest. Repeat this workout 2 to 4 more times. This workout maintains a 1 to 2 work/rest interval so players should be able to recover with the added rest interval provided. Use this workout at the beginning of the summer when conditioning levels may be low (right after your break from the end of the season).

LT #7

A1 Russian Box jumps	20 seconds work, 40 seconds rest
A2 Russian Box jumps	10 seconds work, 20 seconds rest
A3 Russian Box jumps	20 seconds work, 40 seconds rest
A4 Russian Box jumps	10 seconds work, 20 seconds rest
A5 Russian Box jumps	20 seconds work, 40 seconds rest
A6 Russian Box jumps	10 seconds work, 20 seconds rest
A7 Russian Box jumps	20 seconds work, 40 seconds rest
A8 Russian Box jumps	10 seconds work, 20 seconds rest
A9 Russian Box jumps	20 seconds work, 40 seconds rest
A10 Russian Box jumps	10 seconds work

NOTES: Complete all A1-A10 sets and then take a 5 minute rest. Repeat this workout 2 to 4 more times. This workout maintains a 1 to 2 work/rest interval..

LT #8

A1 Russian Box jumps	20 seconds work, 60 seconds rest
A2 Jump Lunges	10 seconds work, 20 seconds rest
A3 Burpees	20 seconds work, 30 seconds rest
A4 Repeated Hurdle Jumps	10 seconds work, 30 seconds rest
A5 Russian Box jumps	20 seconds work, 40 seconds rest
A6 Jump Lunges	10 seconds work, 10 seconds rest
A7 Burpees	20 seconds work, 40 seconds rest
A8 Repeated Hurdle Jumps	10 seconds work

NOTES: Complete all A1-A8 sets and then take a 4 minute rest. Repeat this workout 2 to 4 more times. This workout has a variable work and rest period to simulate the kind of uneven conditions that might be found during a typical hockey shift.

LT #9

A1 Russian Box jumps	30 seconds work, 60 seconds stickhandling
A2 Russian Box jumps	10 seconds work, 20 seconds stickhandling
A3 Russian Box jumps	15 seconds work, 30 seconds stickhandling
A4 Russian Box jumps	30 seconds work, 60 seconds stickhandling
A5 Russian Box jumps	20 seconds work, 40 seconds stickhandling
A6 Russian Box jumps	5 seconds work, 10 seconds stickhandling
A7 Russian Box jumps	20 seconds work, 40 seconds stickhandling
A8 Russian Box jumps	10 seconds work, 20 seconds stickhandling

NOTES: This is another Russian Box drill with variable work periods and "rest" periods. During the work portion of this drill hold a hockey stick for the jumps, and then for the "rest" portion have a Smart hockey ball or puck handy to start stickhandling during this rest break. When the rest break is finished, jump back on the Russian Box and continue with the jumps. Complete 2 to 4 more times.

LT #10

A1	Russian Box jumps	20 seconds work
A2	Frog Squat Jumps	20 seconds work
A3	Russian Box jumps	20 seconds work
A4	Jump Lunges	20 seconds work
A5	Russian Box jumps	20 seconds work
A6	Hindu Squats	20 seconds work

NOTES: This workout is a 2-minute leg killer. Perform all A1-A6 sets without a rest break; just move from exercise to exercise quickly. When finished try not to puke. Rest for 4 minutes (1:2 work/rest ratio), and repeat this again 2 to 4 more times.

Kettlebell Based Workouts

In the kettlebell workouts presented below you will perform one entire set of each exercise, followed by the next set, until you are finished. With all of these workouts you never rest until all the exercises in the giant set are finished.

KB #1

A1 1-Arm Clean & Jerk
A2 1-Arm Overhead Squat, hold the kettlebell overhead to squat
A3 Jerk again

NOTES: Once this set is done switch hands and perform a set on the other side. You would do one of each of these exercises, and then repeat for 5 to 25 full sets of these three exercises (on each hand), depending on your fitness level.

KB #2

Start with 10-kettlebell clean and jerks on each hand, and then follow that up with a 200-meter run as fast as possible (run down your street or around the block). Once you are done with the run take a 60-second rest. Repeat this cycle until the run speed is not fast anymore or you cannot complete the 10 kettlebell clean & jerk repetitions on each hand

KB #3

A1	2-Handed Kettlebell Swings	30 repetitions
A2	Hindu Squats	10 repetitions
A3	2-Handed Kettlebell Swings	25 repetitions
A4	Hindu Squats	15 repetitions
A5	2-Handed Kettlebell Swings	20 repetitions
A6	Hindu Squats	20 repetitions
A7	2-Handed Kettlebell Swings	15 repetitions
A8	Hindu Squats	25 repetitions
A9	2-Handed Kettlebell Swings	10 repetitions
A10	Hindu Squats	30 repetitions

NOTES: Perform this whole set of exercises without resting. At the end of the A10 exercise you can rest for 3 to 5 minutes and then repeat this giant set of exercises. Try timing yourself to see how long it takes you to complete the entire set, and then try to beat that time. If done right this will kill your quads.

KB #4

Set a watch or timer to count down from 60 seconds, and then repeat. Take a kettlebell and perform a set of 5 snatches with each arm, then put the kettlebell down. Wait for the watch to beep (which signals that 60-seconds are up), and then perform another 5 kettlebell snatches with each arm, then put the kettlebell down. Repeat this drill until you cannot complete the 5 snatches per arm in the 60 seconds.

KB #5

A1 One Arm Snatches	10 repetitions/arm
A2 One Arm Clean & Jerks	10 repetitions/arm
A3 One Arm Squat Pulls	10 repetitions/arm
A4 Two Arm Swings	20 repetitions total

NOTES: Move from one exercise to the next with no breaks. When you are done you can repeat this 2 more times for a total of 3 sets. Make sure to use a weight that is difficult to finish this workout (a 35lbs kettlebell will be plenty for most players at first). As you get into better shape keep the repetitions the same but add weight (to the 53lb kettlebell or 72lb kettlebell, or dumbbell).

KB #6

A1 Kettlebell Squat Pulls	20 reps (put your feet out into an Eagle Squat type stance)
A2 One Arm-Rows	15reps/side as fast as possible
A3 Plate Drags	20 reps/side
A4 Hockey Lunges	15 reps/side (holding Kettlebell)
A5 Kettlebell Windmills	10 reps/side

NOTES: This is another timed workout. Complete this giant set of A1 to A4 a total of 5 times without rest. Vomit when finished. If this is not that challenging, then you can up the weight you use during the sets and also add sets to the overall. I only want this workout to last 40 minutes or less.

KB #7

A1 Kettlebell 1-Arm Swings	10 reps/side
A2 Kettlebell Side Abdominals	10 reps/side
A3 Kettlebell 1-Arm Squat Pulls	10 reps/side
A4 Kettlebell Squats	20 reps
A5 Kettlebell 1-Arm Snatches	10 reps/side

NOTES: Do not put the weight down during this entire set, keep moving from exercise to exercise. At the end you can take a 3 minute break and then repeat this 1 to 4 times more.

KB #8

A1 1-Arm Snatches	8 reps/arm
A2 1-Arm Jerks	8 reps/arm
A3 1-Arm Squat Pulls	8 reps/arm
A4 1-Arm Swings	8 reps/arm
A5 1-Arm Cleans	8 reps/arm

NOTES: With this workout you will perform all of the sets (A1 through A5) on one arm, and then after you take a 1 minute rest you will perform all of the sets on the other arm. Take a 3 minute rest and repeat the whole giant set 2 more times (3 total).

KB #9

A1 30 Swings (15 reps per side)
A2 25 Burpees
A3 50 Russian Box Jumps
A4 20 Heavy Rock (or D-Ball) Slams.
A5 20 Box Jumps

NOTES: Complete this workout two more times, (3 total). Time the total workout (and record it in a journal) and try to beat this every time you do this workout. Find a heavy rock or D-ball that is at least 50lbs for this workout.

KB #10 "The Death Mile"

This is a conditioning killer…if you can do this; it will help you with your conditioning. With this circuit you measure out 528 feet at your local park, track or open field (this distance is 1/10th of a mile). Once you have the 528 feet measured out you will perform the following:

- A1 Run 528 feet holding the kettlebell with left hand, then;
- A2 Perform 15 kettlebells Swings per hand, then;
- A3 Run 528 feet holding the kettlebell with right hand, then
- A4 Perform 50 sit-ups and as many push-ups as possible, then;
- A5 Run 528 feet holding the kettlebell with both hands, then;
- A6 Perform 15 kettlebell squat pulls per hand, then;
- A7 Run 528 feet holding the kettlebell overhead with both hands, then;
- A8 Perform 50 squats with the kettlebell, then:
- A9 Run 528 feet holding the kettlebell with both hands behind your back, then;
- A10 Perform 25, 2-Handed kettlebell Swings, then;
- A11 Run 528 feet backwards, holding the kettlebell with both hands, then;
- A12 Perform 15 kettlebell jerks per side, then;
- A13 Travel 528 feet by repeatedly throwing the kettlebell, and running to pick it up, then;
- A14 Perform 15 kettlebell snatches per arm, then;
- A15 Run 528 feet forwards holding kettlebell behind your back, then;
- A16 Perform 50 sit-ups and as many push-ups as possible, then;
- A17 Run 528 feet holding the kettlebell overhead with both hands, then;
- A18 Perform 25, 2-Handed squat pulls, then
- A19 Sprint 528 feet without the kettlebell as fast as possible…
- A20 YOUR DONE…TRY TO KEEP YOUR LUNCH DOWN

NOTES: This is extreme conditioning at its finest. It's only 1 mile…but it will kick your ass if done right. I would strongly suggest you start with a light kettlebell (18lbs to 35lbs) as it gets heavy very quickly. If you can do this entire "Death Mile" twice, then you must be in world class shape or using a kettlebell that is way too small for your abilities… either one!

Strongman Workouts

Strongman workouts are the type of activities you expect to see on the TV show World's Strongest Man. These workouts are a lot of fun but physically demanding as well as mentally taxing. Many times a heavy object such as a large tractor tire, water filled keg, sledgehammer or heavy rock are used as the load that the player must use, move, throw or hit.

SW #1

• Car pushing (forwards)	60 seconds
• Rest 60 seconds	
• 2-handed Kettlebell swings (use a heavy kettlebell)	25 swings
• Rest 30 seconds	
• Car pushing (put your back against the car and push backwards)	60 seconds
• Rest 60 seconds	
• Frog Squat Jumps	25 repetitions

NOTES: Finish this set, rest 3 minutes and then repeat it 4 more times for a total of 5 sets.

SW #2

A1 Heavy Tire Flipping	10 flips
A2 Tire Jumps	6 complete circuits*
A1 Sledgehammer Hits (standing)	20 repetitions/side

NOTES: With tire jumps you will jump from outside the tire to inside the tire, then jump from inside the tire to the other side of the tire. You will repeat this going back and forth until you have completed 6 sets of these jumps. Repeat this entire circuit a total of 5 times, resting 2 minutes between giant sets.

SW #3

A1 Keg Shouldering (heavy keg)	3 repetitions/side
A2 Sledgehammer Hits (on knees)	20 repetitions/side
A3 Sandbag Shouldering	5 repetitions/side

NOTES: Complete this set, take 2 minutes rest, and repeat. Do a total of 2-5 total sets. This is a relatively simple combination of exercises, but it will kick your ass!

SW #4

A1 Sledgehammer Side Hits	20 repetitions/side
A2 Tornado Ball Slams	60 seconds
A3 Medicine Ball Underhand Throws	20 throws
A4 Battling Ropes	60 seconds
A5 Keg Twists	60 seconds

NOTES: Perform this workout outside with all of the equipment set up prior to the start. Make sure to hit the sledgehammer onto a tire to prevent injury to your wrists. Do a total of 2 to 5 sets, with 3 minutes rest in between.

SW #5

A1 Keg Shouldering	5 repetitions/shoulder
A2 Shovelling	30 seconds/side
A3 Tire Flipping	60 seconds
A4 Sled Pushing	60 seconds
A5 Farmers Walk	As long as possible (use heavy dumbbells)

NOTES: Perform this workout outside with all of the equipment set up prior to the start. Do a total of 2 to 5 sets, with 3 minutes rest in between. On the farmers walk exercise use heavy dumbbells and carry them for as long as possible (until they almost fall out of your hands).

SW #6

A1 Tire Flips	10 flips
A2 Kettlebell Snatches	15 repetitions/side
A3 Weighted Push-up Drags	45 seconds
A4 Keg Deadlifts	5 repetitions
A5 Wheelbarrow Running	50 meters out, 50 meters back

NOTES: Perform this workout outside with all of the equipment set up prior to the start. Do a total of 2 to 5 sets, with 3 minutes rest in between. Load the wheelbarrow with cement bags, sand bags, weight plates, dumbbells or kettlebells so the load is around 150-200lbs.

SW #7

A1 Sandbag Shouldering & Squat	5 repetitions/side
A2 Sledgehammer Hits (kneeling)	15 repetitions/side
A3 Tire Rotation Throws	10 throws/side
A4 Battling Ropes	60 seconds
A5 Plyometric Push-ups	Maximum Repetitions

NOTES: Perform this workout outside with all of the equipment set up prior to the start. Do a total of 2 to 5 sets, with 3 minutes rest in between.

SW #8

A1 Keg Shouldering	3 repetitions/side
A2 Sled Pushing	50 feet
A3 Battling Ropes	45 seconds

NOTES: Perform this workout outside with all of the equipment set up prior to the start. Do a total of 2 to 5 sets, with 3 minutes rest in between. With this exercise load up the keg and sled with as much weight as you can manage for the repetitions required…and use a good sized rope for the battling ropes exercise.

SW #9

A1 Heavy Rock Throws	10 repetitions
A2 Kettlebell Swings	10 repetitions/side
A3 Sledgehammer Side Hits	15 repetitions/side
A4 Tire Rotational Throws	10 repetitions/side
A5 Car Pushing	60 seconds

NOTES: Perform this workout outside with all of the equipment set up prior to the start. Do a total of 2 to 5 sets, with 3 minutes rest in between.

SW #10

A1 Backwards Car Pushing	30 seconds
A2 Sandbag Squats (hold sandbag over shoulder)	30 seconds
A3 Sled Pushing	30 seconds
A4 Hindu Squats	30 seconds
A5 Heavy Tire Flips	60 seconds

NOTES: Perform this workout outside with all of the equipment set up prior to the start. Do a total of 2 to 5 sets, with 3 minutes rest in between. This will kill your legs and make your lungs scream for air...enjoy this one!

Running Workouts

Most of the interval workouts I like hockey players to do involve running drills as it is a ground based activity that won't kill your skating stride. Running based workouts are also a great way to condition the legs for acceleration/deceleration, change of direction, sprinting, explosive power and general conditioning. With all of these intervals I want the "hard" cycles to be as fast and as difficult as possible, and the "easy" cycles to be very easy or sitting on the ground if necessary.

RW #1

A1 12' Lateral Agility Drill
A2 Rest 1 minute
A3 3-Cone Agility Drill
A4 Rest 1 minute
A5 10-Repeated Hurdle Jumps
A6 Rest 1 minute
A7 25 Frog Squat Jumps
A8 Jump rope (60 seconds)
A9 Push-ups (as many as possible in 60 seconds)

NOTES: This conditioning drill works all aspects of hockey from lateral agility, sprinting speed, acceleration/deceleration, explosive jumping, cardiovascular conditioning and upper body endurance. Take a 3 minute break when finished and repeat 2 to 4 more times (3 to 5 total sets).

RW #2

A1 30 seconds of running
A2 10 frog squat jumps
A3 30 seconds of running
A4 10 push-ups
A5 30 seconds of running
A6 10 jump lunges/side
A7 30 seconds of running
A8 10 burpees
A9 30 seconds of running
A10 10 sit-ups

NOTES: Complete this workout a total of 3 to 5 times, with a 3 to 5 minute rest between sets. Make sure the running portion of this drill is done as quickly as possible and no rest is taken during the entire set.

RW #3
A1 Forward Backward Sprint Drill
A2 60 seconds rest
A3 5-Line Drill
A4 60 seconds rest
A5 Stop/Start Drill
A6 60 seconds rest
A7 Random 3-Cone Drill
A8 60 seconds rest
A9 60 meter straight sprint

RW #4
A1 200 meter sprint
A2 30 seconds rest
A3 3-Cone Drill
A4 30 seconds rest
A5 20 Frog Squat Jumps
A6 30 seconds rest
A7 Forward/Backward Sprint Drill

NOTES: This workout has lots of sprinting, acceleration, deceleration, and change of direction. The rest interval in between the drills allows a partial recovery before the next drill is attempted. Try to run through each drill as quickly as possible. Repeat 3 to 5 times with a 5 minute rest in between giant sets.

RW #5
A1 50 meter sprint
A2 Stair running (30 seconds)
A3 Burpees
A4 200 meter sprint
A5 Frog Squat Jumps

NOTES: This is a short but killer workout. If you run through the 5 exercises without rest and at full speed your legs and lungs will burn like nothing else. Take a 3 to 5 minute break between giant sets. Time yourself and see how long it takes you to complete each set of this workout.

RW #6 - Interval Runs – 10 repetitions of 200 meters.
After a good warm-up (light jogging and stretching) perform 1 – 200 meter run and then follow that up with 200 meters of slow walking. When you finish the 200 meters of walking run another 200 meters. Repeat this run/walk combination a total of 8 to 15 times. Make sure the runs are as fast as you can go for that distance and the walks in between are very slow to give you the maximum amount of time to recover.

RW #7 - Running Ladders
The running ladder is an interval based workout done on the track. After a good warm-up you will run hard (not sprinting, but close) for a period of time and rest for an equal amount of time (walking or standing in place). The following is the interval times:

-30 seconds hard, 30 seconds rest
-45 seconds hard, 45 seconds rest
-60 seconds hard, 60 seconds rest
-75 seconds hard, 75 seconds rest
-90 seconds hard, 90 seconds rest
-75 seconds hard, 75 seconds rest
-60 seconds hard, 60 seconds rest
-45 seconds hard, 30 seconds rest
-30 seconds hard, 30 seconds rest

NOTES: At the end of the first ladder take 5 minutes rest. Repeat this ladder 1 to 3 more times depending on your level of conditioning. When your "hard" effort becomes a jog rather than a run, your interval workout is over. Cool-down and go home.

RW #8 - Trail, sand or hill Running Intervals

This running workout can be done on any type trail, on the sand at the beach or over a grass hill at the local park. It is based on time rather than distance. I want maximal effort (not sprinting, but run hard) for 30 seconds, followed by 30 seconds rest (sitting down). Repeat this 15 to 30 times, depending on your conditioning. This is the same type of work you perform during a game, with a shorter rest period to help improve your game recovery. By the end of the season you should be recovering very quickly from hockey shifts (which leads to better performance on the ice). As your conditioning improves I increase the amount of time running that a player does from 30 seconds up to a maximum of 45 seconds (always with an equal amount of rest). Please note that with this drill you will want to give up around 8 to 12 sets of time...but hang in there and keep going until you physically cannot perform another set.

RW #9 - Hill/Stair Repeats

Find a local hill or set of stairs that will take you at least 45 seconds to sprint to the top. After a good warm-up of light jogging, jumps, hops, easy stretching run 2 sets of hills/stairs at 80-90% of your maximum speed as a specific warm-up. Now you can begin your work sets of between 5 to 15 hill/stair sprints. If it takes you 45 seconds to sprint up, then walking down will double that time so the work to rest ratio is 1:2 (or close to what a typical hockey shift might look like). Repeat hill sprints for between 15 and 25 total sets (start off slowly and progress). The goal is to sprint as fast as possible but when your speed (and run times to the top) starts to really slow down then cool-down, stretch and go home.

RW #10 - Interval Runs – 400 meter repeats

Go to your local high school 400 meter track (they are all the same distance). Perform your standard warm-up of light running, squats, burpees, jumps, lunges, etc., for 10 full minutes until your muscles are totally warmed up. At this point I want you to take your watch out (to time yourself) and run 1 lap of the track as quickly as possible. Whatever time you finish in is the amount of time you will rest before you run another lap as fast as possible (you will need to reset your watch in between laps).

So, if you first lap you ran the 400 meters in 65 seconds you will get 65 seconds of rest. On the next lap if you run the 400 meters in 73 seconds you get 73 seconds of rest. Repeat this until your 400 meter time hits 90 seconds, because at this point you are not running fast anymore. Cool down with some light exercise and stretching, and go home.

Circuit Based Workouts

I like to put players through short but intense circuit workouts which combine a number of exercises put together to develop conditioning. These will not follow the typical dryland training rules with regard to rest intervals. Basically I want athletes to do these workout circuits as quickly as possible (without rest if possible). If you don't puke or die you can always do 2-sets of circuit, and 3 to 4 total sets if you're in really good shape.

Circuit #1

A1	Repeated Standing Long Jump	10 repetitions total
A2	Eagle Squats	20 repetitions total
A3	Plyometric Push-ups	Max repetitions total
A4	Agility Ladder Drill	30 repetitions total
A5	Frog Squat Jumps	15 repetitions total

NOTES: Complete 3 times total. Rest 3 minutes between giant sets.

Circuit #2

A1	Box Jumps	10 repetitions total
A1	Russian Box Jumps	50 repetitions total
A3	Frog Squat Jumps	20 repetitions total
A2	1-Leg Line Hops	20 repetitions/leg
A4	Hockey Lunges	15 repetitions/leg

NOTES: Complete 3 times total. Rest 3 minutes between giant sets. To complete box jumps find a tall box (24 inches to 40 inches) and jump up onto the box, step down and repeat.

Circuit #4

- 30 KB Swings (15 reps per side)
- 25 Burpees
- 50 Russian Box Jumps
- 30 Medicine Ball Forward Throws (with a 7kg ball)
- 200 Mountain Climbers

NOTES: Complete this workout three times. Time the total workout (record in a logbook at try to beat this time in future workouts). Use challenging weights and rest 5-minutes between giant sets.

Circuit #5

- 40 1-Arm KB Squat Pulls (20 reps per side)
- Jumping rope (200 jumps)
- 40 Push-ups
- 50 Sit-ups
- 100 Jumping Jacks

NOTES: Complete this workout three times. Time the total workout (record in a logbook at try to beat this time in future workouts). Use challenging weights and rest 5-minutes between giant sets.

Circuit #6

• Russian Box Jumps	40 reps total
• Burpees	25 reps
• Sit-ups	25 reps
• Jump Lunges	24 reps total
• Mountain Climbers	50 reps
• Frog Squat Jumps	20 reps
• Plyometric Push-ups	15 reps
• Lying on back, to standing, to lying (as fast as possible)	10 reps
• Pistols	10 reps/side

NOTES: Complete this workout three times in total. Rest 5-minutes between giant sets.

Circuit #7

This is the card workout. Basically you get a deck of cards, shuffle them up and then turn one over at a time. With each card there is a set exercise for each suit and the number on the card represents the number of repetitions. For instance a 5 of clubs would indicate 5 reps of frog squat jumps. The suit and numbers are as follows;

- Hearts = Burpees
- Diamonds = Pushups
- Clubs = Frog Squat Jumps
- Spades = Sit-ups (elbows over the knees on each repetition)
- Jokers = 60 seconds of tornado ball hits

2 = 2 reps	7 = 7 reps	Queen = 12 reps
3 = 3 reps	8 = 8 reps	King = 13 reps
4 = 4 reps	9 = 9 reps	Ace = 14 reps
5 = 5 reps	10 = 10 reps	Jokers = whatever time or reps you wish
6 = 6 reps	Jack = 11 reps	

NOTES: To complete this workout you go through the entire deck as fast as you can (keeping time of the workout). Stop the clock when you're done. If this is done correctly it should be finished in less than 40 minutes. Try to beat the last time each workout.

Circuit #8

A1 20-repetition Squats	20 reps
A2 Weighted Sit-ups	20 reps (anchor feet, add dumbbell)
A3 Plyometric Push-ups	Maximum repetitions
A4 One Arm Rows	15 repetitions/arm
A5 Pistols	Maximum repetitions/leg

NOTES: Complete entire set 3 to 5 times depending on your level. Rest 3 minutes between giant sets.

Circuit #9

A1 Eagle Squats	25 reps (with moderate kettlebell)
A2 Plate Drags	15 reps/leg
A3 Sit-ups	50 reps (anchor your feet)
A4 Hockey Lunges	15reps/leg
A5 Wide Mountain Climbers	50 repetitions

NOTES: Complete 3 times total. Rest 3 minutes between giant sets.

Circuit #10

A1 KB Snatches	10 reps/arm
A2 Tornado Ball Hits	Maximum repetitions/side
A3 Pistols	Maximum repetitions/leg
A4 Water Twists	45 seconds (turn back and forth)
A5 Burpees	25 repetitions

NOTES: Complete 3 times total. Rest 3 minutes between giant sets.

Bike Workouts

The best bikes to use for these following workouts are spin bikes that have a resistance knob that can be turned easily (to increase or decrease tension), like a Monark or a Schwinn. A normal computer type exercise bike will not be very effective for these workouts as it is too hard to change the tension quickly. Enjoy these bike workouts.

BW#1

This workout is on the exercise bike (one of only two bike workouts I allow my athletes, and only in the off-season). Basically you find a stationary bike and after a 5 minute warm-up pedal as fast as hard as possible for 30 seconds followed by 30 seconds rest. Repeat this for 20 to 30 minutes, and then cool-down. Make sure the tension is high enough during the "hard" 30 seconds to make it tough to complete and keep your RPM's (Revolutions Per Minute) of the pedals higher than 90 per minute. If you do this properly your quads will be screaming by the end of the workout and you will be pouring sweat...so bring a towel and some water.

BW #2

A1 Bike	30 seconds work, 30 seconds rest
A2 Bike	10 seconds work, 10 seconds rest
A3 Bike	45 seconds work, 45 seconds rest
A4 Bike	5 seconds work, 5 seconds rest
A5 Bike	15 seconds work, 15 seconds rest
A6 Bike	60 seconds work, 30 seconds rest
A7 Bike	20 seconds work, 10 seconds rest
A8 Bike	10 seconds work, 5 seconds rest
A9 Bike	30 seconds work, 15 seconds rest
A10 Bike	15 seconds work

NOTES: This is a variable work, variable rest program that puts most players into the "red zone" quickly. Make sure the work periods are done at maximal effort (big gear and high RPM), and the rest is with a minimal effort (low gear, 70+ RPM).

BW#3

This is a good conditioning workout for hockey players who want to not only develop strong and powerful quads, but become an anaerobic animal as well. Try this:

- 50 to 100 repetitions of Hindu Squats
- 2 Minutes hard riding on a stationary bike (with the intensity levels cranked up high)

Now repeat this set of two exercises (the Hindu squats and the 2 minutes on the bike) for 3 to 10 sets. Do not take a break between exercises, just move back and forth until you do all of the sets you have planned. With the Hindu squats you can add weight (by holding a dumbbell or with a weight vest) when 100 reps become easy (which it won't). On the bike make sure your RPM's (revolutions per minute) are kept high (90 RPM to 110 RPM). This will make you work like a dog and it reduces most hockey players to a big sweaty mess!

Going into battle... the Banff Hockey Academy take the ice versus the Airdrie Thunder
in the Heritage Junior-B Hockey League

Chapter 28 - Warm-Ups & Cool-Downs

"The highest compliment that you can pay me
is to say that I work hard every day, that I never dog it"

~ Wayne Gretzky, Hall of fame NHL hockey player

Prior to any activity it is important to get the body prepared for the upcoming physical activity. A good warm-up is no longer just some stretching of the muscles before doing something, but rather it involves movement of all the muscles (especially the muscles to be worked) so you prevent injury and get the most out of the workout/practice.

Before Hockey Games or Practices

Before a game it is also important to warm-up as you never know what your previous level of recovery is and you may still be banged up from games, other practices or dryland workouts. About 30-minutes before you get out on the ice you should do a general warm-up with 5 minutes of running and some stairs at the rink or something easy. This should be followed up by a couple (5 to 10) short 30-yard sprints to get the legs used to the quick movements. Some other sprinting type drills such as grapevine, cross-over steps, backwards running, side shuffle steps, quick-feet, and line running will also be useful to prepare the body to move correctly on the ice.

If your team has a slide board this is the perfect time to do some side to side drills to get used to the skating action. For goaltenders I recommend they use a hacky-sack or soccer ball for several minutes to warm-up the hip flexors and hip rotators (this can be done with the other goaltenders on the team, or with a trainer or coach).

On-Ice Warm-ups (Games or Practices)

Warming up on the ice should still follow the dryland guidelines prior to putting on your gear for practice or a game. When a player gets on the ice the first part of the warm-up should be spent with basic skating to warm-up the sport specific muscles. Work the edges, perform C-cuts, pivots, skate backwards, stop & starts, and basic accelerations. After several minutes the warm-up with the team should start where two on one drills, shooting drills, passing drills, etc. help prepare the team and warm up the goaltenders. Near the end of the warm-up players should do several cross ice sprints and some stick-handing with the puck at speed.

Dryland Warm-ups

Prior to **ANY** workout (off-ice, on-ice) it is important to get the body warmed up for physical activity and gradually increase the range of motion of the muscles. Stretching should be used, but sparingly before workouts as the goal should be to increase body temperature with movement such as the hacky sack, light jogging, gradual sprints, explosive kettlebell work (such as swings, snatches or squat pulls). Start slowly and increase the intensity so you ideally end with an intensity that is similar to the upcoming workout. Below are two of the dryland warm-ups that I use with every athlete I train as they work most of the muscles and ensure a good level of activity before strenuous training.

Weight Room Warm-ups

If a workout is in the weight room complete the standard dryland warm-up and then make sure to use lighter weights for the exercises scheduled so that the specific area that is to be trained can get used to the action. For example if you plan to perform squats in the workout then start squatting with just the bar, then add 25lbs to each side for several reps, then take the 25's off and put on 45's for several reps...until you get close to your workout load. That way, when you start the actual work portion of the workout the joints, ligaments and muscles will be used to the heavy weights. Please note that you do not have to use a lighter warm-up for each exercise, but generally just the main exercise in the training session is enough to get the body used to the motion.

Dryland Warm-Up #1

1. Bird Dawgs   10-repetitions/side
2. Fire Hydrants   10-circles each way (forward & back), per leg
3. Dynamic Frog Squat   10-repetitions
4. ABC Cross-Over Drill   4-times each way (3-directions) = 12-total, per leg
5. Push-ups   Maximum repetitions
6. Leg Swings   10-repetitions/leg
7. Windshield Wipers   10-repetitions/leg
8. Jumping Jacks   50-repetitions

#1 Bird Dawgs

Julie completes a full range of motion for best results with this warm-up exercise

The superman exercise is a coordination, balance and stability exercise. You start balancing on one leg and the opposite hand (picture 1), with the knee and elbow of the non-balancing limbs touching. From this position extend both the non-weight bearing arm and leg so that your body creates an X shape (picture 2). Hold this position for 2-seconds and then return to the starting position.

#2 Fire Hydrants

Fire hydrants are a lower body mobility warm-up drill that works to improve the range of motion and strength of the hips. Simply kneel down on a mat with the hands in a push-up position and then rotate the leg in a large circle pattern. Try to make as large a circle as possible so that your hip goes through an extended range of motion. You can perform this exercise standing up (see picture), with an ankle weight or with a light band wrapped around the ankle for more resistance.

Alec warms up the hips using a fire hydrant mobility drill

#3 Dynamic Frog Squat

Squat down into a low squat and with the hands grab the back of the heals or reach back behind the heals as far as possible to really stretch the low back and hips. Hold this position for a couple of seconds and try to lower the butt down into a deep squat.   Release and stand back up, and then squat down again to repeat. Perform 10 of these.

Coach Pollitt warms up with the frog squat (left) to work the flexibility of the hips and low back to a high degree.

#4 ABC Cross-over drill

The ABC cross-over drill dynamically warms up the hamstrings, glutes, back, quads as well as developing balance and proprioception. Start by standing on one leg, and then touch in front of the body in three places (directly in front, to the left side and to the right side).

Professional hockey player Mykul Haun completes the ABC cross-over drill as part of the general warm-up before lifting.

#5 Push-ups
To perform this test players will start flat on the ground, face down with hands under them and with a flat, board like body push themselves up to lock out. Lower yourself down to the starting position without flexing or dipping the middle part of the body.

Start flat on the ground and push up to full extension... repeat

#6 Leg Swings

The leg swing is a dynamic warm-up of the hip flexors, hamstrings, quads, and core area. To start hold on to a fixed object, stand on one leg and swing the other leg (kept nearly straight) front to back and also in a diagonal front to back fashion. Repeatedly swinging the leg and trying to swing through an extended range of motion will dynamically warm-up the entire hip and legs.

Wesley dynamically warming up the hip and hamstrings with the leg swings

#7 Windshield Wipers

261

Lay on your back with one leg extended straight up and from this position rotate this one leg to each side of the body back and forth (see pictures). These dynamic stretches are done slowly so as not to put undue stress on the low back and spine.

#8 Jumping Jacks
Standard jumping jacks are a full body exercise that will help warm up the arms, legs and cardiovascular system all at the same time. In warm-ups I have players do several sets of 50-jumping jacks.

Dryland Warm-Up #2

1. One-Leg Squat & Reach	10-repetitions/leg
2. Scorpions	10-repetitions/leg
3. Lunge & Twist	10-repetitions/leg
4. Mountain Climbers	30-repetitions total
5. Arm Circles	10-repetitions each direction (forward and backwards)
6. Hindu Push-ups	10-repetitions total
7. Overhead Side Bends	10-repetitions/side
8. Burpees (no push-up version)	10-repetitions total

#1 One-Leg Squat & Reach

Bryce shows the one-leg squat and reach warm-up drill

Start by standing on one leg with the hands out in front of the body (picture 1). The goal is to squat as far down as possible and reach as far forward as you can (picture 2). Stand up and repeat for the required number on both sides.

#2 Scorpions
The purpose of the scorpions is to mobilize the glutes and low back to loosen up before activity. Stretch out on your stomach with the arms held to the sides and from this position try to curl the leg towards the opposite hand (as far as possible). As you can see in this picture Clint is not flexible in the low back and therefore he does not complete it as far as some athletes. Ideally the goal should be to touch a toe to the hand.

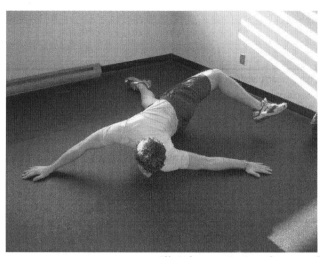
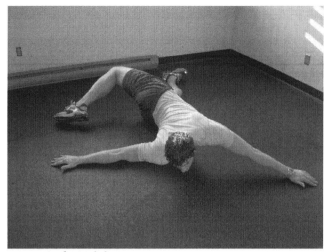

Clint demonstrates the scorpion as part of a training warm-up

#3 Lunge & Twist

For this warm-up I want players to start with hands on their head and lunge forward with the right leg. Bring the left elbow to the right knee by bending at the waist. Return to the starting position and then lunge out to the left side while you bring the right elbow to the left knee. Repeat this alternating right/left lunge for the required number on each leg.

The lunge & twist warm-up exercise

#4 Mountain Climbers

Start in the push-up position with one leg back and one leg up (picture 1). Hope with both legs at the same time and switch them at the same time (picture 2). This is a fast type action so don't drag these out. In the above example of mountain climbers, Kayla does these really quickly to get the blood moving and the muscles firing during warm-ups.

#5 Arm Circles
Arm circles are a basic movement to warm-up the shoulders, chest and upper back muscles. Try to swing the arms in as big of a circle as possible.

 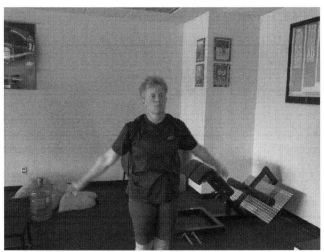

Goaltender Coach Carol Henson demonstrates air circles

#6 Hindu Push-Ups

Slow execution makes this a great warm-up exercise for the chest and shoulder area

Start in a push-up type position with you butt in the air and your upper body/arm in a straight line (figure 1). From this position descend on a angle towards your hands (figure 2), and then push up towards the end of the exercise (figure 3). To get back to the start slowly follow the SAME PATH back to the start.

#7 Overhead Side Bends
With the overhead abs exercise you extend your hands overhead, arms straight and then bend as far as possible from side to side. The goal is the range of motion with this exercise, not the speed of the action. Bend straight to the side without turning the body inward or twisting at all.

Moose Jaw Warriors (WHL) goaltender Brandon Stone moves from side to side while holding a stick overhead

#8 Burpees

From a standing position (picture 1) quickly squat down, kick the legs out so you are in the push-up position (picture 2). Quickly bring the legs into to the body (picture 3) and then jump up to the standing position (picture 4). Repeat for 10-repetitions. Burpees have been used in the military for the training of soldiers for many years as it is a very valuable conditioning exercise for warm-ups and overall training.

Cool-Downs

Following a workout, practice or game this is the time to gradually cool the body down following the activity (rather than hurrying to get out of the rink or gym). Light jogging, stationary cycling, slideboard training or even sled dragging for 5 to 20-minutes is a great way to cool down and help remove lactic acid from the body.

Following the active cool-down players should use a foam roll to help reduce muscle knots and tissue damage created by hard training. At the end of the cool-down players can use a process called Active Isolated Stretching (holding the stretch for 5-seconds and releasing, then repeating) to help keep the range of motion in the muscles. Stretching using the ideas presented in this chapter for the hip flexors, groin, hamstrings, quadriceps, glutes, shoulders, neck, chest, and triceps should be the focus of your stretching routine. Make sure not to stretch too far during this time as following activity the body is in recovery mode and muscles can be stretched too far if not careful.

It is often hard to find space to perform a gradual cool down in many rinks as the dressing rooms are often too small. If this is the case then teams should make arrangements to schedule a dynamic stretching & foam roll session at the hotel. You can find out more about foam roll techniques, active isolated stretching and therapy in our online videos.

Professional hockey player Kevin Flather lights the lamp...

266

Chapter 29 - Flexibility Training

Asked by reporters why he always represented Canada every time he was asked, his response was simple, "Because some day they won't ask."

~ Wayne Gretzky (Hall of fame NHL player)

Flexibility training is the practice of stretching the muscles in an attempt to elongate and improve ranges of motion of the muscles and in hockey related movements. If for example the hamstring muscles had limited mobility it would be very difficult (if not impossible) to get a full extension in the skating stride. Worse yet, if muscles are tight not only does this effect performance of skills, but leads to potential sites for injury and contact trauma due to limited range of motion. An example of this might be if a player gets hit while skating up ice stretching the hip flexor past a "good" range of motion into an area where injury could occur. With a good range of motion in the hips that player might be able to absorb the impact without getting hurt (as the hip would stretch but not enter into the "end point" of muscle). In severe cases, a player may stretch the muscles so far past the functional range of motion that muscles, tendons or ligaments tear away from their attachments and need surgery to be rehabilitated. If this occurs, there is now a chance that this area becomes a permanent point of injury as scar tissue and decreased range of motion now inhibits this muscle from moving in a healthy range of motion.

So, the bottom line is that as athletes we need to stretch. The problem is that most hockey players do NOT stretch nearly enough to make or sustain gains in muscle flexibility. Coaches further this problem by not insisting on stretching before and most importantly after practice. Players need to focus on stretching as much as anything else in hockey or gains in this area simply will not happen and the potential for injury greatly increases. I would say the most groin pulls in hockey (which makes up a large percent of all hockey related trauma), can be solved by flexible and strong groin muscles. Therefore it is CRITICAL to include stretching on a daily basis if you plan to make hockey your career.

The best times to stretch are before activity (very light stretching for 5-minutes or so) and especially after workouts/games/practices for 10 to 15 minutes. Throughout the day players should also stretch upon waking up (15-minutes) and before bed (15 minutes). If you are hanging around the house watching TV this is also a great time to spend stretching.

Stretching Suggestions

- Use a rope with all of your stretching as this will help add a pull on the limb being stretched.

- If possible find a partner and stretch with them. Certain stretches work best when you are being stretched out rather than stretching alone.

- Hold stretches for short periods of 5 to 8-seconds, release slightly, and then stretch again. Repeat this over and over rather than holding a long 20 to 30-second stretch.

- Push the stretch to a point that it is mildly uncomfortable, but not to the point of pain.

- Improving flexibility is a continual process rather than a quick fix. Get used to stretching on a regular basis several times per day for short 15-minute sessions. Think of what dogs and cats do when they move around the first thing they do is perform a mild stretch of the hips or legs...how many sprains or pulls do you ever see with these animals? None.

Hip Stretches

The hip is comprised of many muscles that support, protect and move the hip through a wide range of motion. If one area of the hip is particularly tight, it throws off the other three areas and can lead to potential sites of injury. The hip is not only made up of the four regions (front, back, inside and outside), but is affected by the hamstrings and quadriceps to a great degree. Therefore any stretching protocol for the hip must also include work on the hamstrings and quads. The following are my most used hip stretches:

Skaters Stretch

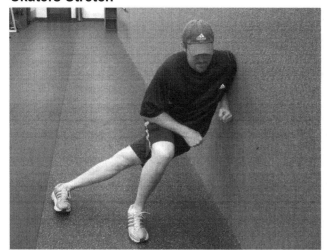

Hockey Coach Steve Phillips performs the skater stretch (picture 1), NHL Linesmen Ryan Galloway uses the skaters stretch in the hotel before and after games (picture 2)

In skating one of the areas that usually gets very little attention is the area on the outside of the leg (tensor fasciae latae and IT band). With most players this area is very tight and filled with muscle knots that pre-dispose them to potential injury. Stretching this area is important for hockey players to keep the range of motion of the hip. Ideally players should also use a foam roll on the outside of the leg to roll out muscle knots.

Hip Flexor/Groin Stretch

Wesley stretches both the hip flexor and groin with these two hockey specific stretches

The hip flexor and groin simply must have good flexibility for skaters. The length of the stride and the potential for contact that might stretch a leg to one side or another is a very real possibility in the sport of hockey. Ensuring that the hip flexor and groin are flexible will help reduce your potential for injuries to this area. Start off with one leg kneeling on an Airex pad and the other leg out in front (see picture). From this position bend the front leg and "sink" the hips downwards so that the hip flexor gets a good stretch. Hold the stretch for 3 to 5-seconds, rise up briefly, and then sink down again. Repeat this short stretch over and over for 10 to 20-repetitions on each leg.

Another variation of this stretch is a stretch with the front leg out to the side of the body so that the groin is stretched to a further degree. Position the front leg facing forward but out to the side and "sink down" into the stretch so that the hip flexor and the groin are stretched at the same time (see picture).

The third variation of this stretch involves sinking into the stretch and then pulling on the ankle of the back leg to stretch the quadriceps muscle. This stretch really hits three areas at once and is a must for players who want to get in a quick stretch after a workout or game.

Floor Hip Flexor Stretch

Done with an exaggerated range of motion the floor hip flexor stretch puts the back leg as far backwards as possible and a large step forward with the front leg. Sink down onto the front leg with hands on the ground to stretch the hip flexor, glutes and calf muscles.

Former WHL goaltender for the Calgary Hitmen and current Calgary Flames prospect Dan Spence stretches the hip flexors following a dryland conditioning workout in Langley, BC.

Hockey Groin Stretch

A variant of some of the other stretches, the hockey groin stretch is a floor based stretch that attempts to stretch the groin and hip in the same range that players use when skating. Start on one knee with the back knee and foot on the ground like a hurdlers stretch. Sink down and forward onto the front leg with the hands to the side for support. This should really be felt on the back leg (groin and hip flexor) and front leg (upper hamstring and calf).

This is a very valuable stretch for all players as it works a wide variety of hip and groin muscles.

Bench Glute Stretch

The bench glute stretch works to stretch the upper hamstrings, IT band, glutes, low back and hip flexors. Start off by sitting down on a bench with one leg curled up in front (see picture) and the other leg held back behind (see picture). Lower the upper body forward over the front leg to feel a good stretch in the glutes and low back. As with other stretches, hold for 3 to 5-seconds and then relax a little bit before repeating many times. Some people will find this stresses the inner part of the knee of the front leg, and for those folks I suggest you move the front leg a little more forward to take the pressure off the knee.

Lying Glute stretch

Lay back on a mat and cross one leg over the other at the knee. From this position reach between the legs and pull on the back leg so as to stretch your glute muscles. Repeat on both sides for several sets for optimal results.

Wesley stretching post workout at Revolution Athletics in Southern California.

Floor Glute Stretch

Much like the bench glute stretch this movement is a more advanced stretch for players who have a wide range of motion in the hips and want to also target the hip flexors of the back leg. Notice in the picture the range of motion that Ryan gets in the hip flexors with this stretch.

Ryan always stretches the hip flexors and glutes with a variety of stretches, including the floor glute stretch in preparation for NHL games.

Side Lunge Stretch

Hockey players need to stretch the inner thigh adductors in a standing position that mimics the side requirements of the goaltender movements and the skating stride. The side lunge stretch shown in the picture helps to improve the flexibility of the adductor leg muscles and the glutes of the opposite leg. Players should look to drop as deeply into the lunge as possible to really develop good range of motion in the hip. This exercise can also be done with the leg being stretched up on a bench or small box so it hits a slightly different angle.

Bulgarian Split Squat Stretch

Similar to the Bulgarian Split Squat exercise, this stretch has the player put the back leg on a high bench or platform (3-feet from the floor is optimal). From this position the player does a single leg squat with the front leg to pull the back legs hip flexor into a good stretch. The further down the player goes while holding the upper body vertical the more the hip flexor stretches on the back leg.

Wall Groin Stretch/Splits

This is the ultimate TV watching stretch as players can move from the first groin stretch into the splits stretch many times without much effort. As the player uses gravity to help stretch the groin it is one of the easier stretches to start off with and master. Make sure to put your butt right against the wall and keep the back flat during these stretches to maximize effectiveness.

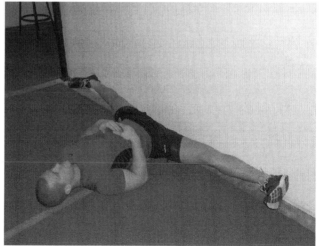

The wall groin stretch into the split stretch is an awesome and relaxing stretch

Babe-Watchers

Nicknamed the "babe-watchers" by junior hockey player John Accardo, this stretch works the glutes, side of the hip and all the rotational muscles of the core. Sit down with the legs straight out in front and then cross one of the legs over the other so the foot of the crossing leg is at the knee of the straight leg. From this position turn the core area so the elbow on the opposite side as the crossed leg touches the leg and you essentially look like you are turning around to look at something.

Julie finds that the babe-watcher stretch really helps the flexibility in her low back and hip.

Frog Squat Stretch

Squatting down and holding onto the back portion of the ankles is a good stretch for most players as they tend to be tight in the hips. This also is a good method to show players the right depth they should try to achieve in the barbell squats exercise.

Coach Pollitt demonstrates the frog squat stretch in the picture as he prepares for an Olympic lifting training session.

Lying Groin Stretch

To complete the lying groin stretch simply lie down, cross one leg over the other and gently push down with the hand to stretch the groin (above picture). If this stretch is easy to perform then move to a flat bench or the side of the bed to allow the leg to be stretched further.

Moose Jaw Warriors (WHL) goaltender Brandon Stone stretching the groin/hip before dryland conditioning.

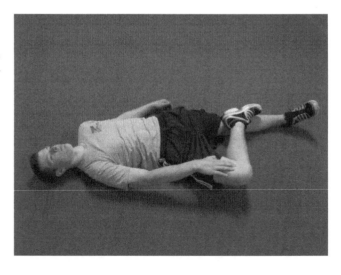

Hip Internal Rotator Stretch

Most hip stretches focus on the external rotators of the hip, but it is important to stretch the smaller internal rotation muscles of the hip. Lying on your back bring one leg up into a bent position. Take the other leg (the one that's to be stretched), up to the chest. Put a band around the foot and from the outside of the leg pull towards the head (see picture below).

Hamstring Stretches

Hamstring rope stretch

Stretching the hamstrings is a key area that all hockey players should focus their attention. The problem is that for years everyone has been taught to flop a leg down on a box or touch their toes to stretch the hamstrings. The new methods of stretching the hamstring muscles is to lie down, bend one leg and hold the other leg straight with a rope or band around the foot. Contract the hip flexor of the leg being stretched and gently pull with the rope. Hold for 3-seconds, release slightly, and then hold for another 3-seconds. Keep repeating this gentle 3-second pull of the straight leg for 15 to 30-total repetitions on both sides.

Standing Hamstring Stretches

Julie stretches the hamstring with leg straight (picture 1), and legs slightly bent (picture 2)

Standing hamstring stretches are a key hamstring stretch that can be done anywhere and as often as possible. Start by keeping your hips closed (simply stand facing a bench and lift a leg up to the bench). Keep the leg straight, toes pointed upward and bend at the waist to stretch the hamstring (picture 1). For a different stretch of the hamstring bend the leg slightly and try to bring the upper body down to the leg (picture 2).

Hurdlers Stretch

The hurdlers stretch is performed by siding down on the floor with one leg straight and the other leg put out to the side with the foot behind you (see picture above). From this position bend forward and with the hands stretch towards the foot on the straight leg. The goal is to get as far towards that straight leg as possible.

Sitting Splits Stretch

With the sitting splits stretch, the idea is to place the legs as far to the sides as possible and then reach from side to side, and then in front to stretch the groin/hamstrings. Dan has pretty solid flexibility in this area as he is a pro goalie, but all players should work towards this type of flexibility.

Double Leg Band Hamstring Stretch

With the double-leg band hamstring stretch I have players wrap a band, towel or rope around the bottom of the feet so they can gently pull their upper body down towards the legs as they stretch the hamstrings in a seated position. Make sure to stretch both with the legs kept straight and then slightly bent so the hamstrings and low back get a good quality stretch. The band/rope/towel is meant to aid in the stretch, not be the source of the stretch by pulling hard on it to bring the upper body down. Ideally you would want to put your chest onto your legs while keeping the knees locked out straight. In this photo Brandon uses a Superband to get a better range of motion.

Quad Stretches

Standing & Lying Quad Stretch

Junior-B player Bryce Nielsen using a traditional quad stretch (picture 1), and a lying quad stretch (picture 2)

This basic exercise is a solid stretch for the quads as you stand on one leg and lift the other leg up by flexing your hamstring muscles. Hold the flexed leg with the same side hand and gently pull upward while keeping the hips straight (picture 1). This stretch can also be performed lying down (picture 2). Try this stretch after using the foam roll (consult the recovery methods chapter), as this provides a deeper stretch and more recovery. In fact the best way to do this is to stretch for 20 to 30 seconds, then foam roll the same area, then stretch again. Repeat until all muscle trauma/knots/tightness is greatly reduced.

Kneeing Quad Stretch

The one-knee quad stretch is a good stretch for the hips and calf muscles as well as a solid stretch for the quad. Bend down on one knee (in a lunge type position), get up on the toes of the leg on the floor and reach back to pull upwards on the other foot to stretch the quad (see picture above).

Calf Stretches

1-Leg Calf Stretching
Stretching the calf muscles (the gastrocnemius and the soleus) should be done regularly by hockey players as this will keep the range of motion in the ankle. Make sure to stretch with the leg straight and leg bent (as with a skating stride) so that the ankle is forced to move in all ranges of motion. If possible, stretch one leg at a time so you can concentrate a proper stretch.

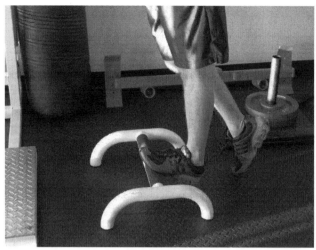 

Stretching the calf should be done with a straight leg (picture 1) and bent knee (picture 2)

Band Ankle Stretching

To stretch the ankle side to side, and even forwards to backwards it is best to take a superband or towel to wrap around the ankle to gently stretch this area. The more the ankle gets used to bending side to side, and up and down the more flexibility and strength a goaltender will have in their ankles.

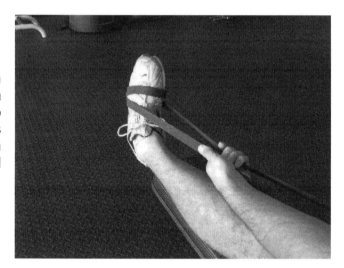

Back Stretches

Lat Stretch

The muscles of the back must also be stretched by holding on to a fixed object, setting the feet away from the hands and then leaning backwards to get a good pull in the posterior should and mid-back. Hold this stretch for several seconds, move around slightly and even change the hand position so that the muscles are pulled differently.

Hanging Back Stretch

This simple back stretch is primarily for the lats in a vertical direction. Hold on to an overhead bar or overhang and raise your feet off the ground so you hang. This will not only stretch muscles in the back (if you relax the upper body muscles), but it will help to build strong gripping muscles as well.

In this picture, William hangs from the squat rack to perform a hanging back stretch.

Chest Stretches

Chest Stretch

Julie hold a straight arm (picture 1), and a bent arm (picture 2), while she rotates away from her arm

The most common type of stretch for the chest is the standard chest stretch. Holding a solid object (such as a wall, pillar, edge of a squat rack, etc.) extend the arm and turn away from the arm as you use leverage to stretch the chest and shoulder area (see picture 1). To add a different element of stretching, bend the arm slightly so that the chest gets a greater stretch without the biceps being stretched as well. Make sure to change the arm angle from time to time (either higher up or lower down) so you stretch from a variety of angles.

Stick Chest Stretch

Stretching out the chest and shoulder areas before workouts, practices and games is very important for range of motion and injury prevention. Start by holding a stick with a wider than shoulder width grip (palms facing downward) and then pull the arms backwards, over the head and facing backwards with the arms straight, while still holding the stick (see picture). Hold this stretch for a few seconds, move the stick around slightly to get a dynamic stretch and then bring the stick back over the head.

Repeat this stretch 5 to 10-times to warm-up and increase the range of motion throughout the chest and shoulder joint. Players can also use a Superband or rope with this stretch as it can be easier to perform and allow more movement in the stretch.

Hockey skills coach Steve Phillips using the stick chest and shoulder stretch prior to dryland shooting drills at the Hockey Contractor Training Facility in Simi Valley, CA.

Shoulder & Arm Stretches
External Rotator Stretch
The external rotator stretch is a dynamic stretch in that players have to use opposite muscle groups to stretch the external rotators of the shoulder. Start with your back against the wall with the hands up to the sides and along the wall as if you were being "held up", (picture 1). Keeping the elbows on the wall, rotate the hands forward and try to put all 5 fingers on the wall (picture 2).

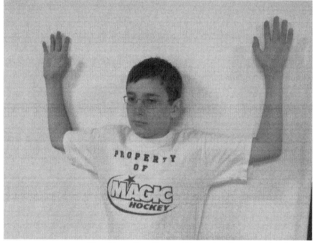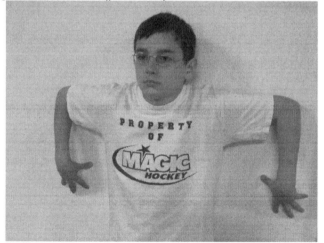

Goaltender Greg Maggio demonstrates good flexibility in the external rotator stretch

Shoulder Traction
The shoulder joint often has range of motion issues and many people are tight in the chest and upper trapezius muscles. Using a Superband fixed to a high position helps an athlete stretch the shoulder and really traction the joint which helps increase blood flow to the area. Make sure to loop the hand through the band without pulling or squeezing with the hands (so the arm stays loose). Bend forward and let the stretching of the band gently pull on the shoulder joint in this position. Do not move around in this position; just let it pull on the joint.

Triceps Stretch

Hold a hockey stick behind your back (as shown in the picture). Use the bottom hand to pull down on the stick and stretch the triceps of the other arm. Switch sides and perform this stretch on both the left and right triceps.

John stretches the triceps of the right arm by pulling down with the left arm.

Core Stretches
Overhead Ab Stretch

Kayla using the overhead ab stretch prior to a workout

Start by interlocking the hands overhead and stretching as far to each side as possible. Make sure to stretch just sideways, without turning as you stretch.

Overhead Stick Twists

The overhead stick twists works to warm-up and stretch the core muscles of the abdominals and low back with a gentle twisting action. Hold a stick overhead and with the feet shoulder width apart. Twist the stick slowly to each side (as pictured above), and hold for a count of 2-seconds. Repeat on both sides until the core feels loose.

Hindu Push-up Ab Stretch

Assume the end position of a Hindu push-up and sink the hips down while holding the arms stretch to stretch the rectus abdominus muscles (above picture). You can hit the sides of the abs by turning away from the stretch with the upper body to the left and the right (not pictured).

Yoga for Hockey Players

For the past few years I have become a huge fan of integrating Yoga into the training programs of all the players and teams I have worked with. Apparently I'm not alone in doing this as I have found out that a number of NHL teams including the Vancouver Canucks, Ottawa Senators, Toronto Maple Leafs, Boston Bruins, Detroit Red Wings, New Jersey Devils, and Tampa Bay Lightning have all adopted Yoga as part of their dryland programs. A number of other NHL players and athletes from other sports have also integrated Yoga into their training.

The reason for teams putting Yoga into their programs is very simple, Yoga has many benefits and can be practiced anywhere with no equipment. Here are some of the beneficial aspects of Yoga:

Pre-Game
Prior to any pre-game warm-up is the perfect time to ease the body into activity, calm the mind and get ready for the game. I recommend a quick 10-minute full body session to activate the muscles and get the blood flowing before the formal pre-game warm-up begins.

Post Game
Yoga in my opinion is most beneficial following a game. Unlike the traditional "flush bike ride" which does not flush the lactic acid out of the muscles (as proven in scientific studies), it also does not loosen up the groin and hip flexor muscles of the legs (which are very tight following a game), and does nothing to calm athletes down to a resting state.

Spending 10 to 20 minutes practicing Yoga will not only calm the body and mind, but will also gently stretch out these tight muscles of the shoulders, neck, lower back, and hips. This will enable a player to return to a normal state and provide recovery that is beneficial...especially if you hop in a car, bus or plane right after a game.

Recovery

With hockey a critical portion of all training should be addressing the need for greater flexibility in the groin, hip flexor and hamstrings. Skating demands a high level of range of motion not only to produce maximal force and agility to the skate blades, but also to provide an element of injury prevention. How many times have we seen players get hit in mid stride, their leg is pushed back and they pull a groin muscle or hip flexor? Hip injuries are the number one injury in hockey.

Adding Yoga into recovery following dryland training, hockey practices, or games provides a gradual increased range of motion that effectively protects the body during impact and allows full power production during movement. The positive effects of Yoga cannot be overstated in the recovery of hockey players.

Relaxation

While many athletes don't pay much attention to relaxation as part of the whole recovery process it's important to note that performing Yoga before bed, prior to a game, or anytime you need to quiet the mind and let the body relax is a really good thing. Ten minutes of relaxation based Yoga might be all you need to get to a place that allows you to sleep or unwind.

Mark Thomas #44, formerly of the London Racers, English Elite Hockey League (EIHL)

281

Chapter 30 - Recovery Methods, Injury Management & Prevention

"Whatever you do, do it with all your might. Work at it, early and late, in season and out of season, not leaving a stone unturned, and never deferring for a single hour that which can be done just as well now".

~ PT Barnum, famous American Showman, Businessman, and Entertainer

Contrary to what people say it is not the amount of exercise you do, but the amount of exercise you can recover from and make progress that is critical to success. Due to all of the various training methods used in training hockey players, the physical nature of the sport and the long competitive season a solid strategy for recovering from workouts is essential. If you cannot recover from these physical stressors, not only will it affect your physical abilities, but it can make you sick, injured, or over-trained (which are similar to a sustained illness caused by prolonged physical stress). You can't play or workout at your best in this condition.

The Anatomy of Soreness
Following any strenuous workout, particularly weight training, plyometric or sprinting exercises you will experience some kind of Delayed Onset of Muscle Soreness, (DOMS). For most people they are stiff or sore in the area that was worked out 12 to 120-hours post exercise. The amount of DOMS you display will be dependent on your general body recovery, recovery methods, type & intensity of the exercise, biological age, training history and the volume of work performed.

The cause of DOMS is micro-trauma or small tears in the muscles (think of your muscles like a palm tree that needs to bend in the wind to stimulate elastic fibres inside the tree to grow tall). While DOMS is not harmful, becoming too sore might reduce the likelihood of returning to regular training and affect your ability to play at a high level. Sometimes if you are really sore you may have to back off training for a day or two, or modify things so you can recover. Ideally I want to hit you with plenty of smaller type workouts throughout the day so you never really develop too much DOMS. That way performance is not affected.

Overtraining
Overtraining is a real problem for most serious athletes and especially junior hockey players who have to deal with traveling to games in addition to all the other stuff that demands your attention (like school, training, work, etc.). In order to keep track of my athletes I ask that they take their heart-rates first thing in the morning before they get out of bed. Use a watch, find your pulse (preferably on your neck) and count the number of beats you get in 15-seconds. Multiply this number by 4 to get your resting heart-rate. Over a couple of weeks you will notice a consistent regular resting heart-rate. If you work too hard one day you might find your heart-rate rises the next morning slightly. This is your body trying to adapt to the stress you put on it by pumping more blood through the system to fix the problem. If you notice a substantial increase (more than 12-beats a minute above "average" then this may be a warning sign to potential over-training). If the high heart-rate is combined with pronounced muscle soreness then the body may not have recovered from previous training. Continual training at a high level in this state may lead to over-training (and ultimately a decrease in your performance).

Forms of Therapy

Light Aerobic Activity
Immediately after exercise, before you leave the gym, the field, arena, etc., make sure you cool down with some light aerobic exercise. The purpose for this is to get the blood flowing which helps to bring nutrients to the muscles and removes toxins that accumulate during exercise. In the NHL they have bikes set up in the dressing rooms so that after practices and games players can do 20 to 40-minutes

of easy exercise for enhanced recovery. The day after a tough training session is also a great time to use light aerobic rhythmical exercises like cycling, swimming, rowing or jogging. This does help speed your recovery so make this happen.

Stretching

After you have finished a workout and done some light aerobic exercise you should take a few minutes to stretch the muscles. Stretching helps to bring blood flow into damaged muscles and works to elongate tissue that can shorten or knot with activity. Progressive stretching for 10 to 15-minutes at the end of exercise will go a long way to help you recovery from the workout.

Later in the day make sure to keep up with some light stretching to keep the muscles long and limber. I would suggest 5 to 10-minutes of stretching first thing in the morning and again before bed, in addition to any other stretching you do during the day. Consult the previous chapter for more information on the correct methods of stretching.

Foam Roll

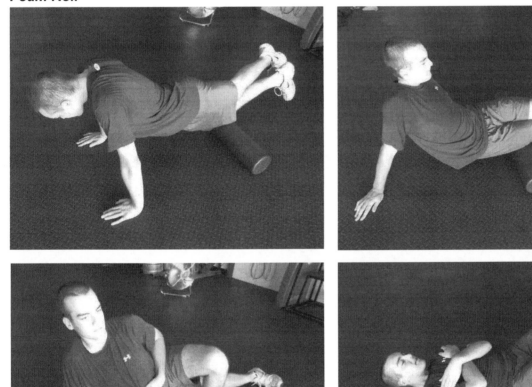

John demonstrates foam rolling of the quadriceps (picture 1),
hamstrings (picture 2), IT band (picture 3) and back (picture 4)

Everyone should buy or have access to a foam roll. This 6-inch round, 3-foot long high density foam roll is a very useful tool following exercise to help break up any residual muscle tension or knots. To use the roll you put it on the ground and then lay on the foam. Moving muscles such as the hamstrings or low back over the roll puts a concentrated pressure on the area and helps to work out the knots or sore areas caused from training. It works like a rolling pin on cookie-dough to hammer out the kinks and scar tissue. Use a slow motion roll for the best results as muscles are made up mostly of water (roughly 70%) and a slower motion causes less disruption of the surrounding area which helps to heal the muscle. Start out with light pressure on the roll and gradually use more body weight as the pain dissipates. Often times I like to use a Lacrosse ball (no pictured but demonstrated in the online videos) much like a foam roll to help workout concentrated areas of pain.

The Stick

Similar to the foam roll, using the stick helps to work out muscle knots, sore spots and injuries by rolling the stick back and forth over the area. By changing the angle and the way the stick is held players can roll out a number of areas in the quadriceps, hamstrings, calfs, and groin.

On my website DP Hockey I include the plans to build your own version of the stick for much less than buying the real plastic version in the stores. Visit **www.dphockey.com** for more information.

Cold Therapy
Post workout the muscles are in a state of stress due to increased inflammatory markers such as creatine kinase and cytokines. Studies have shown to help reduce overall muscle and tissue inflammation using a cold water bath at 50°F for 15 to 20-minutes helps to restore muscles by reducing inflammation and promoting muscle repair.

Using ice packs (or ice in a bag) on muscles following a workout is not recommended however as the ice will raise cortisol levels in the body which leads to a lowered testosterone to cortisol ratio. This shifts the body out of an anabolic state and the ability to recover from exercise and build muscle mass is severely depressed.

If however you become injured from training or competition it is more important to reduce the inflammation at all cost to the anabolic state and at this time icing is highly recommended. My preferred method of icing is using a bucket or bath tub filled with cool water, having the athlete immerse the limb or body parts into the water and then slowly adding ice (and stay there for 15 to 20-minutes). For more acute injuries an ice pack that is wrapped onto the limb or area (with a thin layer of material between the ice and the skin) is sufficient. Ice can and should be used often (up to 8-times per day) as a method to treat all injuries (not just in the first 24-hours post injury).

Post Workout Nutrition
Perhaps one of the most important recovery strategies after a workout is to use a high quality meal that will give the body the tools it needs to rebuild and recover from the inside out. You see after a workout the muscle cells are like a sponge that has been rung dry. There is a period of **less than 45-minutes** after the workout to ingest these nutrients as the cells are very responsive at this time. After that the cells rapidly decrease their ability to absorb and utilize this energy, until they return to baseline levels of nutrient absorption. Since our goal is high speed recovery, I suggest using a liquid medium (a protein & carbohydrate shake) that is absorbed much quicker verses regular food. The optimal range is 50-grams of high quality protein (whey protein) and 100-grams of a high glycemic index carbohydrate (like maltodextrin or dextrose). I would have these shakes pre-made and cold so after a game or a workout you can drink it down and start to recover that much faster. Find out more in my upcoming book *The Hockey Nutrition Manual* at **www.dphockey.com**.

Re-Hydration

Water accounts for over 70% of your body weight, and needs to be replaced on a constant basis. Failure to do this <u>will</u> lead to decreased performance. In a typical game you can lose up to 5lbs from water loss. Drinking cold water (temperature does matter for best results) not only throughout the game but for several hours before and afterwards will re-hydrate the cells and help remove any harmful toxins that may have accumulated from the physical stress. Consuming 2-4 cups (500-1000 ml) after activity (and more if you sweat a lot) is suggested to help re-hydrate the body.

When preparing programs for hockey players I am always asked my daily recommendations for water intake. I use a formula to estimate water needs per day based on work by Charles Poliquin. The equation looks like this (Body weight in pounds/2) + (Body weight x 20%) = number of ounces per day. Therefore a 180lb hockey player would need 126 oz/day (just under a gallon/day).

Alternating Shower Therapy

A very effective way to rejuvenate the body after a hard training session is to use alternating hot and cold showers. The process acts like a "pump" as the hot and cold action dilates and constricts the muscles to move blood through the body faster than normal. This technique speeds the removal of toxins in the blood, and brings nutrients and oxygen to the muscle cells. This 6 to 15-minute process is a very refreshing way to finish a workout session and aid the relaxation process.

The shower should start off with relatively hot water and after 2-minutes switch to water as cold as possible for 1-minute. Repeat these processes 2 to 5-times or until you are sufficiently refreshed. This type of recovery can be difficult to get used to, but the results and post-therapy feeling will make up for the uncomfortable process.

Sauna/Cold Shower Therapy

A coach with the Finnish National cross-country ski team told me of this sauna/shower therapy technique for its relaxing and restorative properties. The deep heating action of the sauna into the muscles acts to stimulate perspiration and remove toxins from the body for improved recovery. When a cool shower is added to the sauna, this therapy is very similar to the alternating shower therapy, only much more effective.

Start off in the sauna or steam room for 5-15-minutes until you have worked up a good sweat, and then move to the shower room for a 2 to 3-minute cold shower. Return to the sauna and repeat 3 to 5- times. Be prepared for a major shock to your system when that cool water hits your body. In any event, the practice is very refreshing and will certainly help you recover from a workout.

Do not use this type of therapy immediately after a game as you will further dehydrate yourself. Instead save this therapy for after traditional strength training. Make sure you have had your protein shake first and bring a water bottle into the sauna to keep hydrated. Keep drinking water for at least an hour after the sauna to ensure you are properly hydrated.

Massage

Over the years massage has become one of the most important methods of recovery for athletes. The benefits include greater relaxation, reduced stress, removal of toxins, elimination of muscle knots and improved circulation. While a professional massage is highly advisable, you can learn the basic techniques from a massage book or by watching a quality professional in action.

Generally it is recommended to rub the muscles towards the heart, then across the muscle in a wringing action, and then back towards the heart. Start off lightly, and as the muscle relaxes, increase the intensity of the action. Spend some time working out various knots (see Active Release section for more information on knots), or sore spots by pressing firmly on the spot for a couple of seconds or using the palm of your hand on the area in a circular motion. The use of your thumb or fingers in a kneading action (pretend your muscle is bread dough) where one hand scoops the other hand is a useful way to treat knots. Pinching the knot between several fingers and the thumb for 10 to 20-seconds is also valuable for knot reduction. After this you can strip the muscle using direct long strokes with several fingers in a cupping manner along the muscle. For a more specific therapy try working between the muscle groups such as between the quadriceps and the IT band on the upper outward side of your leg (should be noticeable by the increase in sharp increase in pain). At this point you can use tapotement therapy (karate chop motions with the edge of the hand or fist) for a stimulating effect. Always end the massage with slight vibrating or shaking of the muscle for a soothing effect, and a gentle rub towards the heart to help the blood circulation.

Using a quality massage oil, or vegetable oil with some essential oils mixed is always advisable to improve the therapeutic process. Have a towel handy to prevent any spillage onto the floor or bed. It is recommended to have a massage once every two weeks to prevent any tissue binding or knots that do occur from time to time from stressful training.

Hot baths
Hot water therapies will help to relax the body and bring an increased blood flow to the area or areas that receive the heat. Depending on the temperature of the water, the effects can penetrate deeply into the muscles. Staying in the hot water or using the pad for 15 to 20-minutes is an appropriate technique for workout recoveries. The addition of Epson salts or essential oils to the hot bath helps to stimulate toxin removal or offers a measure of aromatherapy that can greatly improve the therapy.

Stopain

Stopain is a natural herbal spray that provides temporary relief of many different muscle and joint ailments. Folks who also suffer pain from carpal tunnel syndrome, arthritis, tendonitis, basic muscle sprains and back pain may find this remedy an immediate source of pain relief.

Introduced to me by senior USA weightlifting coach William Johnson, this product really works as the advertisements claim. The fast acting spray penetrates deep into the skin without rubbing or massaging, and it dries quickly so you can put clothes over the area and carry on with your day.

The substance has a strong concentration of menthol with glucosamine and MSM added. I recommend this product and use it myself after difficult training sessions in which I have pushed too far or have sustained a minor injury. I would recommend buying the extra strength formula over the regular strength formula as it gives you more bang for your buck. You can find out more about Stopain at **www.stopain.com**, or it can be bought at a variety of drugs stores.

Traumeel
Over the years I have used and suggested Traumeel with my athletes extensively as a means to help treat minor injuries, bruises or inflammations. Rub the preparation into the skin for 60-seconds and

repeat every 2-hours or as required. Unlike normal creams such as A5-35 or Deep Cold (which are terrible), this preparation helps to heal the damaged tissue.

Traumeel (pictured above) is produced by the Heel Company in Germany, and can be purchased at most health-food stores or online through Nutrition Dynamics (which offer a complete description and details of Traumeel) at www.drmorrow.com/featured_product/ .

Sleep
Quality sleep is an important part of the recovery process that most players take for granted. Only when we have a bad sleep or feel fatigued the next day do we start to put a value on proper sleep. A good sleep keeps our immune system in balance, restores muscles, bones and organs, is necessary for growth hormone production, and improves brain functioning. In terms of sport performance a well-rested hockey players should find that they recover more quickly from workouts, and perform skills better on the ice with greater proficiency. According to Art Horne, Associate Director of Sports Medicine at Northeastern University, "studies showed that teenagers and college-age athletes performed at an optimal level both physically and mentally with approximately **9-hours of sleep per night**". With all the training and games you need at least 9-hours of quality sleep a day, without exception.

Forms of Physical Therapy Treatment

Chiropractic
The basic idea of chiropractic treatment is to diagnose, treat and help prevent future pain in the back and limbs by use of manual manipulation of the spine and other joints that affect soft tissues areas in the body. Many chiropractors use additional procedures in their treatment such as heat, ice, light massage, ultrasound, Electro Muscle Stimulation (EMS), and forms of acupuncture. All of these treatments are geared towards relieving pain caused by a compression of the central nervous system at some point in the spine, or to relieve joint pain by allowing pressure to be released.

Chiropractors must be licensed, which requires 2 to 4-years of undergraduate education, the completion of a 4-year chiropractic college course, and passing scores on National and State board examinations. Satisfaction rates are typically higher for chiropractic care compared to medical care, with a 1998 U.S. survey reporting 83% of respondents satisfied or very satisfied with their care. In my personal experience with chiropractic care I have felt that for back pain that is structural (meaning that the spine is out of alignment) the services of a qualified chiropractor are essential. If part of the central nervous system is being pinched by the spine it is critical that this pressure be relieved within 2-months or permanent damage may occur. Therefore I highly recommend chiropractic treatment when other forms of therapy such as stretching, icing, foam rolling, and even a doctor's visit fail to fix the back problem or issues with the limbs (like sciatic nerve pain or other forms of radiating pain).

Cold Laser Therapy
This form of therapy is primarily used in physical therapy clinics to aid in the healing of various injuries such as sprains, ligament damage, inflammation, etc. The cold laser's function is to stimulate the mitochondria (the powerhouse of the cell) to produce more ATP and increase protein synthesis (more energy becomes available to the cell to aid in healing). A secondary response to the laser is the relief of pain due to an increasing release of endorphins (natural pain relieving hormones). If you need physical therapy make sure to ask about the laser as part of a complete treatment.

Ultrasound Therapy
If you have an injury that requires the help of a physiotherapist you might come in contact with Ultrasound therapy. In simple terms a high frequency sound wave (that humans cannot hear) is directed into the body to help promote blood flow and soften scar tissue that is usually present with an injury. This treatment can be useful in bringing about a reduced healing time for your injury.

Electro Muscle Stimulation (EMS)

Alternating currents of electricity are shot through the muscle to help increase blood flow to injured areas, break adhesions, relax muscle spasms, increase range of motion and lose any muscle tension. These machines are used by a physical therapist and have been used in athletics for years to bring back athletes quickly. If you have a soft tissue injury I suggest you try this treatment.

Active Release Techniques (ART)

Over the time an athlete trains inevitably they will encounter a variety of muscle pulls, sprains, tears, collisions, micro-trauma and hypoxia that will damage soft tissue and create dense scar tissue. This scar tissue (that everyone has) binds up and ties down tissues that need to move freely. With the build-up of this scar tissue muscles can become shorter and weaker (causing reduced range of motion), tendons can develop tendonitis and nerves can become trapped leading to radiating pain.

Founded by Dr. Michael Leahy, an ART practitioner uses over 500-unique moves to evaluate, identify and correct specific problems in the soft tissues by applying direct pressure and then having the patient perform different movements. This helps drive a wedge into the tissue and helps release or reduce scar tissue. By observing how muscles, fascia, tendons, ligaments and nerves responded to different types of work and creating a new form of treatment, Dr. Leahy was able to consistently resolve over 90% of his patients' problems. As I have had a number of injuries throughout my athletic life I have used and highly recommend ART as a treatment because it works very well.

Exercise as a Treatment

Light exercise is a great way to move the blood through the body and allows your natural painkillers (endorphins) to work their magic. The protocol for this therapy is to promote general range of motion and move the limbs or area. Start off ridiculously slow. Make sure you don't over-exert yourself and stay within a comfortable range of pain. Slight pain is alright, but moderate pain and above is not recommended. Once again, check with you doctor or trainer to confirm that light exercise is appropriate for your injury.

Corticosteroids

Sometimes an injury can be so debilitating and painful that the doctor might suggest an injection shot into the inflamed joint, tendon or bursa of a corticosteroid (examples include: Prednisone, Cortisone, Decadron, or Hydrocortisone). The purpose of using such drugs is to achieve an immediate reduction of localized inflammation. Such a treatment can provide months of relief if used correctly and with some conditions such as bursitis and tendonitis a corticosteroid can offer a permanent solution for the injury. While the upside of these drugs can be significant, the downside is that repeated injections to a particular sight can cause cartilage damage and weakened ligaments in joints or weakening of the tendons, (which is not good for exercise purposes). In order to avoid this doctors usually only allow up to 3-injections in a particular area over the course of a year. Make sure you talk to several doctors, coaches and of course your athletic trainer before considering a corticosteroid treatment.

Another thing you might want to consider when taking a corticosteroid is that it may affect drug testing for hockey (if you do in fact ever get tested). If you are in doubt about the drug, supplement or method of therapy you are using a quick email or call to your National Anti-Drug Organization might be in order. The following website address will provide you a list of all the NADA's and their contact information, http://www.wada-ama.org/en/Anti-Doping-Community/NADOs/List-of-NADOs/. Make sure you provide them with the exact drug or supplement and brand so as to provide specific information.

Surgery

Many injuries can be treated with some or all of the above treatments. Surgery however is thought of as a permanent "fix" for traditional injuries. While it is beyond the scope of this chapter to advise when and how you should decide to use surgery as an injury treatment option, it is important to note that you need to get as much information as possible before deciding which treatment option is best. If possible, seek a second and third opinion. Search the web. Talk to other experts. Generally in my experience I consider surgery to be an absolute last resort and not recommended until other forms of treatment have been tried. If you think your case can benefit from surgery and the procedure is valid, then go for it. Just make sure you know all the facts and the recovery times for your procedure.

Coming Back from Injury
Every hockey player we know wants to get back on the ice as soon as possible after an injury. The need to show your coaches you're alright and the peer pressure you face from other team-mates is huge. Letting coaches, trainers or team-mates convince you to come back before you are good to go is not advised. Many times players come back too early, and end up hurting themselves even worse. Instead, try working with your coaches and trainers (keeping them informed) and make sure you do everything you can do get back on the ice.

Dealing with Injuries
In hockey it's a matter of when you'll get injured, not if you'll get injured. At the junior level and above, nearly every player has some kind of injury each season. The most common areas for injury in hockey are the groin, hip flexor, knee, shoulder, neck, low back, concussions and ankle injuries. With the exception of head trauma, these can all be strengthened with specific exercises (see below or in the strength training chapter), but require a great deal of time to heal if injured. If an injury does happen to strike, here is a list of things I recommend you follow to get back on the ice quickly.

- Following an injury on the ice or during dryland training it is essential to have it evaluated by a doctor so as to determine the extent of the injury and potential treatment. Having x-rays or an MRI done can be very helpful to diagnose the injury correctly.

- With some injuries, it is important to get a second opinion or diagnosis of the area as mistakes can be made even by qualified professionals. This is especially important when looking at having surgery to correct a major injury.

- Keep a file of all your injuries in case you need to show them to a doctor or trainer at some point in your hockey career.

- Follow all of the kinds of treatment in this chapter such as icing, heat, massage, along with stretching (when appropriate) in order to rehab an injury.

- Work hard with rehab to get back into practicing with the team so you can feel a part of the team again, but realize that coming back too soon can have negative consequences. Follow the advice of your trainers and doctors who know the body and what can be accomplished.

- Try not to get discouraged if injuries do not heal on time or as well as planned. Sometimes life throws us a curve ball and it's up to us to take the hand that is dealt to us and do the best we can to make it work. This is especially true for athletes and injuries.

Injury Prevention
In order to keep the body ready and prepared to play hockey at the highest level I encourage all my players to perform daily injury prevention exercises that work the ankle, neck, shoulder, groin and hip. These are the most vulnerable areas of injury, and making them all as strong as possible is highly appropriate to protect these areas in the net.

Start off with light loads and slow movements for high repetitions (15 to 50). As your strength increases vary this with higher loads for less reps (8 to 15). It is NOT important how much weight you lift each workout, but rather how regularly you work these areas. Personally I have my players pick one exercise from each of the five areas below and train that each day for 2-sets. It takes 10-minutes, but adds up to help armour the body for hockey.

- Ankle training (dard II, band ankle circles, balance board, etc.)
- Neck training (neck harness, towel neck work, stability ball neck work extension, etc.)
- Shoulder training (Cuban press, external rotations on knee, etc.)
- Groin (plate drags, stability ball adductions, cable adduction, etc.)
- Hip Flexor (band hip flexion, assisted band hip flexion, cable hip flexion, etc.)

In addition to all of the above I cannot stress enough that a properly designed training program will go a long way to balancing the muscles in the body, provide armour in the form of muscle mass to help reduce injuries, and allow a full range of motion due to a consistent and correct flexibility and recovery program performed each and every day!

Illnesses
Nothing stops a player faster than a cold or flu. It affects your ability to breathe and weakens the muscles (not good for hockey). A quick trip to the doctors may not be such a bad idea. If you decide to stick it out at home like most folks then here are my recommendations;

- Use a decongestant to reduce the phlegm and get that cold moving along. There is a product on the market called "Ocean" which is a salt water type of nasal spray that can be effective moving the garbage out of your sinus passages.

- Get plenty of sleep. Trying to tough out a cold with your usual routine is usually the wrong move and it can make everyone you work with sick as well. Stay at home and sleep.

- Get plenty of food and water. Foods high in vitamins and minerals are valuable to maintaining the strength of your immune system. Staying hydrated is very important (especially if we have a fever) as we lose a lot of fluids when we are sick (sweating, vomit, etc.)

- Up the amount of vitamin-C you consume each day (from 3-grams to at least 5-grams).

- Take herbal mixtures such as Echinacea, Astragalus, Garlic, Ginger Root, and Golden Seal which all have shown evidence of being effective for fighting off an infection.

- Use humidity in your room when sleeping by plugging in a humidifier. The moist air will not allow your throat to dry out (which starts the onset of the coughing and poor sleep).

- As the cold is starting to break try some light exercise to improve blood circulation and to "sweat the cold out" as they say in hockey. At the very least this will improve your view (compared to the bedroom), and your mood as you get out to exercise. Pick activities such as walking, light jogging, skating, or cycling that are not overly stressful on the system. The goal is to reduce the cold, not try to get any type of training effect, go slow.

Medical Professionals
Nobody likes to go to the doctor, but they are a very important part in the immediate treatment of injuries or illnesses. Hockey players avoid the doctor more than the average person as they want to show the coaches they are fine, and tend to believe they are invulnerable. Doctor's however, are the only people who can refer you to a specialist, or prescribe any kind drugs that may improve your healing time. Find a good medical professional you trust (shop around just like if you were buying a car) and one who's office is relatively close to home (otherwise you won't go to them). The bottom line is that they can help you, but only if you go to them.

Chapter 31 - Traveling & Game Day Preparation

"Aut Viam Inveniam aut Faciam"
"I will find a way or make one."

~ unknown

There are times when the team must go on extended road trips over several days, a week or even more. Miles of traveling, multiple games, uncomfortable hotel rooms and unhealthy food all can make a road trip difficult. When playing games at home everything is easy. You have a routine and then if something goes wrong you know where to go, or what to do to fix it.

On the road however, things are different. I have seen players forget skates, break laces, crack a blade during the trip or lose luggage in transit. Nothing upsets a coach like a player who can't perform well due to travel related problems. Most coaches never go over what they expect from players on the road, and then wonder why players make mistakes. Here are some suggestions that will allow you the best chance to show up and perform at your best, no matter where you play.

Stuff to do at Home

As you usually don't know what services may be available on the road here is a list of stuff to do at home so you don't have to worry about these issues while traveling.

- Fix any broken equipment before you pack it for the trip.

- Sharpen you skates at home with your regular skate sharpener (the trainer or local pro-shop) and then put a skate guard on so you keep them sharp. If you play multiple road games ask you're coaching staff to bring along a skate sharpener or ask your trainer to find locations on the road where you can sharpen dull skates. If necessary use the internet phone books available to find information on skate sharpening and equipment shops where you are going.

- Bring along extra skate laces, helmet clips, helmet straps, extra stick blades, towels, ace bandages, stick and clear pad tape, and team socks. Replace these if you use them so you always have a backup. If your team is on the road for extended periods you will no doubt have one or two practices during the trip so pack your practice gear just in case. This might include extra socks, practice jersey, warm-up gear, stick blades, etc.

- Pack all of the food and water you may need for the entire trip. Include enough bottles of water, energy bars, sandwiches, cans of tuna, fruit and vegetables, etc. Prepare for the unexpected by bringing along extra food in case the team doesn't stop at a restaurant or is in a hurry after a late game.

- Take some extra money in case of emergency.

- Charge your cell phone before the trip. If you play in the junior leagues you need to have a cell phone and it has to be charged before you leave. Bring your charger along and a portable car adaptor to make sure you are covered.

- Take along an iPod, Gameboy, a good book or whatever else you need to relax.

- Take your homework if you are still in school. You can often get a lot done during the trip.

- If you are traveling internationally or boarding a plane make sure you have identification such as a driver's license, passport and a visa if you need one.

On the Road
The coaching staff should work with the team to develop a routine and "culture" for travel days so that everyone on the team is on the same page. Setting up a regular routine takes the pressure and stress off of players (and staff) because everything is always done the same for each trip.

Getting Ready on Game Day
On game day it's important to have everything hammered out so you can hit the ice and play at your best. If you are on the road you may also have to adjust to many things such as traveling to the rink, setting up shop in a new rink, coordinating team meals, and changing the warm-up for the facilities at hand.

Here is a timeline breakdown of what should go on for a typical junior away game (you should adjust this schedule for your particular level of play). Games played at home may have a different timeline but should be similar.

For a 7:30pm game here is a sample schedule you should employ.

- (3:00pm) Eat a decent sized pre-game meal such as spaghetti with meat sauce, stir-fry with rice, vegetables and meat, or a serving of chicken with lots of vegetables.

- (4:30pm) Arrive at the rink at least 3-hours before game time. Bring in your gear, talk to coaches, lay out your gear and start to get mentally prepared.

- (5:00pm) Prepare your sticks, touch up your skates, and repair anything that is damaged.

- (5:30pm) Eat your pre-game snack. This meal should be a smaller meal high in protein and carbohydrates such as a tuna sandwich, protein shake and some fruit. Do not have any milk, beans, soda, candy, or junk food. Usually the coach will have a pre-game strategy talk with the team before the dryland warm-up. Eat while they talk.

- (6:00pm) Dryland warm-up. Do a light 5-minute team jog, run some stairs (most rinks have stairs), complete 5 to 8 sprints in the tunnels below the rink, finish 2-sets of 15-burpees and perhaps play 5 to 10 minutes of hacky-sack or ball hockey with teammates to warm-up the hip flexors and your agility before you do some light stretching (mostly the shoulders and groin areas) before heading back to the locker room.

- (6:30pm) Put on your gear.

- (7:00pm) On-ice warm-up. Don't just go out there, take a couple shots and skate around like most players. Make sure you do some short sprints and quick feet work on the ice to warm-up the skating muscles. Avoid stretching on the ice as this isn't the best surface to stretch on anyways (cold won't loosen the muscles). Remember to touch the puck lots and move lots.

- (7:15pm) When the on-ice warm-up is over, the coach should have a final word with the team. Keep loose in the dressing room by putting on your skate guards to do some easy squats, lunges, push-ups, etc. to keep the blood flowing. Many coaches fail to keep the players loose during this part in the pre-game preparation (instead they like to talk and talk).

- (7:30pm) Game time.

Between the Periods
After each period of play you need to replace some of the energy you have drained from playing. I recommend either a power-gel type energy source or at the very least a 6 to 8-ounce serving of orange juice (hall of fame player Mark Messier used to drink orange juice between periods) or watered down Gatorade with protein powder. You don't want to eat anything that might upset your stomach, but you do need to replenish energy levels. I suggest you try various things during practices so that when you get to the games it will be no big deal.

Post Game Activities
When you are a visitor in another team's barn, they don't usually provide the facilities to warm-down from the game. Aside from this, you need to take this time to cool off from the game. Here are some suggestions:

- After you finish getting chewed out from the coach or listening to the post game speech (depending on how the team played) take off your gear and get into warm-up gear.

- If you are hurt it's time to see the trainer and get injuries evaluated, wrapped and iced. You might need a trip to the hospital, but the trainer and coach will see to this.

- If you aren't hurt, jump on the exercise bike for only a few minutes (at a light pace), and then break out a travel sized foam roll and get to work rolling all of your tight spots out (the hip, groin, low back, quads and IT band are essential to roll out). If no exercise bikes are available then perform another dynamic warm-up before foam rolling.

- Easy stretching for 10-minutes of the groin and hip flexors is necessary following any game as this area will be tight and overworked. Other areas such as the chest, shoulders, low back, hamstrings, glutes, ankles and quads will also need stretching. If possible a light massage will really help speed the recovery process.

- Eat your post game meal (high protein and carbohydrates) such as a protein shake with fruit, a turkey sandwich or an energy bar. Try to get at least 50-grams of protein and 100- grams of carbohydrate into your body at this time. You need to consume this within 45-minutes of the finish of the game to get the maximum recovery benefits so bring this with you in your hockey bag.

- Consume some post game vitamins/minerals (in a liquid form if possible). Another great product is Emergen-C (a vitamin-C powder) that can be added to water.

- When you leave the rink dry out your gear at the hotel (either in a conference room that the coaching staff sets up, or in your hotel room) or if at home in an area that you won't mind the smell. If you can, wash out your socks and jersey (or have the trainer do this).

Sleep
As I talked about in the recovery chapter getting enough sleep (at least 9 hours) is very important after a game (or trip). If you get on the bus and ride to the next town then try to sleep on the bus before you get to the hotel. You might want to bring an MP3 player or IPod and ear plugs to ensure you have undisturbed shut eye.

Conditioning
Unless your team pays for a hotel with a gym or the team you play against has enough money for a gym at the rink then you have to improvise to get in your regular conditioning. For this reason I suggest the team (or you) bring along kettlebells (one of either a 53lb, 63lb or 72lb are the best options), an ab roller and a skipping rope.

Along with kettlebells I suggest bringing several of the following; jump ropes, ab rollers, Superbands (2" wide or more), hacky sacks, and 20 cones. All of this stuff can fit into a large duffle bag and works great when you want to turn a dressing room, storage area or conference room into an effective strength training circuit. There is no reason not to continue with basic conditioning work on the road (something that most teams forget).

Team Meals

Most teams I know only provide 3-meals a day while on the road. This old school thinking of three squares a day is not right for a hockey player. Bring along your own energy bars, protein powder (and shaker bottle), beef jerky, fruit, cut up vegetables, or other pre-packaged foods so that you can maintain your 5+ meals a day eating plan. If you stop at a restaurant on the road, try to eat something healthy from the menu (items with fruits, vegetables, brown rice, lean meats, etc). Here are some other suggestions for road meals:

- Always drink a glass of water before every meal. By getting into that habit players can make sure they stay hydrated while traveling.

- Prior to and after games make sure to get in enough carbohydrates to replenish glycogen stores. At this time foods such as rice, pasta, and potatoes are good to eat in addition to all the fruits and vegetables recommended earlier.

- Bring along a vitamin/mineral supplement, in addition to vitamin-C supplements to make sure you get your daily recommended allowances of vitamins/minerals.

- At many restaurants you can order off the menu if you don't find any suitable healthy options.

- Stay away from empty calories such as sodas, candy, deserts, and other type snacks.

Jet Lag

When teams travel to games the issue of jet lag always comes up with the coaching staff as it really does have a big impact on performance if players are tired and their internal clock is out of sink. Here are some tips on dealing with jet lag:

- Jet lag is worse when traveling eastward because you "lose hours". Traveling westward will often not be too much of a problem (depending on the distance traveled) as you "gain hours" which can help athletes actually get a good nights sleep.

- If possible arrange flight times so that players get a full night's sleep in the new time zone the first night.

- Plane flights dehydrate everyone so it is important to drink water throughout the trip and avoid caffeine as this will further dehydrate players.

- Short naps should be avoided if possible as this prolongs the player's ability to integrate into the new time zone.

- Coaches should adjust the practice schedule in the first few days to accommodate the internal clock of the athletes. Therefore if you usually practice at 7am in Vancouver you would want to schedule practice at 10am in Boston for a couple of days so players get used to the new time zone and players can perform at their best. As everyone acclimates the practice times can be adjusted over several days to the regular time.

Chapter 32 - Mental Preparation

"Whether you think you can or whether you think you can't, you're right!"

~ Henry Ford

Most hockey players I know think that mental training is a supreme waste of time. It has been drilled into their heads that practice, practice and more practice is the best course of action to improve hockey performance. Ask any person who has achieved any measure of success what the key is and they will undoubtedly mention persistence, dedication or grit as some of the words. The trouble for most folks is they have no idea how to go about setting themselves up for success. They think that hard work solves everything, which is untrue. Hard work in a focused manner, done correctly over and over again is much more powerful.

With mental training we gain the insight to harness our mental focus and turn this energy into a razor sharp tool that will help elevate your game. The process of finding out where we are, assessing our weaknesses, taking a planned direction and then getting feedback to assess our situation is the key to success. In the next section I want you to get out a notebook and map your 5-step mental model that will direct your energy towards a hockey goal.

The 5-Step Mental Model
There are 5 key areas with changing your mental focus that will ensure you make the most out of your goals. You can use it for anything in your life, but for our purposes let's stick to hockey. To illustrate what the 5-step mental model approach looks like I have included my own 5-step model for writing my first book (the one you are holding in your hands).

Choose your Ultimate Goals
So what is your ultimate goal? Do you want to play professional hockey (get to the show)? Play NCAA or Canadian college hockey and get an education? When choosing your ultimate goal you have to find something that lights a fire under your butt. Something you can really sink your teeth into. It can't be easily attainable and there has to be a measure of sacrifice in order for you to achieve the goal. In addition to the ultimate goal you need to decide on smaller goals that (if accomplished) will lead you to your ultimate goal.

Whatever these goals are it has to be specific and measurable. Now take out that notebook as I indicated earlier and write down 1-dream goal, 2-medium term goals (things you might accomplish this season) and 2-short term goals (something you can do in the next month or two). Don't wait, do this now! Make sure you put a time sensitive date on it so it forces you to do something right away (like cramming for an important exam in school).

Current Status
Now that you have an idea of what you want, how do you get there? We need to take stock of our current situation and see where we are compared to what we want to achieve. In this step we have to come face to face with the truth and be brutally honest. When I consult with clients this often becomes my job to hold up the mirror and force them to take a long hard look at their strengths and weaknesses. In reality, this is and should be your job.

When you take a look at yourself find out what it is you need to complete your goal. Do you need to alter your mental approach, your attitude or perhaps work ethic? What are you missing that holds you back from achieving your goals? For the junior hockey player I strongly suggest some type of physical testing as part of this process. Testing things like your 40-meter sprint time, shuttle run, 1RM incline bench press, weighted sled drag, standing long jump, front squat test, power snatch, etc., are invaluable. I would also enlist the help of a coach or friend who can point out areas that need improvement on the ice. Once you get a true picture of your current situation then it's easy to start planning to complete your goal. Find out all of this information in the next couple of days and write this down in your notebook along with all the other mental preparation skills.

What do you Intend to Do?

You know what you want and what your problems are; let's develop a game plan that can help you get to where you want to be. We must use specific and measurable methods to achieve our goal with clear intentions. Simply working harder isn't enough.

With some hockey teams I have seen the players unite to form a team contract for what they wanted to accomplish during the season and how they were going to make that happen. If someone wasn't pulling their weight, they simply reminded them of the team goals and what everyone was doing to accomplish it. If that didn't work, then the players took action in the best interests of the team. When you have clear intentions it creates confidence in your ability to take risks, make hard decisions and act without fear. It's cut and dry, because you know if you're on track with these goals or not.

What you need to do is determine the key values you must implement in order to increase your performance. Write out a contract for yourself that has a set of intentions to keep you on track. This should include time spent training (how many hours per week), how you will improve on the ice (such as will you spend 20-minutes after practice working on your skating or passing skills), will you read other hockey books to improve your knowledge for the sport, etc. You need to create a list of things that you will do every day to make you a better player (which is essentially what your intentions really are). Put a time frame on this so that you develop a sense of urgency.

Take Action

You have a plan of attack, now execute it! Brilliant planning is nothing without action (a lesson I am still learning). The problem is that our actions are often in many different directions at the same time. We tend to get excited about something and then run around like a chicken with its head cut off trying to achieve it. You have a blueprint for what you need to do with your hockey career, just use it.

Get Feedback

The last step in this sequence of events is after taking action you need clear feedback to determine if your intentions and actions are really working. Look at this step critically and objectively so you don't skew the results of your overall plan. See what's working and what's not. Talk to friends, coaches, team-mates, or an expert in the field you are lacking for clear feedback.

If you are successful with your actions then this will lead to increased confidence in your plan and can help you stay on top of your training. If the plan leads to little or no progress then you have to either step up your determination and fight harder, or simply modify your plan so that you will be successful. Either way, we do it with a plan of attack and with the knowledge that the greater goal is all important. This is an ongoing process that will need to be done hundreds if not thousands of times before you finally get to the ultimate goal.

A Sample 5-step Mental Model

My own 5-step mental model came about while I was working with hockey players in the late 90's and several of them suggested I should write a kick-ass hockey book based on all my dryland training methodologies and ideas. I kicked around that idea for a while and in 2000 I started off with this mental model so I could focus my attention on this project and make it happen.

Choosing my Goal
- Write a book on dryland training for hockey based on my training philosophies & experience.

Current Status (in the year 2000)
- Have never published anything (other than basic articles for a skiing newsletter).

- Lack the writing experience to submit anything to a journal or editor.
- Don't know anyone in the writing world (magazines, journals or books).
- Have no idea how to review, edit or publish a book.

My Intensions
- Read as much as I can on the subject of writing.
- Start writing my training and fitness ideas down into the computer.
- Begin writing articles for peer reviewed journals and magazines.
- Stay in contact with editors to see if they need an article done on a certain topic.
- Collect, research and obtain as much information as I can on hockey related topics by reading trade journals, magazines and books so I know what I want to talk about in my book.
- Sit down for a minimum of 2-hours a week to write (articles or on the book).
- Talk to other professionals and experts at trade shows and conferences on how best to start off in the fitness writing business.

Taking Actions (what happened during these 13+ years)
- Writing a minimum of 2-hours per week was the goal. (During this time I ended up writing more than 10-hours a week for 3 ½ years).
- Limited holidays and days off to focus on writing.
- Read related industry and trade journals 1-hour per day minimum.
- Contacted as many authors as I could to improve my skills.
- I ended up on the editorial panel for the Performance Training Journal and a peer reviewer for the Strength & Conditioning Journal.
- Submitted articles to journals as planned. I ended up having more than 25-articles published in journals, magazines and online over a 10-year period. My first article took me over two years to finish and get a favorable review from peers. I learned a lot on the first article.
- I researched topics and collected information at the University of Manitoba, University of Calgary, University of British Columbia, University of Alberta, University of California at Riverside, California Baptist University…and a number of public libraries.
- I ended up buying a laptop computer to write when I had a free hour at the gym or on the road.
- I downsized my client list for the last 6-months of writing the book to get all of the necessary pre-production stuff done (pictures, printing, cover work, etc).

Getting Feedback (these were my clear feedback goals)
- Find a minimum of 5 proofreaders for every article and chapter I created
- Ask every editor and peer reviewer for feedback on how to improve my writing
- Volunteer as a peer reviewer for the National Strength and Conditioning Association so I can review other authors and learn to improve my craft of writing by helping others
- Have all of my clients review, edit (if necessary) and provide feedback for my book
- I took this book to many different hockey experts and coaches to get feedback and refine it (including many NHL strength & conditioning coaches), who all offered great advice.
- Enlist the help of 3 different English teachers/professors to evaluate and provide feedback for each chapter of this book
- Have the book professionally edited

In my original 5-step mental model I had this project pegged at 2-years. A host of things delayed the eventual goal, but I kept on track the best I could. During this process I would get feedback from a many sources, plug that information into the 5-step mental model and adjust my strategy as necessary. Even though you have an outline of a plan, it is by no means etched in stone. This fluid progress has to be flexible to setbacks, challenges, and harsh feedback or it will fail. The point of all of this is to show that you can and should map out your goals, take action, get necessary feedback on your plan, make changes (if needed) and keep pounding away until you achieve it!

Mental Imagery

With a solid plan in place for your goals you need to know how to conjure up the ability to perform at your best every time you workout. Mental imagery is the practice of creating a perfect picture in your mind (complete with sounds, smells, tastes, and touch if you can muster that sensation). The famous professional golfer Jack Nicklaus once said that he made a mental picture of the ball flight and landing spot for every shot he ever took, before it physically happened. If you ever watch downhill ski racers or ski jumpers they do the same thing. They will close their eyes and you can see them racing the course before it happens. In talks with members of the Canadian National Ski Team they try to make the imagery as real as possible so they essentially race the course hundreds of times before actually performing it in real competition.

Now how does this help you? I want you to push yourself past your comfort zone and put forth a decent effort with all training. You won't accomplish your goals otherwise. This might occur when you are carrying the puck into the opposition zone, during overtime in a big game or even during training as you get under a heavy barbell. You need to see yourself completing the task in a positive light or it may not happen. Make it as real as possible with sounds, sights, smells, even your sense of touch. Get used to using mental imagery for all of your training and it will help you carry over into game time. Just make sure you strive to achieve something more from yourself each day and you'll do fine.

Be There Now!

Several Christmas's ago, one of my gifts was a t-shirt for the 2010 Olympics. As I am a big fan of the Olympics and am a member of the Canadian Olympic Association I welcome these types of gifts. While I sat there and looked at the shirt I started thinking that many people in the world had already started to celebrate the Vancouver Olympics at least 3-years early. The marketing of the shirts was meant to get people excited to plan ahead and then come to the city to take part in the games.

Our life is something like that. We have big dreams but we keep them on a wish list without really acting on them. Our goal of playing professional hockey is just that...a goal.

What do you think would happen if you picked a spot in the future and started getting excited about it NOW. Don't wait until you have actually achieved the dream, but start thinking about it today.

My friend & former training partner Duff Gibson (2006 Olympic Gold Medalist in Skeleton), (photo by Dave O)

Imagine getting drafted by an NHL team. Next you go to training camp and impress the coaching staff with your skilled play. After being chosen to the team you get your first big check (more money then you ever made in your whole life), and have the task of finding a sick lake house, buying a new sports car, and setting up your investments. Your games are played in front of thousands of fans (in a pro-arena that seats 18,000+ people), while many other fans watch you on TV, After games, you are interviewed by CBC hockey announcer Ron Maclean, talked about by Scott Ferrall on Sirius satellite radio, written about in the *Hockey News* or mentioned by Don Cherry on "Coaches Corner". This is your life!

Nice feeling isn't it? Now what do you think would happen if you felt that way all the time? Remember, you **are** a professional athlete. You may not be at the moment but in your mind, you are. "Act as if". Act as if you are a professional hockey player. Take the doubt, the fear and the negative out of your feelings and just play the game. Now that's something powerful...

Final Thoughts

Banff Hockey Academy coach Billy Doherty draws out drills during Junior practice at the Banff Rec Centre

Over the past 23+ years I have worked with some amazing players, coaches and officials in this great game of hockey and hope to for many, many more years. The most important thing to remember when training for hockey is that only an extreme effort, combined with great skill and tremendous heart will allow players to move to the highest levels.

In the words of Navy SEAL Commander Chuck Pfarrer talking about SEAL team training at BUDS he says *"students emerge with the realization that the human body is capable of ten times the output previously thought possible. There are few limits and no limitations to what a determined individual can accomplish."*

It is with that statement I will suggest that if you want to play hockey at the highest level...get to work. Leave no stone unturned. Work tirelessly to make your dreams come true. Contact coaches to see what you can do to develop your skills (preferably LTAD qualified coaches). Take some private lessons from a hockey skills coach (such as my buddy Steve Phillips at Hockey Contractor). Seek out a quality strength coach and learn as much as you can from them. Squat...lots, and then squat some more until you can't feel your legs. Work on your shooting (all variations under different conditions), and shoot lots of pucks. Take up ball hockey for dryland training (without having to worry about skating) so you can focus on stick-handling and play development. Improve your skating with a respected skating expert (Steffany Hanlen, Vanessa Hettinger & Laura Stamm immediately come to mind, but there are others). Play 3-on-3 hockey on a mini-rink or small area games as much as possible. Go to pick-up hockey or shinny to learn how to dangle. Study hard in school, and ask for help if you need it. Get a good SAT score. Make sure to go to college. Talk to other pros and learn from them. Take a coaching or officiating course so you can give back to the great game of hockey. Get a job so your parents don't have to pay for all your hockey expenses. Speaking of parents, say "thank you" to them for supporting your hockey career...its time consuming, expensive and draining but they have done this for you consistently over the years. Live the hockey life and do the work it takes to play at the highest level. Enjoy being an elite athlete...it only lasts so long. Do this now...and when you do make it, shoot me an email to tell me how hard you worked to get there!

Cheers!

APPENDIX A - DP Hockey Physical Testing Form

You may photocopy these appendix pages only to use for recording physical fitness data, monthly hours and workout log. If possible create a binder with your filled in data sheets so you can look back on your training history from time to time to problem solve issues and/or gain future insight.

Player Name: _____   Date: _____   Age: _____

Team Name/Camp: _____   Level: _____

Body Composition

Height: _____Inches   Body Weight: _____lbs

Body Fat: _____%   Body Fat: _____lbs

Basic Strength Testing

2-Minute Push-up Test: _____repetitions   2-Minute Sit-up Test: _____repetitions

Maximum Number of Pull-ups: _____repetitions   Standing Long Jump: _____Inches

1-Leg Lateral Long Jump: _____Inches   Sled Pull: _____seconds

Grip Test: _____lbs Right, _____lbs Left

Advanced Strength Testing

1RM Power Snatch: _____lbs   1RM Front Squat: _____lbs

1RM Incline Bench Press: _____lbs   1RM Deadlift: _____lbs

Speed & Agility Tests

40-Yard Sprint: _____seconds   12" Agility Test: _____seconds

Conditioning Tests

Shuttle Run Test: _____seconds   300-Yard Shuttle Run: _____seconds

KB Snatch Test (5mins): _____Number, _____lbs KB   20 Meter Beep Test: _____level

On-Ice Skating Tests

T-Skating Test: _____seconds   Banff Agility Test: _____seconds

MA Skating Test: _____seconds

Comments

APPENDIX B - DP Hockey Workout Log Sheet

Order	Exercise	Sets	Reps	Load	Comments

APPENDIX C - DP Hockey Monthly Program Hours Sheet

Date	Strength	Cardio	Speed	GPP	SPP	Ice	Flexibility	Totals
1								
2								
3								
4								
5								
6								
7								
8								
9								
10								
11								
12								
13								
14								
15								
16								
17								
18								
19								
20								
21								
22								
23								
24								
25								
26								
27								
28								
29								
30								
31								
Total								

APPENDIX D - Weight Training Percentage Chart

100%	95%	92.5%	90%	87.5%	85%	82.5%	80%	77.5%	75%	72.5%	70%	67.5%	65%	62.5%	60%	57.5%	55%	52.5%	50%
1RM	2RM	3RM	4RM	5RM	6RM	7RM	8RM	9RM	10RM	11RM	12RM	13RM	14RM	15RM	16RM	17RM	18RM	19RM	20RM
100	95	92	90	87	85	82	80	77	75	72	70	67	65	62	60	57	55	52	50
105	99	97	94	91	89	86	84	81	78	76	73	70	68	65	63	60	57	55	52
110	104	101	99	96	93	90	88	85	82	79	77	74	71	68	66	63	60	57	55
115	109	106	103	100	97	94	92	89	86	83	80	77	74	71	69	66	63	60	57
120	114	111	108	105	102	99	96	93	90	87	84	81	78	75	72	69	66	63	60
125	118	115	112	19	106	103	100	96	93	90	87	84	81	78	75	71	68	65	62
130	123	120	117	113	110	107	104	100	97	94	91	87	84	81	78	74	71	68	65
135	128	124	121	118	114	111	108	104	101	97	94	91	87	84	81	77	74	70	67
140	133	129	126	122	119	115	112	108	105	101	98	94	91	87	84	80	77	73	70
145	137	134	130	126	123	119	116	112	108	105	101	97	94	90	87	83	79	76	72
150	142	138	135	131	127	123	120	116	112	108	105	101	97	93	90	86	82	78	75
155	147	143	139	135	131	127	124	120	116	112	108	104	100	96	93	89	85	81	77
160	152	148	144	140	136	132	128	124	120	116	112	108	104	100	96	92	88	84	80
165	156	152	148	144	140	136	132	127	123	119	115	111	107	103	99	94	90	86	82
170	161	157	153	148	144	140	136	131	127	123	119	114	110	106	102	97	93	89	85
175	166	161	157	153	148	144	140	135	131	126	122	118	113	109	105	100	96	91	87
180	171	166	162	157	153	148	144	139	135	130	126	121	117	112	108	103	99	94	90
185	175	171	166	161	157	152	148	143	138	134	129	124	120	115	111	106	101	97	92
190	180	175	171	166	161	156	152	147	142	137	133	128	124	118	114	109	104	99	95
195	185	180	175	170	165	160	156	151	146	1410	136	131	126	121	117	112	107	102	97
200	190	185	180	175	170	165	160	155	150	145	140	135	130	125	120	115	110	105	100
205	194	189	184	179	174	169	164	158	153	148	143	138	133	128	123	117	112	107	102
210	199	194	189	183	178	173	168	162	157	152	147	141	136	131	126	120	115	110	105
215	204	198	193	188	182	177	172	166	161	155	150	145	139	134	129	123	118	112	107
220	209	203	195	192	187	181	176	170	165	159	154	148	143	137	132	126	121	115	110
225	213	208	202	196	191	185	180	174	168	163	157	151	146	140	135	129	123	118	112
230	218	212	207	201	195	189	184	178	172	166	161	155	149	143	138	132	126	120	115
235	223	217	211	205	199	193	188	182	176	170	164	158	152	146	141	135	129	123	117
240	228	222	216	210	204	198	192	186	180	174	168	162	156	150	144	138	132	126	120
245	232	226	220	214	208	202	196	189	183	177	171	165	159	153	147	140	134	128	122
250	237	231	225	218	212	206	200	193	187	181	175	168	162	156	150	143	137	131	125
255	242	235	229	223	216	210	204	197	191	184	178	172	165	159	153	146	140	133	127
260	247	240	234	227	221	214	208	201	195	188	182	175	169	162	156	149	143	136	130
265	251	245	238	231	225	218	212	205	198	192	185	178	172	165	159	152	145	139	132
270	265	249	243	236	229	222	216	209	202	195	189	182	175	168	162	155	148	141	135
275	261	254	247	240	233	226	220	213	206	199	192	185	178	171	165	158	151	144	137
280	266	259	252	245	238	231	224	217	210	203	196	189	182	175	168	161	154	147	140
285	270	263	256	249	242	235	228	220	213	206	199	192	185	178	171	163	156	149	142
290	275	268	261	253	246	239	232	224	217	210	203	195	188	181	174	166	159	152	145
295	280.2	272.8	265	258	250	24	236	228	221	213	206	199	191	184	177	169	162	154	147
300	285	277	270	262	255	247	240	232	225	217	210	202	195	187	180	172	165	157	150
305	289	282	274	266	259	251	244	236	228	221	213	205	198	190	183	175	167	160	152
310	294	286	279	271	263	255	248	240	232	224	217	209	201	193	186	178	170	162	155
315	299	291	283	275	267	259	525	244	236	228	220	212	204	196	189	181	173	165	157
320	304	296	288	280	272	264	256	248	240	232	224	216	208	200	192	184	176	168	160
325	308	300	292	284	276	268	260	251	243	235	227	219	211	203	195	186	178	170	162
330	313	305	297	288	280	272	264	255	247	239	231	222	214	206	198	189	181	173	165
335	318	309	301	293	284	276	268	259	251	242	234	226	217	209	201	192	184	175	167
340	323	314	306	297	289	280	272	263	255	246	238	229	221	212	204	195	187	178	170
345	327	319	310	301	293	284	276	267	258	250	241	232	224	215	207	198	189	181	172
350	332	323	315	306	297	288	280	271	262	253	245	236	227	218	210	201	192	183	175
355	337	328	319	310	301	292	284	275	266	257	248	239	230	221	231	204	195	186	177
360	342	333	324	315	306	297	288	279	270	261	252	243	234	225	216	207	198	189	180
365	346	337	328	319	310	301	292	282	273	264	255	246	237	228	219	209	200	191	182
370	351	342	333	323	314	305	296	286	277	268	259	249	240	231	222	212	203	194	185
375	356	346	337	328	318	309	300	290	281	271	262	253	243	234	225	215	206	196	187
380	361	351	342	332	323	313	304	294	285	275	266	256	247	237	228	218	209	199	190

100%	95%	.92.5%	90%	.87.5%	85%	.82.5%	80%	.77.5%	75%	.72.5%	70%	.67.5%	65%	.62.5%	60%	.57.5%	55%	.52.5%	50%
1RM	2RM	3RM	4RM	5RM	6RM	7RM	8RM	9RM	10RM	11RM	12RM	13RM	14RM	15RM	16RM	17RM	18RM	19RM	20RM
385	365	356	346	336	327	317	308	298	288	279	269	259	250	240	231	221	211	202	192
390	370	360	350	341	331	321	312	302	292	282	273	263	253	243	234	224	214	204	195
395	375	365	355	345	335	325	315	306	296	286	276	266	256	246	237	227	217	207	197
400	380	370	360	350	340	330	320	310	300	290	280	270	260	250	240	230	220	210	200
405	384	374	364	354	344	334	324	313	303	293	283	273	263	253	243	232	222	212	202
410	389	379	369	358	348	338	328	317	307	297	287	276	266	256	246	235	225	215	205
415	394	383	373	363	352	342	332	321	311	300	290	280	269	259	249	238	228	217	207
420	399	388	378	367	357	346	336	325	315	304	294	283	273	262	252	241	231	220	210
425	403	393	382	371	361	350	340	329	318	308	297	286	276	265	255	244	233	223	212
430	408	397	387	376	365	354	344	333	322	311	301	290	279	268	258	247	236	255	215
435	413	402	391	380	369	358	348	337	326	315	304	293	282	271	261	250	239	228	217
440	418	407	396	385	374	363	352	341	330	319	308	297	286	275	264	253	242	231	220
445	422	411	400	389	378	367	356	344	333	322	311	300	289	278	267	255	244	233	222
450	427	416	405	393	382	371	360	348	337	326	315	303	292	281	270	258	247	236	225

Mitch Hughes (#24) of the Sioux Falls Stampede (USHL)

DP Hockey Products & Services

DP Hockey is committed to providing the best training services and products in hockey! Our goal is to make better hockey players and outfit them correctly with the training tools they need to succeed. Visit us online at www.dphockey.com, for more information.

Services

Team Training
Most junior and semi-professional hockey teams do not have the resources to put together, implement and monitor a dryland training program. Simply buying players a pass at the local gym or following some NHL workout routine is not enough and often leads to poor performance and injuries.

At DP Hockey Coach Pollitt will work with teams at any level, anywhere in North America and can produce a complete team training program, monitor the progress and teach our methods to coaches and players for a very reasonable yearly cost. Visit www.dphockey.com for more information on Team Training.

Products

Just Hockey Programs *(Expected Release, fall of 2013)*
For players looking for just hockey programs this book is for them. I took a collection of my best programs that have been tried and tested over a 23+ career and put them all in one book. Instead of paying thousands of dollars for personal consultations and custom designed programs you can buy this book which details everything. Learn more at www.dphockey.com.

Hockey Nutrition Manual *(Expected Release, spring of 2014)*
Good nutrition makes up a big part of the results and recovery you can achieve during training and in games. As players need to add muscle mass, lose body fat, or simply learn the important methods of performance nutrition it is key that you consult accurate and detailed sources. In preparing this *Hockey Nutrition Manual* I looked at all the situations that a player will need performance nutrition from pre & post workout/games, during training camps, in the off-season to manipulate body composition and information regarding supplementation. Visit www.dphockey.com for more information.

Sixth Warrior – Goaltender Development Manual *(Expected Release, winter of 2013)*
Goaltenders need specific training both on and off the ice. In this manual I consulted with numerous goaltending experts over a 10-year period to develop this revolutionary goaltender manual. Find out more at www.dphockey.com.

Junior hockey goaltender David Sargent in action with the Laconia Leafs of the MJHL

About the Author - David Pollitt

- Born & raised in Canada with hockey experience as a strength coach, hockey coach, athletic trainer (over 350-games at the Midget & Junior level), on-ice official, player, volunteer, and a fan!

- Bachelor of Physical Education Degree (BPE), from the University of Manitoba.

- Graduate of the Olympic Academy of Canada.

- Certified Strength & Conditioning Coach (CSCS) with distinction from the *National Strength & Conditioning Association*.

- Certified Fitness Consultant from *the Canadian Society for Exercise Physiology*.

- Professional Coaching Certifications in Olympic Weightlifting (in Canada & the USA).

- Internships with the Calgary Olympic Development Association, National Team Development Centre (Canmore, AB), and the Manitoba Ski Team.

- 23+ years' experience as a Strength & Conditioning Coach to elite hockey players at the amateur, junior, college and professional level throughout North America & Europe.

- Award winning Strength & Conditioning Coach.

- Advanced Level-4 USA Hockey Coach & Intermediate (NCCP Level-2) Hockey Coach (Canada).

- Coach Pollitt has written over 30-hockey articles published in peer reviewed journals, magazines, on the internet and his blog (www.dphockey.com). He has authored three other books that are in the final stages of development including: *The Sixth Warrior - Goaltender Development Manual*, *Just Hockey Workouts*, and *The Hockey Nutrition Manual*, soon available at DP Hockey.

- Former Assistant Editor of the *Performance Training Journal* (now a peer reviewer), and peer reviewer for the *Strength & Conditioning Journal*.

- Owner of www.dphockey.com.

- Co-owner & Director of Training for Chalk Fitness (www.chalkfitness.com), in Orange County, California.

- Certified Athletic First Aider (*Manitoba Athletic Trainers Association*), the Hockey Trainers Development Program (*Canadian Hockey Association*), and Speak Out (*Canadian Hockey Association*)

- Elected to the Board of Directors for the *Coaches Association of Manitoba* (1992-96).

- Former Strength & Conditioning Coach for the Duquesne University Ice Dukes (2003 to 2006).

- Strength & Conditioning Coach for the Banff Hockey Academy (1999-2003, 2009-12).

- Trainer of US Special Forces soldiers, Paramilitary personnel & elite athletes in 8-other sports.

- Consultant to a number of sports teams, professional organizations and ABHES.

Made in the USA
San Bernardino, CA
07 December 2013